King Alfred's
Winchester

Martial Rose Library
Tel: 01962 827306

2 7 MAR 2009

To be returned on or before the day marked above, subject to recall.

D1615180

WITHDRAWN FROM
THE LIBRARY
UNIVERSITY OF
WINCHESTER

KA 0334611 0

Studies in Renaissance Literature

Volume 21

STAGING ISLAM IN ENGLAND
DRAMA AND CULTURE, 1640–1685

Transmitted via the mechanisms of trade and diplomacy and reflected through stage and press, England's cultural encounters with Islam – its peoples, its history, its territories – were fundamental to the ways in which the nation constructed itself through all the tribulations of the seventeenth century; a preoccupation with Islam permeated religious, political, diplomatic and commercial discourses to a degree that has not been recognised by standard accounts of the period.

This book traces engagement with Islam in English political and dramatic life from the inauguration of the Long Parliament until the death of Charles II. It explores the reception and representation of Islam in a wide range of English writings of the period, employing close textual and historical research to trace the development of the 'Turk' from the archetype of cruelty and treachery to the complex and often contradictory figure of mid-century discourse. Throughout, it argues that Islam provided a repository of meanings ripe for transposition to Revolutionary and Restoration England, a process that transfigured the 'East' through the lens of English politics and vice-versa.

MATTHEW BIRCHWOOD is Lecturer in English Literature at Kingston University.

Studies in Renaissance Literature

ISSN 1465–6310

General Editors
David Colclough
Raphael Lyne
Sean Keilen

Studies in Renaissance Literature offers investigations of topics in English literature focussed in the sixteenth and seventeenth centuries; its scope extends from early Tudor writing, including works reflecting medieval concerns, to the Restoration period. Studies exploring the interplay between the literature of the English Renaissance and its cultural history are particularly welcomed.

Proposals or queries should be sent in the first instance to the editors, or to the publisher, at the addresses given below; all submissions receive prompt and informed consideration.

Dr David Colclough, School of English and Drama, Queen Mary, University of London, Mile End Road, London, E1 4NS

Dr Raphael Lyne, New Hall, Cambridge, CB3 0DF

Dr Sean Keilen, English Department, University of Pennsylvania, Fisher-Bennett Hall, 3340 Walnut Street, Philadephia, PA 19104–6273, USA

Boydell & Brewer Limited, PO Box 9, Woodbridge, Suffolk, IP12 3DF

Previously published titles in this series are listed at the back of this volume

STAGING ISLAM IN ENGLAND
DRAMA AND CULTURE, 1640–1685

Matthew Birchwood

D. S. BREWER

© Matthew Birchwood 2007

All Rights Reserved. Except as permitted under current legislation
no part of this work may be photocopied, stored in a retrieval system,
published, performed in public, adapted, broadcast,
transmitted, recorded or reproduced in any form or by any means,
without the prior permission of the copyright owner

The right of Matthew Birchwood to be identified as
the author of this work has been asserted in accordance with
sections 77 and 78 of the Copyright, Designs and Patents Act 1998

First published 2007
D. S. Brewer, Cambridge

ISBN 978–1–84384–127–2

D. S. Brewer is an imprint of Boydell & Brewer Ltd
PO Box 9, Woodbridge, Suffolk IP12 3DF, UK
and of Boydell & Brewer Inc.
668 Mt Hope Avenue, Rochester, NY 14620, USA
website: www.boydellandbrewer.com

A catalogue record for this title is available
from the British Library

This publication is printed on acid-free paper

Printed in Great Britain by
Antony Rowe Ltd, Chippenham, Wiltshire

CONTENTS

ILLUSTRATIONS

ACKNOWLEDGEMENTS

I have incurred many debts in the research and writing of *Staging Islam*. Early research was made possible by the institutional support of Royal Holloway and the AHRC and latterly, Queen Mary, University of London.

At Queen Mary, Lisa Jardine, Warren Boutcher and David Colclough have been fathomless wellsprings of advice and encouragement. Individually, they have read and commented upon sections of the work in its various phases, providing insightful answers to particular questions. Collectively, their innovative approach to the study and teaching of early modern drama has been a motivating example and reassuring proof of the possibilities of reading old plays in ways both historically informed and culturally relevant. My especial thanks, though, must go to Jerry Brotton who has acted as a matchless guide since the project's inception and continues to show the way, not least by setting the highest standards of dynamic scholarship. This book, quite simply, would have not been written without his help.

My thanks also to the numerous scholars working in this and related fields who have commented on aspects of the developing work as presented at various seminars and conferences, many of whose names appear herein as authors of studies indispensable to my own. In the earliest stages, Tom Healy and Sue Owen acted as critical readers while Gerald MacLean's sharp-eyed reading and unparalleled expertise in all things Anglo-Ottoman were invaluable in the final stages. Matthew Dimmock has long been a fellow traveller along East-West borders and I look forward to future and productive exchanges. Thanks also to my new colleagues and friends at Kingston for contributing to such a conducive working environment. For their patience and effortless efficiency, my grateful acknowledgement to all at Boydell and Brewer. For permission to reproduce images my thanks to the Guildhall Art Gallery, English Heritage, Cambridge University Library and, particularly to Rosemary Triffitt at Newby Hall for her generous help. Elements of chapters four and five have appeared elsewhere in Goran Stanivukovic's *Remapping the Mediterranean World* and Elaine Hobby's special issue of *Prose Studies* – my thanks to them both for their interest and expert suggestions.

Outside academic circles, valued friends have lent support and encouragement on many levels. Damian Roberts, John Roscoe, Rowland Hughes Richard Gould and Martin Rack have all contributed in ways that may not be very evident to them here. Likewise, Helen Stratton and Emily Gee have both been there from the outset. The Gribbon family have also closely followed the progress of the book with interest and have helped towards its appearance in many ways.

To my own family, I owe a special vote of thanks. My parents and sister Sarah have shown support and unquestioning belief in my chosen course for which I hope they know I am eternally grateful. It seems fitting also to express my admiration for my grandparents who gave me opportunities I would not have otherwise had and who, I know, expect no thanks.

One person has, however, been with me every step of the way and without whose love and support I would not have come this far. To Michelle, my true inspiration, I dedicate the following.

INTRODUCTION

In a poem composed in 1676 two horses debate the political climate of the day, denouncing the government of Charles II both in terms of a legacy of Stuart tyranny and an anticipated betrayal at the hands of the Catholic James:

> [*W.*]   Though the father and son be different rods,
>   Between the two scourges we find little odds…
>   One of the two tyrants must still be our case
>   Under all that shall reign of the false Scottish race.
> *C.*   De Witt and Cromwell had each a brave soul:
>   I freely declare, I am for old Noll.
> *W.*   Though his government did a tyrant's resemble,
>   He made England great and its enemies tremble…
> *C.*   What is thy opinion of James Duke of York?
> *W.*   The same that the frogs had of Jupiter's stork:
>   With the Turk in his head and the Pope in his heart.
>   Father Patrick's disciple will make England smart.
>   *A Dialogue Between the Two Horses*[1]

The two horses in question were the equestrian statues erected at Charing Cross (the '*C*' of the poem) and Stocks Market (also known as '*W*oolchurch'), both well-known landmarks of Restoration London depicting Charles I in bronze and Charles II in white marble respectively (see Fig. 1). The anonymous poem, tentatively associated with Marvell by some editors, seizes upon the irresistible opportunity to make a historical comparison between the two monarchs that undercuts the self-confident civic authority apparently proclaimed by the two monuments.[2] As well as inspiring a spate of satires, the history or perhaps mythology of the two statues is intriguingly bound up with that of the Civil

---

[1] 'A Dialogue between the Two Horses', in *Poems on Affairs of State: Augustan Satirical Verse 1660–1714*, ed. George Deforest Lord, 7 vols. (New Haven and London: Yale University Press, 1963), vol. 1, p. 281 (ll. 127–46).

[2] Other satirical poems on the statues include *On the Statue Erected by Sir Robert Viner* (1675) and *The Statue at Charing Cross* (1675). As Deforest Lord points out, both of these may be more readily attributed to Marvell since they appear in the Bodleian Marvell manuscript whereas *A Dialogue Between the Two Horses*, quoted above, does not. Deforest Lord, ed., *Poems on Affairs of State*, vol. 1, pp. 274–5. For attribution, see also H. M. Margoliouth, ed., *The Poems and Letters of Andrew Marvell*, 2 vols. (Oxford: Clarendon Press, 1971), vol. 1, p. 414.

Figure 1. View of the Stocks Market, Poultry, looking from the west.

War itself. Whilst that of the elder Charles had been ostensibly destroyed at the outbreak of hostilities, only to miraculously reappear at the Restoration,[3] that of Charles II was, upon closer inspection, a curious composite of images. Sir Robert Viner, soon to be Lord Mayor of London, presented the statue to the King on 29 May 1672 in honour of the royal birthday and ordered it to be erected in Stocks Market, the site of the present Mansion House. According to Viner's entry in the *Dictionary of National Biography*,

> it originally represented John Sobieski, King of Poland, trampling a Turk beneath his horse's feet. To save time and expense, the Polish king was converted into Charles, and the Turk into Oliver Cromwell, unfortunately the turban on the Turk's head was overlooked and remained as proof of the conversion.

Now, as the story has it, this visual pun, no doubt unconsciously perpetrated on the part of the staunchly loyal Viner, would overlook the entrance

---

[3] In a recent biography Nicholas Murray retells the story that, in 1633, the king's Lord Treasurer Richard Weston commissioned Le Sueur to cast a bronze statue of Charles I to be erected at Charing Cross, only to be thwarted by Parliament before the project could be completed. They 'sold it contemptuously to a brazier called Rivet who, after the King's execution, made a profitable sideline in bronze-handled knives and forks that he persuaded ardent Royalists to buy. ... In fact, Rivet had kept the statue intact, producing it after the Restoration and eventually selling it to Danby.' *World Enough and Time: The Life of Andrew Marvell* (London: Little, Brown, 1999), pp. 218–19. See Martin Dzelzainis '"Incendiaries of the State": Charles I and Tyranny' in Thomas N. Corns, ed., *The Royal Image: Representations of Charles I* (Cambridge: Cambridge University Press, 1999), pp. 74–5.

Figure 2. Marble Equestrian Statue of Charles II at
Newby Hall, Yorkshire.

to Cornhill for the next sixty two years. In fact, the statue's provenance is
rather more murky than the *DNB* confidently reports.[4] The first mention of
the Polish king in connection with Viner's statue is made in Benjamin Ralph's
1734 review of London architecture, some sixty years after its erection.[5] Moreover, it seems improbable that a statue would be commissioned to celebrate a

---

4   The contested history of the monument and its convoluted travels from Stocks Market to
    its present location in the grounds of Newby Hall, Yorkshire are documented in Maurice
    Exwood, 'The Equestrian Statue of Charles II at Gautby', *Lincolnshire Past & Present* 25
    (Autumn 1996), pp. 4–8.
5   Ralph's scathing review describes the statue as 'a thing in itself so exceeding ridiculous and
    absurd, that 'tis not in one's power to look upon it without reflecting on the tastes of those
    who set it up: but, when we enquire into the history of it, the farce improves upon our hands,
    and, what was before contemptible grows entertaining'. Benjamin Ralph, *A Critical Review
    of the publick buildings, statues and ornaments in and about London and Westminster, etc.*
    (London, 1734), p. 12.

man who had not yet succeeded to the throne; Sobieski was not elected king until 1674, two years after the dedication of the equestrian statue and a full eleven years before his defeat of the Ottomans at Vienna, upon which his fame was principally based. Judging from the available evidence, it seems most likely that Viner acquired a generic statue perhaps in lieu of one of his many debts and paid for its alteration by Jasper Latham. Only subsequently did the story of the Sobieski connection grow up. Nevertheless, apocrypha apart, one of the most prominent monuments of Restoration London depicted the English monarch trampling a turbaned figure who might be construed as either 'Turk' or Cromwell or both. To passers-by, Cromwell's 'conversion' must have seemed a humorous testament to the Lord Mayor's enthusiastic, if thrifty royalism. On another level, however, the suggested analogy would have provoked a whole nexus of religious and political associations directly contingent upon the experience of civil war and its aftermath. For any who, like the two horses of the *Dialogue*, had occasion to reflect upon the unprecedented transformations wrought since the breakdown of monarchical rule some thirty years earlier, the notion that an Englishman might be represented by a 'Turk' was both culturally familiar and powerfully resonant.

On the face of it, statue and poem appear to offer ideologically conflicting constructions of English 'Turks'. Fashioned in stone, the statue embodies an analogy that is, at its most basic level, between two infidels, one the archetypal enemy of monarchy, the other of Christendom itself. Certainly, an equation of Cromwell with the Ottoman sultan might be termed a commonplace of mid-century polemic and, although the original identity of the prostrate figure is shrouded in anecdotal speculation, it is entirely plausible that the monument invited such an interpretation. Fashioned in verse, however, the poem makes an equally recognisable correlation between Ottoman sultan and English king that calls upon an opposite set of ideas relating monarchical tyranny with oriental despotism. This apparent contradiction, encoded in the visual puzzle of the statue and its attendant poem, lies at the very heart of English engagement with what might be called the idea of the East in the period of Revolution and Restoration. To denounce a political enemy for having 'the Turk in his head' in 1676 was not simply to allege a proverbial treachery (to 'turn Turk') but to invoke a wider and more complex history of cultural negotiation between East and West, both real and notional. Crucially, however, this is a history wide open to interpretation. By deploying 'the Turk' in commemoration of the nation's recent turbulent past, the poem and statue reveal both the prevalence and thoroughgoing politicisation of this familiar figure in the discourse of the mid-century onwards. The comparison points to the extraordinarily protean character of the figure of 'the Turk' and Islam in general in the wake of civil war, available to both republican and royalist versions of history as either tyrant or turncoat or both. As the enigmatic significance of the Stocks Market statue indicates, far from being set in stone, English representations of Islam were ideologically fluid and utterly resist monolithic interpretation. Instead,

4

confronted with the spiritual and political crises of civil war, the Islamic paradigm was seductive to writers of every political complexion precisely because of this indeterminacy. Islam presented a repository of meanings apparently ripe for transposition to the particular contingencies of the time, a process that transfigured the East through the lens of English politics and vice-versa. It is the aim of this study to trace the development of that transfiguration in the literary–political expression of the period 1640–1685.

In English historiography the significance of these dates would seem to require little explanation. In 1640, the inauguration of the Long Parliament challenged the institutionalised authority of Charles I and set in motion a revolution that would culminate in the unthinkable: the state-sanctioned death of a divinely instituted monarch. If Charles' execution symbolised the ultimate destruction of the old order, then the death of his restored heir in 1685 appeared to bring the country full circle – with the prospect of an openly Catholic king, England seemed to be on the verge of betraying the very principles that had motivated opposition to monarchy in the first place. To widen the perspective, however, this period was also formative in the development of the Ottoman Empire, the most immediate manifestation of Islamic nationhood. The year 1640 also marked the accession of Ibrahim I to the Ottoman throne, the sultan who would be overthrown and executed after an uprising by his Janissaries eight years later in an uncanny paralleling of English events. His successor, Sultan Mehmed IV, oversaw a period of civil turmoil and foreign conflict that marked the final phase of Ottoman territorial expansion. By the end of the period under consideration, the territorial ambitions of the Porte were finally checked following the defeat of Ottoman forces at Vienna (1683) after which the empire would not regain its former eminence. As succeeding chapters will show, to many English commentators this symmetry was the stimulus for correlative interpretations and became further confirmation for a reciprocity that ran deep in the national consciousness. Transmitted via the mechanisms of trade and diplomacy and refracted through stage and press, England's cultural encounters with Islam – its peoples, its history, its territories – were fundamental to the ways in which the nation constructed itself through all the tribulations of this revolutionary century. Moreover, growing cultural contact with the East and in particular the Ottoman domain made for frequent news reports from the sultan's territories and an unprecedented awareness in London of affairs in Istanbul. As one empire reached its zenith, the foundations for another were being laid in the cultural and constitutional transformations experienced in England in the second half of the century. The degree to which the idea of Islam helped to shape the nation that emerged from the 'Glorious Revolution' is a hidden chapter in that history.

In recent years, the pioneering work of Nabil Matar has begun to address this blind spot in our understanding of the period. Making impressive and comprehensive use of documentary resources, his overarching account, encompassing both Tudor and Stuart eras, has provided compelling evidence for the significance of Islam to English literary and political culture and has pointed the way for further critical inquiry.[6] Other studies of the final period of Matar's remit, that is, specifically the period of Anglo-Islamic interaction after the outbreak of the English Civil War, are few and far between and do not seek to address the literary and dramatic dimension at all. Constructed through diplomatic and other archival records, for example, the work of Daniel Goffman has placed the commercial activities of the English merchants at the Porte and elsewhere in the Levant firmly in the context of the domestic political situation and supplements Robert Brenner's authoritative ground-work, *Merchants and Revolution* in several areas.[7] Similarly, on the question of England's intellectual engagement with Islamic culture, G. J. Toomer's *Eastern Wisdome and Learning* offers a detailed discussion of the rise and demise of English 'Arabism' in the century. With these exceptions, though, there remain few specialised historical accounts of the role of Islam in England of the mid-century onwards. In the literary sphere, the dearth of criticism alive to the cultural and historical specificities of Islam is even more striking and it is astonishing that the only large scale study to describe the place of Islam on the English stage throughout the period remains Samuel Chew's *The Crescent and the Rose*, first published in 1937.[8] Other early summaries are to be found in Louis Wann's article, 'The Oriental in Elizabethan Drama' (1915) and Warner Grenelle Rice's unpublished dissertation, 'Turk, Moor, and Persian in English Literature from 1550–1660' (1927) although these are concerned largely with aesthetic observations about the plays they address and are steeped in the orientalist critical preconceptions of their day.[9]

In marked contrast to this anomalous lacuna, much recent scholarly energy has been invested in describing the place of Islam in the culture and literature of the period immediately preceding the remit of this study. In what might almost be termed a vogue for Renaissance revisions of 'Orientalism', the last ten years have seen a sustained examination of the role of Europe's cultural encounter with the East in the Early Modern period as, broadly speaking, the attention of new historicists has shifted from fashionings of the New World

---

6   Nabil Matar, *Islam in Britain 1558–1685* (Cambridge: Cambridge University Press, 1998).
7   See Daniel Goffman, *Britons in the Ottoman Empire 1642–1660* (London and Seattle: University of Washington Press, 1998) and *Izmir and the Levantine World, 1550–1650* (London and Seattle: University of Washington Press, 1990); Robert Brenner, *Merchants and Revolution: Commercial Change, Political Conflict, and London's Overseas Traders, 1550–1653* (Princeton: Princeton University Press, 1993). Goffman disagrees with Brenner over the political makeup of the Levant Company at the outbreak of the Civil War, arguing for the existence of a significant section of Parliamentary sympathisers.
8   Samuel Chew, *The Crescent and the Rose: Islam and England During the Renaissance* (New York: Oxford University Press, 1937).
9   Louis Wann, 'The Oriental in Elizabethan Drama', *Modern Philology* 12 (January 1915), pp. 163–87; Warner Grenelle Rice, 'Turk, Moor, and Persian in English Literature from 1550–1660 with Particular Reference to the Drama' (PhD dissertation, Harvard University, 1927).

to those of Orient.[10] Inevitably, much of this attention has focused upon the relatively contested field of Elizabethan and early Jacobean drama, also known as the Age of Shakespeare.[11] The gravitational pull of Shakespeare and his immediate contemporaries has therefore tended to warp our understanding of the larger impact of Islam, and particularly the Ottoman Empire, upon the Early Modern period as a whole. To take a well-rehearsed example, the dualistic nature of Othello as both 'Turk' and convert, 'servant and enemy of the Christian state',[12] has become a commonplace of criticism of the play and yet the historical context of anxiety aroused by renegade and apostate routinely invoked to cement such a reading is equally, if not more germane to the period following civil war, as I shall discuss further in Chapter 4. Following on from Matar's reading of plays such as Robert Daborne's *A Christian turn'd Turke* (1612) and Philip Massinger's *The Renegadoe* (1624) in the context of actual conversion narratives, a spate of critical work attending to 'Turk plays' of the early seventeenth century has followed, a trend most visible in the appearance of Daniel Vitkus' collection of three previously unedited dramatic texts.[13] His subsequent study, *Turning Turk*, consolidated the thesis that English theatre of the late sixteenth and early seventeenth centuries had been profoundly shaped by its representation of the 'multicultural Mediterranean' and in particular by commercial contexts.[14] Whilst attendance to Islam has opened up new horizons in the study of Renaissance drama, virtually all critical attention has been paid to the relatively narrow period roughly beginning with Marlowe's *Tamburlaine* (1587) and ending with the appearance of Shakespeare's First Folio in 1623.

A parallel and interconnected body of work has been simultaneously and variously devoted to critiquing, defending, but in some way engaging Edward Said's profoundly important study *Orientalism* (1978). Primarily considering

---

10 A natural development of these two approaches has been combinatory, relating exploration of the New World to the context of oriental encounters and vice versa. See Barbara Fuchs, *Mimesis and Empire: The New World, Islam and European Identities* (Cambridge: Cambridge University Press, 2001); Nabil Matar, *Turks, Moors and Englishmen in the Age of Discovery* (New York: Columbia University Press, 1999).

11 For example, Barbara Fuchs, 'Conquering Islands: Contextualizing *The Tempest*', *Shakespeare Quarterly* 48, no. 1 (Spring 1997), pp. 45–62; Emily Bartels, *Spectacles of Strangeness: Imperialism, Alienation, and Marlowe* (Philadelphia: University of Pennsylvania Press, 1993); 'Pirates and "turning Turk" in Renaissance drama', in *Travel and Drama in Shakespeare's Time*, eds. Jean-Pierre Maquerlot and Michèle Willems (Cambridge: Cambridge University Press, 1996), pp. 124–40.

12 Walter Cohen, introduction to *Othello* in *The Norton Shakespeare*, eds. Stephen Greenblatt, Walter Cohen, Jean E. Howard, and Katharine E. Maus (New York and London: Norton, 1997), p. 2098.

13 Daniel Vitkus, ed., *Three Turk Plays From Early Modern England* (New York: Columbia University Press, 2000).

14 Daniel Vitkus, *Turning Turk: English Theater and the Multicultural Mediterranean, 1570–1630* (New York: Palgrave Macmillan, 2003).

the history of his subject from the eighteenth century onwards, Said originally describes Orientalism as

> the corporate institution for dealing with the Orient – dealing with it by making statements about it, authorizing views of it, describing it, by teaching it, settling it, ruling over it: in short, as a Western style for dominating, restructuring, and having authority over the Orient.[15]

What is striking about the period immediately preceding that of Said's remit is precisely the impossibility of such a coherent strategy. Since its conquest of Constantinople in 1453, the Ottoman Empire had been a constant and real threat on the margins of Western Europe, traditionally inimical and militarily formidable. English writers might zealously refute the teachings of the Prophet and the civilisation and empire that espoused them but they could not, in Said's phrase, have 'authority' over them. Instead, a reverse process appears to be under way, at least in England of the mid-seventeenth century. In this sense, writers call upon Islam precisely *because* it is and persists in being a serious source of ideological and cultural opposition to Christendom, despite the best efforts of European soldiers and writers to contain 'the East' in one way or another. Conventional histories of the Ottoman Empire tend to designate the century as one of inevitable decline, reading in the series of bloody internecine struggles for the succession that followed the death of Ahmed I in 1617, the fatal weakening of the sinews of imperial hegemony.[16] This is, however, to impose a teleological coherence upon events that has tended to homogenise the true situation as English contemporaries perceived it, downplaying the influence of the Ottoman Empire almost in anticipation of a Saidian conception of East–West power relations. Indeed, the potency of Said's thesis has made it tempting for literary scholars with one eye on the historical sweep to see in seventeenth-century representations the precursors of Orientalist discourse proper, resulting in the argument that fascination with the Orient increases in direct proportion to the relative weakness of its projected political power. Of course, at specific moments in the turbulent history of the Ottoman Empire, English observers *were* fascinated by the spectacle of domestic turmoil and foreign setbacks, but it is an underlying principle of this book that English fascination with the Orient may be indexed not to perceived weaknesses there, but to religious and political anxieties at home. Few anticipated the imminent collapse of fabled Ottoman supremacy, and it was not until the Ottoman Empire tried its strength against Vienna in 1683 that the prospect of a Western European order of power with any kind of 'authority' over the Orient became conceivable.

And yet, this is only half the story. Another strand of recent scholarship

---

[15] Edward Said, *Orientalism* (London: Routledge & Kegan Paul, 1978), p. 3.
[16] See, for example, the chapter entitled 'Seeds of Decline' in Lord Kinross, *The Ottoman Centuries: The Rise and Fall of the Turkish Empire* (London: Jonathan Cape, 1977).

has done much to correct the view that Early Modern Europe's relationship with the East was defined primarily by hostility and anxiety aroused by territorial ambitions. For example, Palmira Brummett's study of the importance of trading relations to the sustenance of the Ottoman Empire in the sixteenth century depicts a political entity dependent more upon a commercial cooperation than military subjugation.[17] Similarly, by tracking the complex artistic transactions made between East and West in the period 1450–1550, the revisionist work of Jerry Brotton and Lisa Jardine has overturned the assumption that the Western aesthetic tradition of Renaissance Europe flourished in glorious isolation from the commercial and political pressures of the wider world and has revealed the degree of cultural prestige accorded to the Ottomans through that material exchange.[18] In *The Renaissance Bazaar*, Jerry Brotton consolidates and broadens these arguments to draw vital connections between the 'vigorously traded art, ideas, and luxury goods' and the 'impact of these exchanges between east and west that created the culture, art, and scholarship that have been popularly associated with the Renaissance'.[19] That most defining moment of 'western' civilisation and achievement, in other words, might be a more global and far-reaching phenomenon than traditionally admitted.

In many ways, these sophistications of the orthodox history of Europe's relationship with its eastern neighbours foreshadow England's own deeply ambivalent engagement with the empires of Islam in the succeeding century and are directly pertinent to my own study. In the field of Ottoman studies, though, this corrective has hardly been necessary, for the 'existence of such Eurocentric mythologizing in scholarship is almost axiomatic'.[20] By comparison, however, the impact of new perspectives in literary studies remains relatively recent. Both Vitkus' *Turning Turk* and Richmond Barbour's recent study *Before Orientalism: London's Theatre of the East, 1576–1626* adopt theoretical positions that are to various extents syntheses of established critical approaches. Vitkus rejects the post-colonial appropriation of the psychoanalytic term of 'othering' by cultural historians, with its intrinsic binary opposition in favour of a 'post-structuralist theory of alterity', which admits a more complex and fragmented model of cultural representation. The theatre is imagined as a site of cultural production that responds directly to the flow of material commodities between East and West or, more specifically, between England and the Mediterranean, as well as being a commercial enterprise in its own right. Barbour insists upon

---

[17] Palmira Brummett, *Ottoman Seapower and Levantine Diplomacy in the Age of Discovery* (Albany, NY: State University of New York Press, 1994).

[18] See Lisa Jardine and Jerry Brotton, *Global Interests: Renaissance Art Between East and West* (London: Reaktion, 2000).

[19] Jerry Brotton, *The Renaissance Bazaar: From the Silk Road to Michelangelo* (Oxford: Oxford University Press, 2002), p. 1.

[20] Daniel Goffman, *The Ottoman Empire and Early Modern Europe* (Cambridge: Cambridge University Press, 2002), p. 4.

the same material agency in his formulation of what he calls 'cultural logistics', that is, broadly, an approach to texts that emphasises the strong correlation between 'material and discursive practises'.[21]

In common with other recent commentaries, both also take issue with Said's *Orientalism* and, as Gerald MacLean has summed up in an important recent collection,

> Scholars are generally agreed that we need a better way of thinking about East–West relations before the Napoleonic invasion of Egypt, the event that initiates the period of most interest to Said. The earlier precolonial period receives very little attention in Said's book, while the Ottoman Empire receives none at all.[22]

And yet Said does offer a suggestive account of the relationship between encounter and a peculiarly dramatic kind of representation. Describing a fifteenth-century attempt by the Christian Church to publicly confute Islam and bring about the wholesale conversion of Muslims, Said identifies

> … part of a general European attempt from Bede to Luther – to put a representative Orient in front of Europe, to *stage* the Orient and Europe together in some coherent way, the idea being for Christians to make it clear to Muslims that Islam was just a misguided version of Christianity.[23]

This notion of theatrical representation is suggestive because it allows Islam and Christianity to share the stage 'together', albeit for propagandistic purposes. Said picks up the same metaphor in attempting to define the primary target of his condemnation: the Orientalist as author and prescriber of his own learned field:

> A field is often an enclosed space. The idea of representation is a theatrical one: the Orient is the stage on which the whole East is confined. On this stage will appear figures whose role is to represent the larger whole from which they emanate. The Orient then seems to be, not an unlimited extension beyond the familiar European world, but rather a closed field, a theatrical stage affixed to Europe. An Orientalist is but the particular specialist in knowledge for which Europe at large is responsible for (and responsive to) dramas technically put together by the dramatist.[24]

Such a construction imagines a very particular relationship between dramatist, audience and performers in which all the roles are fixed. Above all, the

---

21 Richmond Barbour, *Before Orientalism: London's Theatre of the East 1576–1626* (Cambridge: Cambridge University Press, 2003), p. 7.

22 Gerald MacLean, ed., *Reorienting the Renaissance: Cultural Exchanges with the East* (New York and Basingstoke: Palgrave Macmillan, 2005), p. 7. See also Matthew Birchwood and Matthew Dimmock, eds., *Cultural Encounters Between East and West: 1453–1699* (Newcastle: Cambridge Scholars Press, 2005).

23 Said, *Orientalism*, p. 61.

24 Said, *Orientalism*, p. 63.

Orientalist or 'dramatist' is responsible for orchestrating the entire action, designing a stage upon which any authentic 'performance' of the East can be 'technically' contained, directed and subsumed. Some degree of self-reflexivity is admitted – Europe as audience are 'responsive to' those performances – but the perspective and portrayal are entirely Eurocentric. Such subjectivity is, of course, intrinsic to the nature of dramatic representation, but it is the contention of this study that dramatic writings of the mid to late seventeenth century reveal a far more complex and mobile relationship between dramatist, audience and performer and between East and West more generally. To stage Orient in this period is not to circumscribe its identity but rather to appropriate *its* authority, to mobilise not only the performers but also the audience in a show of politicised other worlds that self-consciously and inevitably reflect back on their orchestrators.

As the best work of the preceding period has demonstrated, the boundaries between East and West were thoroughly permeable and constantly shifting. In England, the disruption of what might be termed the crusader binary – or in modern parlance, the 'clash of civilisations' model – can be traced back to the Reformation. Following the break with Rome there was a new demonic infidel to assimilate, and it is no coincidence that the first real cracks to appear in straightforward representations of the mythological eastern enemy may be traced to this moment of both political and religious realignment. By Elizabeth's reign, in nuanced ways, both Ottomans and Persians had begun to occupy a rather more ambivalent position in relation to the Protestant English, sharing not only a natural enemy in Catholic Europe but also an officially sanctioned trade agreement.[25] Again, however, this well-rehearsed thesis of sixteenth-century studies of Islam has as much if not more relevance when related to the later period. By the middle of the next century, as Brenner has shown, the Levant traders had supplanted the Merchant Adventurers as the most influential section of the merchant community. As traditional markets declined, the lucrative trade in silk and currant imports became of increasing economic importance and, as both merchants and monarchs were aware, cordial relations with the Porte were an essential prerequisite of Mediterranean commerce. Thus, growing numbers of Englishmen were in direct contact with Muslim peoples, in a context whereby they and not their powerful hosts were the cultural and religious outsider. Clearly though, this is not to argue that this mere fact led to a universal enlightenment in attitudes towards Islam itself. This holds particularly true for those for whom cultural encounter was indivisible from religious antagonism. Judging from the evidence of printed sermons and theological tracts, the overwhelming response throughout the

---

[25] The charter of the Turkey Company, later the Levant Company, was granted in 1581. For a detailed contextualisation of English drama and the Anglo-Ottoman Capitulations, see Matthew Dimmock, *New Turkes: Dramatizing Islam and the Ottomans in Early Modern England* (Aldershot: Ashgate, 2005), particularly ch. 2.

period under consideration was censorious, with the vehemence of the attack rising proportionately to the perceived need to defend the true faith. Writing in 1697, the Dean of Norwich, Humphrey Prideaux, summed up the position of the English Church throughout the century in his dogmatically entitled, *The True Nature of Imposture fully display'd in the life of Mahomet. With a discourse annex'd, for the vindication of Christianity from this charge.* With one notable and radical exception, examined further here in a later chapter of this study, this remained the conditioned response of English Christians to the rival doctrine of the Prophet. However, a clear subtext for this religious enmity was political and cultural envy. Officially vilified at the pulpit, the civilisation of Islam was nevertheless the object of study and admiration as the account of the rise of Arabic studies in Chapter 1 will suggest.

The development of commercial ties with the Levant and the polarisation of religious rivalries within Christian Europe engendered a doubleness in English comprehension of the Islamic other that could only deepen as the ideological stakes were raised. With the onset of the Civil War, England's longstanding fascination with the Orient, or rather with its own construction of Orient became dislocated, fragmented and rechannelled under the revolutionary pressures of internalised division. As the political and religious certainties upon which old convictions had been built began to crumble, so imaginative engagement with the East was reinvigorated. The result was a radically current, if bewilderingly diverse array of appropriations and representations. As this book will argue, a preoccupation with Islam permeated religious, political, diplomatic and commercial discourses to a degree that has not been recognised by standard accounts of this period. In theological and political animadversions 'the Turk' and his religion could be requisitioned in an apparently limitless number of ways; in questions of natural religion, free will, divine revelation, ecclesiastical sovereignty, liberty of conscience, tyranny and toleration, Islam was repeatedly treated. The overall effect was frequently contradictory but, crucially, always carefully tailored to suit the ideological exigencies of the moment.

The period's drama is a particularly good place to investigate the shifting significance of Islam primarily because of its own protean qualities. Following the official closure of the theatres in 1642, dramatic expression is rendered not only intensely politicised but radically indeterminate, its form and function merging with those of other modes, most notably printed pamphlets and newsbooks. Poised somewhere between the currency of political propaganda and the legacy of theatrical tradition, drama of the 1640s and 1650s is ideally placed to contain and respond to the multiplicity of Islamic representations fashioned by war and revolution. The fluctuating conditions of authorship are thus directly implicated in the changing significance of these representations.

To stage an episode in Persian history in 1641 (John Denham's *The Sophy*) means something radically different from scripting the same episode in printed dialogue in 1655 (Robert Baron's *Mirza*). Similarly sharing the same immediate source material, the differences, but also the similarities, between the first full play to be licitly performed in public under the Protectorate in 1656 (William Davenant's *The Siege of Rhodes*) and in 1665, one of the most popular plays of the early Restoration stage (Roger Boyle's *Mustapha*) are telling indicators of the political and cultural transformations to have taken place in the intervening period. A subsequent revisitation to the same characters in 1676 with the Exclusion Crisis in full swing (Elkanah Settle's *Ibrahim the Illustrious Bassa*) vividly demonstrates the elasticity of such histories. Indeed, a sign of the intimate correlation between theatre and Orient in this period is the fact that the history of its dramatic representation is closely entwined with that of English theatre itself. In this sense, my own study intersects with and corroborates many recent attempts to track broad generic shifts within the drama – the sublimation of tragedy in the 1650s, or the development of the heroic play in the 1660s for example – through their explicit political contexts.[26] As this also suggests, I work from the premise that drama is incontrovertibly political *throughout* this period, albeit far from straightforwardly. Not only were partisan audiences and readers sophisticatedly attuned to the radical potentiality of the drama, but they were positively expected to perform interpretations of their own. Close reading of these plays in the light of English fascination with Islam will go some way towards resuscitating their original significance – indeed attentive and sustained acts of narrative interpretation were part and parcel of the new conditions of reading and writing after the revolution.[27] Allegory may have been as old as literature itself, but the political immediacy of those parallels was felt as never before. Given the close linkage between the seditious connotations of dramatic expression in a time of prohibition and more conventionally political forms of writing, such as the pamphlet, these observations may seem self-evident for the period of Civil War and Protectorate. I shall argue, however, that they are equally applicable after the return of public theatre in 1660. It seems deeply ironic that to take the traditional view of literary critics that the Restoration signalled the triumph of aesthetics over politics is itself uncritically to accept a calculatedly political and specifically royalist version of history. As more recent contributions to our understanding of the period have illustrated, the politics of the Restoration were deeply invested in the conflicts of the mid-century, an intractability that is inevitably reflected in the drama.[28] Despite and perhaps partly

---

[26] Most emphatically, perhaps, Nancy Klein Maguire, *Regicide and Restoration: English Tragicomedy, 1660–1671* (Cambridge: Cambridge University Press, 1992).

[27] For a wide-ranging account of the relationship between revolution and literary dissidence, see Christopher Hill, *A Nation of Change and Novelty: Radical Politics, Religion and Literature in Seventeenth-Century England* (London: Routledge, 1990).

[28] The titles of two recent works suggest the determination of both historians and literary critics to erode the conventional divide of 1660: John Morrill, *After the Civil Wars: English Politics and Government in the Reign of Charles II* (Harlow: Longman, 2000) and Maguire, *Regicide and Restoration*.

because of their status as royally countenanced events, the performances of the new theatre companies were invested with a political currency that could not be simply erased by the outward show of national consensus. Similarly, although highly contingent upon the historical moment of their production and the particular affiliations of the author, dramatic representations of Islam in the Restoration can only be understood in the light of their revolutionary forebears. From Davenant's *Siege of Rhodes* on, the cultural resonance of Islam was instrumental to the ways in which restored drama negotiated the dialectic between past and present, republic and monarchy that persisted long after the king's triumphant return.

To call the drama political, however, is not to presuppose a transparency of purpose or a consistently identifiable credo in any of the plays I shall discuss. Rather, as a site for the playing out of multiple and potentially conflictive ideologies, drama is specifically able to represent the multivalent model of Islam outlined above. Functioning in this way, the Islamic metaphor is a malleable and powerful political weapon precisely because it resists, disrupts and short-circuits uni-dimensional interpretation. Constructs of Islam were not only deployed for use by royalists and republicans to attack each other but admitted a remarkable degree of self-scrutiny. The availability of Islam to dramatists as a means for critiquing their own ideologies and public positions becomes increasingly important with every change in the political scenery. This political multivalence in part derives from the geographical and religious complexities of Islam in the period, which further complicate the task of interpretation. As this suggests, the sheer scope and diversity of ideas available to contemporary writers presents the modern-day historian or literary scholar with a problem of terminology that requires some explanation. The designation 'Turk' so frequently alluded to in the sixteenth and seventeenth centuries is often used as a cover-all term that might mean Muslim or Ottoman or some conflation of the two. Notwithstanding the religious, ethnic and linguistic diversity of the constituents of the polity of the Ottoman Empire, 'Turk' in this latter sense could include any or all peoples inhabiting a vast range of territories, including both Christians and Muslims. Thus, 'Mahometans', or occasionally 'Mussulmen' in contemporary usage, were particularly identified with the extensive Ottoman Empire, reaching its furthest extent in the later seventeenth century and stretching from Hungary to the shores of the Gulf and included the regencies of the North African coast. Further east there was a rival Islamic empire in Persia, which perennially fascinated English writers as a source of doctrinal and military opposition to the Ottomans, as I shall explore in relation to specific plays of the period. 'Orient' goes some way towards encompassing all these meanings but with its post-Romantic connotations of fantastic and exotic otherness, also implying a clear-cut division from 'Occident', is somewhat distant from the sense of political and cultural proximity in the 'here and now' with which I aim to resituate East–West encounters of the seventeenth century. As a conceptual space, despite the often conflatory impulse of English writers, Islam in the sense of 'Dar ul-Islam', the abode of the faithful, was as varied as 'Christendom' and might signify a host of ethnic groups, cultural traditions and geographical locales. I have attempted to encompass this multitude of connotations and distinguish between the various religious and geopolitical senses of the term as befits the context. As I shall argue, the various geographic locations of the plays treating Islam are often highly specific to the political significance of the action.[29]

A focus upon Islam in drama and its political contexts has, therefore, defined to a large extent the historical parameters of the study. The reconstruction of this context is a key element in my reading of specific plays, which focuses quite deliberately upon pivotal moments in that history, an organising theme that has been dictated as much by the positioning of the material as it appears in the archives as the conventional boundaries of historiography. Indeed, although prevalent throughout the period, it is striking to note the correspondence between intense recourse to Islam in the literature, particularly in the drama under consideration, and the crisis points of Revolution, Regicide, Restoration and Exclusion. This is no coincidence, of course, and the overall patterning reveals the recurring eruptions of Islam, as it were along the ideological fault lines of the century's history.

As this implies, this study shares the conviction of many recent literary–historical accounts of the mid-century, manifest for example in the work of David Norbrook and Nigel Smith, whose studies have highlighted ways in which literature was truly revolutionary, not only reflecting the crises in authority that define the period but also were actively and intimately engaged in formulating the very processes of revolution. In this sense, social and political breakdown can be seen as a liberating force, allowing, in Smith's words, for the 'rapid cross-fertilisation of rhetorical components' whereby 'hostile images of the enemy were developed and traded by all interests'.[30] Throughout the military and political confrontation of the 1640s, Islamic representations certainly operated in this way. With the royalist defeat, however, English engagement with Islam was set to intensify still further, culminating in one of the most extraordinary documents of the entire period. Barely four months after the regicide appeared the first full English translation of the Qur'an, fully entitled *The Alcoran of Mahomet, Translated out of Arabique into French; By the Sieur du Ryer, Lord of Malezair, and Resident for the King of France, at Alexandria.* As the title indicates, the translator had no direct knowledge of the text in its original language, but relied on one of the several translations that had been

---

29 The term 'Turk' had already acquired an astonishing multivalency in the political writings of the English Reformation. As Matthew Dimmock has show in his study of Islam and the Ottomans in the earlier period, 'notions of the "turke" and Islam … take a central position in so many aspects of English cultural life in the sixteenth century'. Dimmock, *New Turkes*, p. 16.

30 Nigel Smith, *Literature and Revolution in England 1640–1660* (New Haven and London: Yale University Press, 1994), p. 360.

made from the Arabic into other European languages throughout the century, the Sieur de Ryer's being merely the most recent. Nevertheless, *The Alcoran of Mahomet* is at the epicentre of the explosive fusion of Islam and English politics and is the key textual point of reference to which this study returns in a number of differing contexts. As a translation of a rival sacred text, the traditional embodiment of the Prophet's imposture, the radical implications of the publication are manifold. As subsequent chapters will demonstrate, its initial reception and accompanying polemic leave the political import of the work in little doubt. Yet the epochal appearance of the Qur'an also reflects an increasing bifurcation in English understanding of Islam. The intellectual turmoil of the revolutionary decades was instrumental in sparking a new wave of scholarly interest in the intellectual and religious possibilities of transla- tions from the Arabic, and yet under the pressures of domestic politics the gap between Islam's representation and demonstrable reality seemed to be widening. In one sense, the appearance of the 1649 translation can be seen as a logical step in the process of a new appraisal of Islamic history and culture. In another, however, it symbolised the inevitable conflation and subsequent confusion of the two worlds.

In the language of politics, however, the correlation could articulate alter- native possibilities as well as straightforward enmity. Suggestive in this regard is Steven Zwicker's formulation of the relationship between literature and conflict:

> With the raising of arms in civil combat the verbal stakes had been altered. Literature assumed increasing importance both as a site for and as a way of giving shape and authority to the conduct of polemical argument: to moral triumphalism, to the expression of political resistance, to the assertion of political elevation and authority, to the articulation not simply of criticism within the commonwealth but of alternative social and political orders.[31]

That same function of radicalised literature – to imagine 'alternative social and political orders' – helps towards an understanding of Islam's significance in the constitutional uncertainty of the early Commonwealth and Protectorate.

The degree to which the legitimising precedents of classical history and literary forms were called upon, particularly in the service of the republican cause, has been extensively discussed in recent studies.[32] Hobbes famously denounced access to classical texts as a catalyst for dissent and war:

---

31 Steven N. Zwicker, *Lines of Authority: Politics and English Literary Culture, 1649–1689* (Ithaca and London: Cornell University Press, 1993), p. 10.

32 See particularly David Norbrook, *Writing the English Republic: Poetry, Rhetoric and Politics, 1627–1660* (Cambridge: Cambridge University Press, 1999); Blair Worden, 'Marchamont Nedham and the Beginnings of English Republicanism, 1649–1656', in David Wootton, ed., *Republicanism, Liberty, and Commercial Society, 1649–1776* (Stanford: Stanford University Press, 1994), pp. 45–81.

In these western parts of the world we are made to receive our opinions concerning the institution and rights of Commonwealths from Aristotle, Cicero, and other men, Greeks and Romans, that, living under popular states, derived those rights, not from the principles of nature, but transcribed them into their books out of the practice of their own Commonwealths. ... And by reading of these Greek and Latin authors, men from their childhood have gotten a habit, under a false show of liberty, of favouring tumults, and of licentious controlling the actions of their sovereigns; and again of controlling those controllers; with the effusion of so much blood, as I think I may truly say there was never anything so dearly bought as these western parts have bought the learning of the Greek and Latin tongues.[33]

As Hobbes' qualifier – 'these western parts' – implies, however, there was a different tradition and an alternative model of government to be found in the East. Francis Osborne's *Politicall Reflections upon the Government of the Turks* (1656) is an important example of this comparative strategy. Within the framework of Osborne's critique, the sultan's infamous tyranny was reinterpreted as a paradigm of absolute monarchy, a representation of an effective, even desirable manifestation of the sovereign will over emulous factions. Unlike European monarchies, the author asserts, the Ottoman government fosters a meritocracy in which religious and military authority are made subordinate to that of the sultan. Of course, the idea that the Ottoman polity might be an instructive source for Western statesmanship was nothing new. The identification of the Ottoman sultan as an autocrat *par excellence* was to be found in *Il Principe*, and it is telling that the first edition of Osborne's treatise was accompanied by a discourse upon Machiavelli, a key author for republican theorists of the 1650s, as Jonathan Scott and others have tracked.[34] The Ottoman example was deeply fissured, not least by the fact that, unlike the theory of ancient 'Commonwealths' indicted by Hobbes, this was a political theory in action, visibly and explosively evolving. In its recent history the Ottoman Empire had twice succumbed to the insurrection of both ecclesiastical and military factions, a fact that seemed to belie the exemplary cohesion of Ottoman society as posited by Machiavelli. In his own political manifesto, *Oceana* (1656), James Harrington makes extensive reference to the government of the 'Turks' but significantly modifies his classification of the source of the sultan's personal authority:

---

[33] Thomas Hobbes, *Leviathan*, II.21, ed. C. B. Macpherson (Harmondsworth: Penguin, 1968), p. 268.

[34] Niccolò Machiavelli, *The Prince*, trans., George Bull (Harmondsworth: Penguin, 1981), ch. 4. See Jonathan Scott, *Algernon Sidney and the English Republic, 1623–1677* (Cambridge: Cambridge University Press, 1988); also Gisela Bock, Quentin Skinner and Maurizio Viroli, eds., *Machiavelli and Republicanism* (Cambridge: Cambridge University Press, 1990).

> If one man be sole landlord of a territory, or overbalance the people, for example, three parts in four, he is grand seignior; for so the Turk is called from his property, and his empire is absolute monarchy.[35]

By shifting the emphasis from an empire built upon dominion over the hearts and minds of its people, to one of 'property' ownership, Harrington is able to maintain the absolutism of the sultan. Nevertheless, he identifies a dangerous 'flaw' that characterised comparisons between English and Ottoman political systems in the recurring debates over the presence of a standing army:

> But for a monarchy by arms, as that of the Turk (which, of all models that ever were, comes up to the perfection of the kind), it is not in the wit or power of man to cure it of this dangerous flaw, that the Janizaries have frequent interest and perpetual power to raise sedition, and to tear the magistrate, even the prince himself, in pieces. Therefore the monarchy of Turkey is no perfect government.[36]

When the English republic finally collapsed, the acquiescence of the army under General Monck would prove instrumental in reconstituting monarchical authority. Widely expressed anxieties aroused by the role of military power in the projection of national identity are once again mediated through the figure of the Turk both on and off the Restoration stage. Even more fundamentally though, tropes of conversion and apostasy, specifically situated in Islamic history, are at the forefront of ways in which English writers addressed the problem of rapidly altered public loyalties in the early years of Restoration. Whilst ostensibly celebrating a new and renewed political and moral order, dramatists were inevitably caught up in the process of obsessive retrospection.

When political events of the 1670s seemed to many to replay those of the 1640s, drama returned once again to Islam. At the centre of this crisis was liberty of conscience, although its meaning had radically shifted from the rallying call of puritan revolutionaries to the suspected means by which popery and arbitrary government might be stealthily introduced. With a renewed emphasis upon the fragility of the succession, models of Islamic sovereignty and familial rivalries are appropriated by both emergent oppositional factions and loyalists determined to defend the sacred institution of monarchy against those who would apparently seek to plunge the nation once more into the abyss of a second civil war.

In the intervening period, the nation had undergone unprecedented upheaval and transformation in the space of what, it is astonishing to remember, is not much more than a single generation. Indeed, several of the protagonists of the story told in the succeeding pages not only witnessed but also actively

[35] James Harrington, *Commonwealth of Oceana*, in *Political Works of James Harrington*, ed. J. G. A. Pocock (Cambridge: Cambridge University Press, 1977), p. 163.
[36] Harrington, *Commonwealth of Oceana*, p. 179.

participated in every stage of that transformation through Civil War, Republic and Restoration. Playwrights like Davenant and Boyle were soldiers in the armed conflict whilst others like Settle were active propagandists as well as popular dramatists. Some, like the Arabist Edward Pococke and the diplomat Paul Rycaut, were informed by their own travels in the Levant whilst others like Francis Osborne and Robert Baron considered themselves thoroughly conversant in the culture and history of Islam without ever setting foot out of the study. The mobility of ideas between these ostensibly disparate forms is perhaps best exemplified by the life and writings of Henry Stubbe, sometime soldier for Cromwell, and apologist for Charles II, correspondent with Pococke and Hobbes and biographer of the Prophet. Through such networks, ideas of Islam were transmitted through every stratum of English society, vitally connecting drama, diplomacy, political philosophy and propaganda.

The first chapter surveys Anglo-Islamic encounters in the period, demonstrating the correlation between trade and diplomatic exchange and intellectual and religious transmissions, revealing not only the sustained engagement with the East in the literary–political expression but the exhilarating valency of the Islamic metaphor, a set of complex and often contradictory ideas deployed by writers of every political complexion. One encounter in particular, the celebrated visit of the Moroccan ambassador Kaid Mohammed ben Hadu in 1682, recorded in Evelyn's diary and elsewhere, provides further evidence for the perceived reciprocity between the two cultures. Reports of the embassy are read in the context of ongoing clashes with pirates from the North African ports as well as the precarious position of the beleaguered English garrison at Tangiers, the only English toehold on Muslim territory, and offer an insight into the cultural, religious and political considerations underpinning English representations throughout the period.

In Chapter 2, the anonymous pamphlet play *The Famous Tragedie of King Charles I* (1649) is read in the context of the first English translation of the Qur'an, contemporaneously published and defended in print by Charles' former chaplain Alexander Ross, four months after the king's execution. Whilst the play's enthusiastic appropriation of a range of ideas deriving from Islam points to the disruption of traditional representations in the wake of the regicide, the circumstances surrounding the translation itself underline the radical implications of its appearance in the volatile climate of 1649.

Chapter 3 turns to the political currency of Islam in the Protectorate, examining Robert Baron's *Mirza* (1655), a closet drama treating Persian history; a comparison with an earlier rendition of the story by John Denham in *The Sophy* (1642) draws out some crucial differences between the two responses situated at either end of a political and dramatic revolution in England. A close textual reading of *Mirza* demonstrates ways in which the Persian model provided a means to address contested and unstable notions of tyranny and religious conscience in the 1650s.

Pursuant to this, Chapter 4 reappraises William Davenant's *The Siege of Rhodes* (1663), which spans the gap between Protectorate and Restoration renditions of the Ottoman Empire, representing a critical departure in treatments of Islamic history, with a radically 'Christian Turk' at its heart. With the reopening of the public stage, Islam continues to play a prominent part in the drama, and Davenant's play inaugurates a re-evaluation of longstanding tropes of conversion and, in particular, the figure of the English renegade, in relation to the political exigencies of the day.

Chapter 5 takes Robert Boyle's *Mustapha* (1668) as an example of how the Islamic model became newly compelling to English writers prompted to address the vexed questions of allegiance and apostasy that plagued public life. Returning to the interrelationship between trade and politics, the chapter also examines the writings of Paul Rycaut, representative of the Levant Company and secretary of the ambassador at Constantinople in the 1660s. His continuation of Richard Knolles' influential *General Historie of the Turkes* indicates a continuing fascination with Islamic history, recapitulated in the light of domestic upheaval and burgeoning trade. The first of Elkanah Settle's 'Oriental' tragedies, *Cambyses King of Persia* (1667), links the perennial problem of loyalty with that of legitimacy and is an early example of the role of Islam in the oppositional cause. These themes are consolidated through an analysis of Henry Stubbe's revolutionary tract, *An Account of the Rise of Mahometanism* (c.1673). Circulated in manuscript, Stubbe's *Account* represents the most sympathetic and radical treatment of Islam in English to date.

The final chapter develops the argument by reading Settle's preoccupation with political orients manifest in his spectacularly successful *Empress of Morocco* (1673) and *Ibrahim the Illustrious Bassa* (1676) in the light of the renewed significance of Islam in the Exclusion Crisis of the 1670s. The enduring universality of Islam is evinced in a play that responds directly to the attempts of exclusionists to discredit the Duke of York as a Catholic despot in waiting. Unlike Settle's popular spectacles, however, Nevil Payne's *Siege of Constantinople* (1675) remains staunchly supportive of the Stuart monarchy, portraying the notorious fall of this Christian outpost as the handiwork of a scheming chancellor, whose ambition is unchecked by a factious and ineffectual counsel. Outside the drama, the remarkable prevalence of the Turk in the bitter polemical exchanges that accompanied the revelations of Titus Oates and his Popish Plot is analysed in the context of the news of the final Ottoman advance westwards. Following the subsequent destruction of Islam's most vaunted imperial army at the gates of Vienna, this extraordinary period in England's self-reflexive engagement with a supposedly alien historical and cultural tradition begins to draw to a close.

Chapter 1

CULTURAL ENCOUNTERS BETWEEN ENGLAND AND ISLAM IN THE SEVENTEENTH CENTURY: A TOPOGRAPHY

WHEN NEWS OF THE death of James I reached the sublime Porte, Sultan Murad IV formally conveyed his condolences to the English residency there in what Sir Thomas Roe describes as 'a civility and honour never formerly used to any Christian prince'.[1] Roe, English ambassador at Constantinople between 1621 and 1628, had adroitly managed English affairs, renegotiating a favourable trade agreement (the so-called 'capitulations'), and winning the gratitude of the Levant Company and the esteem of his Ottoman hosts. Notwithstanding the celebrated (and chiefly rhetorical) zeal of his sovereign against the 'infidel Turk',[2] Roe had overseen a period of mutually lucrative cooperation between the two nations: by 1626 the Levant Company was exporting £250,000 of goods per annum, reciprocated by an equally valuable amount of imports.[3] Whilst frequently interfering with the affairs of the Company, however, it seems that Charles was content to leave direct diplomatic representations to his official envoys, that is until 1642.

> We understand by Our Embassadour Resident with You, with how much Honour and respect, the death of Our dear Lord and Father (of ever glorious memory) was condoled at your Imperiall Port : and if the signification thereof, and of Our peacable succession to these Crownes, have not in all this time come unto you immediately from Our self, it hath not been through any default of Our affection, or respect to You, but many important affairs upon *Our* first Access, and the dangerous troubles wherewith *Our* City of *London* and many other principall parts of our Kingdome have been (and at this time are) infected with; have diverted Us, and forced Us to defer these offices longer than we intended or

---

[1] Sir Thomas Roe, *The Negotiations in his embassy to the Ottoman Porte from 1621 to 1628* (London: 1740), p. 412; Dorothy M. Vaughan, *Europe and the Turk: A Pattern of Alliances 1350–1700* (Liverpool: University Press, 1954), p. 241.

[2] As a boy, James had composed an encomium of the famous victory of the Holy League over the Turks at Lepanto.

[3] Alfred C. Wood, *A History of the Levant Company* (Oxford: Oxford University Press, 1935), p. 42.

desired; and as we hope You will : For these important Reasons, readily and freely execute those omissions which in so weighty occasions may well be dispersed withal.[4]

In reality, such sentiments were rather more belated than Charles apparently realised: 'Sultan Morat Han', or Murad IV, had died more than two years before. Dated 1 August 1642, Charles' letter goes on to ratify the treaties negotiated by Roe with Algiers and Tunis, urging the sultan to uphold the customs agreements in his dominions whilst protesting at the actions of Barbary corsairs in the region. A frequent bone of contention in diplomatic exchanges of the period, the prevalent threat of piracy forms a continual backdrop to the practice of Mediterranean trade, irrespective of nominal nationality – the sultan's original address to Charles had itself included a complaint against English privateering. Most intriguing of all, however, is the reason intimated for this sudden recollection of diplomatic manners. Those 'dangerous troubles' to which the king refers are plainly not the cause of his delay in responding, but the incentive for responding at all. Equally disingenuous is Charles' somewhat anachronistic characterisation of English representation at the Porte. As I shall later discuss in more detail, by the time of writing, English prestige was waning and with Roe having long since relinquished the embassy, the controversial Sir Sackville Crowe was proving a source of friction between the Crown, the Company and its merchants.

Even as the letter was making its way to Constantinople, the prospect of civil war at home was looming large. A month earlier, Parliament had voted to raise an army in order to protect 'the safety of the King's person', and on 22 August the royal standard was itself raised in Nottingham. Taken in isolation, the full implications of Charles' tentative approach to 'the Ottoman Kingdom' remain inconclusive. Nevertheless, and despite his apparent ignorance of the latest incumbent, like every Englishman exposed to the media of newsbook and sermon, play and pamphlet, the king was well aware that the empire had only recently undergone its own ordeal of civil turmoil.[5] Perhaps rather ominously for Charles, the single event continually remembered and rehearsed by English writers was the regicide of Sultan Osman II. Following the death of Ahmed I in 1617, the throne was briefly taken by his brother Mustafa I who, having escaped the traditional law of fratricide, had been confined in the imperial palace for much of his life and soon proved himself incapable of government. Returning Mustafa to his prison after only three months, the

4 *King Charles his Letter to the Great Turk: the High and Mighty Emperour Sultan Morat Han: Chiefe Lord and Commander of the Ottoman Kingdom* (London, 1642), A2r–A3v.
5 For a recent and authoritative account of Ottoman rivalries in the region that also incorporates much valuable information concerning domestic events, see Kenneth M. Setton, *Venice, Austria, and the Turks in the Seventeenth Century* (Philadelphia: The American Philosophical Society, 1991). A broader overview is offered in Paul Coles, *The Ottoman Impact on Europe* (London: Thames & Hudson, 1968).

Janissaries imposed Osman, Ahmed's fourteen-year-old son, in his place. Following an unsuccessful campaign against Poland in 1621, however, the young sultan's authority was being seriously undermined by sedition within the Ottoman army. In what was later to be recounted as a salutary example to English governments, the standing army that had been traditionally perceived as the backbone of Ottoman imperialism was now a civil liability. Pointedly rehearsing the political tumults of 1620s Turkey from the vantage point of late Protectorate England, an unidentified pamphleteer takes up the story:

> *Sed fourtuna vitrea est, cum splendet maxima frangitur.* This young Prince was scarce well warm in his fathers Seat: But taking discontent at his souldiery, especially the Janizaries, he had a design upon them to disband and disarme them, if not wholly destroy them, and erect another Militia in their roome. To cover which designe of his the better, he gave out a pretension of a *Voiage to Mecha*, to visit the Sepulchre of their great Prophet, from which undertaking no Reasons, Advises, Petitions could disswade him, although the souldiery passed so far, as to threaten publickly, and to protest they would not follow, but rather set up another King in his absence. ... On *Wednesday* the seventh of *May* in the year of 1622, while his Tents and other accomodations for his journey were passing over unto *Asia*-side, the *Janizaries* and *Spahies* suddenly met at the *Hyppodrome* in the City, upon a word given, and from thence ran to the *Seraglio*, which is the great *Turks* palace, in tumult, and there cryed out for the King, who appeared to them, asked what this insolency meant, and what they pretended? ... But the *Aga* of the *Janizaries* thinking to merit of the king, and beginning to plead unseasonably for him, with some harsh words of upbraidure, anew moved their fury, so that they cryed out TREASON, and fell upon him and *Huzein Bassa*, and cut them in pieces. ... Now the poor *Osman* saw his friends slain, and knew not which way to turne himself; but binding up his eyes with a napkin, expected death as the last of their fury. ... At last they consulted with themselves ... and sent him away prisoner to the seven Towers. ...The souldiers now thought all was done, and onely sacking the houses of Huzein Bassa, and some others, returned in quiet to their lodgings, and had no further malice. But the new Vizier *Daout Bassa* made by *Mustapha*, knew well if Osman lived, that this storm might passe over ... the Vizier went himself to the prison with a pack of hangmen, and gave order to strangle the unfortunate Prince. ... Thus one of the greatest Monarchs in the world was first *affronted* by his mutinied Troops, his own slaves, almost unarm'd, and few in number, no man taking up sword to defend him; and they who first began this madnesse, not meaning to *hurt him*, by the encrease of their own fury, which had no bounds, *deposed him against their own purpose*; and at *last exposed his life against their will, to the counsels of other men, whom they equally hated.*[6]

---

[6] *Learne of a Turk or Instructions and Advice sent from the* Turkish *Army at* Constantinople, *to the* English *army at* London. *Faithfully and Impartially communicated by M.B. one of the Attendants of the* English *agent there* (London, 1660), pp. 1–6.

The circumstances of Osman's demise were most likely gleaned from Roe's contemporary account, which was specifically directed to the attention of the king[7], a version of which featured in Samuel Purchas' *Pilgrimes*. According to Roe, the precedent of king-killing and its attendant blood bath signalled the end of Ottoman hegemony:

> Your Lordship may behold in a dymme glasse our motions: fit matter for Ben Jonson. If I durst augure, I would, by these beastes entrails, that are daily butchered, pronounce the imminent ruine of this great monarchy, now, I think, yrrecouerably sick.[8]

In the context of the 1620s, the notion that the political intrigue at the Porte might provide 'fit matter' for the English stage is both current and extraordinarily prescient. The easy slippage between political and theatrical stages is characteristic of representations of Islam throughout the century, but Roe's prophecy that the bloody tribulations of Empire might offer a 'dymme glasse' to English spectators was to be fulfilled in ways unimaginable to the king's ambassador.

In the years immediately following the army's insurrection, Roe's diagnosis looked to be borne out. The so-called 'mad' Sultan Mustafa was installed on the throne once more and yet again proved incapable of uniting an increasingly factious militia. As successive grand viziers fell and the court became increasingly susceptible to intrigue and venality, a rebellion in Anatolia prompted a new consensus in Istanbul, born of self-preservation. In 1623, Mustafa was once again deposed, this time in favour of Murad, younger brother of the assassinated Osman. Whilst the new sultan waited to attain his majority, effective power lay in the hands of his mother Kösem and crises continued to beset the empire both at home and abroad. Under the command of Abaza Mehemmed, rebel forces in Asia Minor continued to defy the jurisdiction of the central authorities whilst a renewal of war with Persia led to the loss of Baghdad. However, by the time of the publication of Charles' letter to the sultan, the empire, under the ruthless charge of the mature Murad IV, had undergone somewhat of a revival. In 1632, rebel Janissaries once more invaded the sacred precincts of the Seraglio, demanding the execution of Murad's favourites in an uncanny repetition of the events leading up to the murder of his brother ten years before. Having been initially forced to concede the execution of his Grand Vizier Hafiz Pasha, however, the enraged sultan countered by luring the rebel leader to his own death, effectively strangling any further resistance to his authority. From this point on, Murad ruled with a severe and often arbitrary sway, fulfilling the European archetype of the Turkish tyrant perhaps more

7   Sir Thomas Roe, *A true and faithfull relation, presented to his Maiestie and the prince ... concerning the death of Sultan Osman, and the setting up of Mustafa his uncle. Together with other memorable occurrents worthy of obseruation* (London, 1622).
8   Sir Thomas Roe, *The Negotiations*, p. 126.

potently than any sultan since Mehmet III.[9] Unflinching repression at home was accompanied by a newly invigorated foreign policy; in 1635, the province of Erivan was recaptured from the Persians and three years later, Baghdad itself was recovered after a bloody massacre of its inhabitants.

The extraordinary events leading up to Murad's accession and the notoriety of his reign left a unique and indelible print on the imaginations of seventeenth-century Englishmen. After his death in 1640, Ahmed's youngest son, Ibrahim, succeeded to the sultanate, but failed to maintain the disciplined government of his brother. Once again, eight years into his reign, the Janissaries challenged the authority of the sultan, although this time their calls for reform of the harem and the execution of the grand vizier were joined by those of both the Mufti and sipahis. However, details of the latest constitutional crisis appear to have reached England only slowly. Whilst the State Papers do not record any particular acknowledgement of the events of 1648, the newsbook *The Moderate Intelligencer* for the week commencing 5 October, could only report that 'Two ships arrived here from *Constantinople* the eleventh of this instant, make no mention of the rising of the Janizaries, against the great Turke; although that here 'tis confirmed both from *Buda*, and *Bosnia*, that he hath been deposed by reason of his Incapacity.'[10] Meanwhile, the domestic news was dominated by the final manoeuvrings of those determined to bring the king to account. Parliament's vote of 'No Address' had broken off negotiations with the imprisoned monarch, branding him a 'Man of Blood'. The revelation that the king had been engaged in last-ditch negotiations with Presbyterian members of the house only strengthened the resolve of Cromwell, who, with the weight of the army behind him, purged the parliament of meaningful opposition and, in effect, sealed the king's fate. In the wake of Charles' execution, however, a pamphlet did finally appear, containing *A True Relation of what passed in Constantinople, In August last, about the deposing of the Great Emperour Sultan Hibraim, And the crowning of his Sonne Sultan Mehemet in his place.* According to the anonymous author,

> As the evill carriage of the *Sultan Hibraim*, Emperour of the *Turks*, had of long time alienated from him the hearts of the most parts of his Subjects, and chiefly of his Militia, not accustomed to endure : So their discontents being come to a greater height by extraordinary oppressions, this Militia resolved to free themselves from them by making away the first *Vizier* and by deposing of the grand *Seignior* himselfe ... [relates the strangulation of the Vizier and the setting up of Ibrahim's seven-year-old son as sultan]. ... The whole Militia being in the Courts of the *Seralia* and there-about, cryed presently, GOD SAVE SULTAN MEHEMET : Which being done, every one went home; And the 9th of the said

---

9   Upon his accession in 1595, Mehmet had ordered the executions of nineteen of his younger
    brothers, after which the policy of fratricide was abandoned by the Ottoman constitution.

10   *The Moderate Intelligencer: Impartially communicating Martiall Affairs to the kingdom of
     England. From Th. Oct. 5 to Th. Oct. 12, 1648,* no. 180, p. 1681.

month *August* last, the conclusion of the businesse was, That the new *Vizier*, and the Officers of the Militia, with a great number of *Janizaries* and *Spatris* came backe againe to the *Seralia*, where they confined the unhappy *Sultan Hibraim* to a chamber; which is the same prison where he hath been kept many years in the reign of *Sultan Amura*.[11]

What is glaringly, and surely deliberately, omitted from the account is the sultan's murder. Ibrahim was indeed imprisoned in the Seraglio, but threatened by a resurgence of support for his reinstatement, the Mufti sanctioned a death sentence; the ultimate 'conclusion of the businesse' was not imprisonment but regicide. The author (or perhaps authoriser) of this particularly sanitised version of events is clearly anxious to downplay any suggestion of a correlation between the virtually contemporaneous execution of two monarchs, one English, one Ottoman. In the observation that Ibrahim's 'evill carriage … had of long time alienated from him the hearts of the most parts of his Subjects', there is perhaps a faint echo of the charges levied against Charles, but on the subject of England's new order the pamphlet is deafeningly silent. Nevertheless, it is hard to imagine that in 1649 an English reader of *A True Relation* could fail to read between these lines. Instead, the kind of explicit paralleling that events at Constantinople and London seemed to invite so irresistibly surfaced across the Channel where many of the late king's supporters found themselves in exile. Published in Paris, also in 1649, the verse dialogue *L'entreueue du Sultan Hibrim Empereur des Turcs: et du roy d'angleterre* imagines a meeting between the two murdered monarchs in the Elysian fields.[12] Charles greets the sultan with a conventional taunt:

> *Le Roy:* Ou courrez vous donc Empereur,
> Vous qui sustes nostre terreur,
> Qui nous faisiez tousiours la guerre
> Soit sur la mer ou sur la terre,
> Que faites vous parmy ces lieux,
> Deuiez vous pas monter aux Cieux,
> Auev Mahomet le prophete?[13]

Here are two of the attributes most commonly ascribed to the Ottoman Turk by Western writers: the 'terreur' of his military puissance and the fraudulence of his religion, based upon the teachings of a false prophet. As the two tell their stories, however, differences in religious ideology are soon forgotten in

[11] *A True Relation of what passed in Constantinople, In August last, about the deposing of the Great Emperour Sultan Hibraim, And the crowning of his Sonne Sultan Mehemet in his place. Printed in the year MDCXLIX* (London, 1649), pp. 1–6.
[12] A brief account of the poem is given in C. D. Rouillard, *The Turk in French History, Thought and Literature 1520–1660* (Paris: Boivin & Co., 1940).
[13] 'The King: Where are you running to Emperor,/ You who have been our terror,/ Who was always making war,/ Whether at sea or on land,/ What are you doing here in these environs,/ Should you not rise to Heaven,/ With Mahomet the prophet?', A2r.

lieu of a general condemnation of the treason by which the two sovereigns were betrayed; Cromwell is singled out with especial vitriol as a perfidious malefactor, unique amongst 'les peoples d'Occident'.

At first glance, the fact that such a provocative comparison should not appear in London but abroad would seem self-explanatory. Having briefly repealed state control of the press with the abolition of the Star Chamber in 1641, by 1649 Parliament was vigorously enforcing its own censorship legislation, authorizing the Stationer's Company to destroy unlicensed presses and publications, and to arrest printers and authors involved in the production and distribution of 'forged, scandalous, seditious, libellous, and unlicensed Papers, Pamphlets, and Books to the great defamation of Religion and government'.[14] The anomaly, however, is also indicative of a more general trend in the formulation of English representations of Islam in the period.

'[T]HE WEALTH OF ARABY': INTELLECTUAL AND RELIGIOUS TRANSMISSIONS

As the Parisian dialogue suggests, when employed in the service of polemic, religious differences between East and West could often be crudely delineated. From the sixteenth century, however, Western Europe had seen the emergence of a distinct group of writers and theologians who were equipped, ostensibly at least, for a more informed appreciation of this rival religion: the Arabists. The first centres for the study of Arabic grew up in Catholic Europe. In Paris, Hebrew and Arabic had been taught at the University since at least 1517 when the Italian scholar Agostino Giustiniani was invited to lecture there; by 1538, Arabic studies were firmly established with the installation of Guillaume Postel who took the first Arabic chair in Europe. In Rome, where a substantial collection of Oriental manuscripts was already being accumulated, the foundation of the first Arabic printing press, under the patronage of Cardinal Ferdinand de Medici in 1584, signalled the Vatican's commitment to the production and dissemination of Arabic texts. Approximately ten years later, Franciscus Raphelengius set up a second press in Leiden and held the professorship there himself.[15] Thus, representatives of both Catholic and Protestant Europe

---

[14] *Order for the Regulation of Printing* (14 June, 1643). This ordinance was the occasion for Milton's celebrated defence of a free press, *Areopagitica* (1644). Characteristically, Milton conflates the 'Antichristian' forces of Catholic Europe with those of the Ottoman Empire in his indictment of licensing, which, with 'malice and mystery on set purpose to extinguish, if it were possible, the light of Reformation, and to settle falsehood; little differing from that policy wherewith the Turk upholds his Alcoran, by the prohibition of printing'. John Milton, *Areopagitica*, in *The Complete Prose Works of John Milton*, ed. D. M. Wolfe, 8 vols. (New Haven and London: Yale University Press, 1966), vol. 2, p. 505.

[15] The most comprehensive account of Arabic study in the period is that of Toomer, *Eastern Wisedome and Learning*.

showed themselves deeply invested in the intellectual and perhaps economic benefits to be reaped from Arabic learning.

In comparison to its continental neighbours, however, England was slow to embrace this burgeoning discipline. It was not until 1612 that an English writer made the first published contribution to Arabic scholarship in the form of a translation of the Epistles of John. William Bedwell did not, however, benefit from the logistical or institutional support of his European counterparts and was forced to make the journey to Leiden in order to publish both the Arabic original and his Latin translation. In fact, despite Bedwell's attempt to procure an intact set of Arabic types from the Raphelengius brothers (who had inherited the press from their father), the facilities to produce Arabic type were not to exist in England for at least another thirty-five years. When Bedwell died in 1632, his life's work, an expansive Arabic dictionary, remained unpublished.[16] In 1615, however, Bedwell had published a curious treatise that, in typical English fashion, was poised somewhere between an attack on Islam and a call for a greater understanding of its language and religion. Entitled *Mohammedis Imposturae: That is, A Discovery of the Manifold Forgeries, Falshoods, and horrible impieties of the blasphemous seducer MOHAMMED* [etc.], the main body of the work consists of a translation of an ancient Arabic text reporting a conference purportedly '*had between two Mohametans, in their return from Mecha*'. Naturally enough, their conversation turns into a refutation of the Prophet and the Qur'an. Also typical of English treatments in the period, however, is the impulse to compare the 'Falshoods' of Islam with other examples of professed wisdom, both political and religious. In his preface 'To the Christian Reader', Bedwell adopts a rhetorical positioning that would recur throughout the century:

> For in the Alkoran, saith a learned Divine, there is no one opinion so impious & wicked, which may not be found in the bookes of those writers which I have before spoken of; to wit, *Irenaeus, Tertullian*, The Ecclesiastical historians, *Epiphanius, Philastrius*, and *Augustine*; whose bookes do breed well nere as oft as conies: And the printers do thereby reape no small gaines, and withal do deserve very well of all good students. Some things also, in the discoveries of old heresies, are met withal, more absurd and grosse, then the Alkoran doth afford any.[17]

Thus, alongside the conventional condemnation of the heretical 'Alkoran' is a defiant justification for its study. Appended to the dialogue are two more treatises, *The Arabian Trudgman* and an *Index of the Chapters of the Alkoran*, making Bedwell's publication a seminal point in the history of English Qur'anic studies. The former simply constitutes a glossary of offices held in Islamic society. His *Index*, however, with its translation and occasional anno-

---

16 See Alistair Hamilton, *William Bedwell the Arabist, 1563–1632* (Leiden: E. J. Brill, 1985).
17 William Bedwell, *Mohammedis Imposturae* (London, 1615), A3r–A4v.

tation of each 'Assurat' of the Qur'an, was the first step towards the organised study of the Islamic holy text in England.

However, it was not until 1632 that the nascent study of Arabic was finally secured a future with the foundation of the first chair of Arabic at Cambridge. Inaugurated by Thomas Adams, a wealthy London merchant, the first professorship was awarded to Abraham Wheelocke, a fellow graduate of Trinity College. Two years later, Oxford followed suit with the appointment of Edward Pococke, a former pupil of Bedwell's, and chaplain to the Aleppo factory of the Levant Company. This time, the endowment was made by Archbishop Laud, then chancellor of Oxford University, who seems to have been a keen collector of Arabic manuscripts in his own right. An entry in the *Calendar of State Papers* for February 1634 entitled 'The King to the Turkey Company' demonstrates the prelate's willingness to commandeer the resources of state and private enterprise in order to augment his own, and ultimately the Bodleian's collection:

> The King has also considered that there is a great deal of learning fit to be known written in Arabic, and great scarcity of Arabic and Persian books in this country, wherefore he requires that every ship of that company at every voyage shall bring home one Arabic or Persian manuscript book, to be delivered to the master of the company, and by him to the Archbishop of Canterbury, who shall dispose of them as the King shall think fit, provided that the books so to be brought be any other than Alkarons, because there is a great choice of them here already.[18]

Clearly, the activities of the Levant Company were crucial in the propagation of the texts required to feed the new intellectual industry and, in Pococke's case, to the actual acquisition of the requisite linguistic skills. When Pococke was elected to the chaplaincy of the Levant Company in 1629, his Oriental studies had already benefited from the lectures of the German Arabist Matthew Pasor at Oxford as well as the supervision of Bedwell himself, and had resulted in the publication of his first work in the field, *Versio et notae ad quatuor epistolas Syricae* (1630), an edition of the previously unpublished four parts of the Syriac version of the New Testament. Now from his residency at Aleppo, Pococke had the opportunity to develop his proficiency in spoken as well as written Arabic.[19] It was here too, that Pococke pursued his lifelong devotion to

---

18 *Calendar of State Papers, Domestic, Charles I. 1633–34*, ed. Mary Anne Everett Green (London: HMSO, 1878), pp. 476–7. All subsequent footnoted references will be abbreviated to C.S.P. and will include the relevant year and page number.

19 According to his eighteenth-century biographer, in Aleppo, Pococke learned both 'Syriack' and 'Ethiopick', 'But Arabick, the most learned and general Language of the East, was the subject of his greatest Industry and Application, for farther instruction in which, he agreed with a *Sheikh* or Doctor, call'd *Phatallah*, to come to him frequently, and entertain'd, as a Servant, by the Year, one *Hamet*, chiefly for this End, I suppose, that he might on every Occasion converse familiarly in it.' Leonard Twells, *The Theological Works of the Learned Dr. Pocock. … To which is prefixed, An Account of his Life and Writings never before printed* (London, 1740), vol. 1, p. 6.

the collection of Eastern manuscripts, many commissioned by Laud himself. By the time Pococke was to return to England in 1641, the state of the nation had radically altered, and with it, the apparent future of Arabic studies in England. Earlier in the year, Laud had moved to safeguard the professorship by extending the endowment in perpetuity, prompting the following tribute from the university:

> You have greatly enriched the Bodleia-Laudian treasury, by importing Araby to Oxford, but when this store of literature reached us, being confined to books it remained mute, being restrained by its unknown characters; but when a stipend was attached as a key, with a lecturer to unlock the learning of Barbary, the tongue was loosed. Even so it was not made immortal, as it hung on the single thread of your existence, which we hope indeed may be immortal. Then this difficulty was remedied by your untiring munificence, an annual rent from your ancestral lands being conferred upon it. Your patronage of the Arabic language far surpasses the wealth of Araby; being Arabized by you we must necessarily be either happy Arabians or Rocky Arabians; happy if we yield due obedience to your mandates, but otherwise stony and arid.[20]

In only a matter of months, platitudinous hopes for the archbishop's immortality would seem absurdly misplaced; in December of that year Laud was impeached for treason, subsequently imprisoned in the Tower and finally executed in 1644. Just as the study of Arabic was beginning to establish itself in England, it looked set to be uprooted by the maelstrom of civil war. Following Edgehill and the king's retreat to Oxford, the rarefied environs of the colleges had been transformed into virtual garrisons. The college where Pococke had probably delivered his first lecture, Christ Church, was designated as the royal residence and whilst the great hall hosted meetings of the king's counsel, the college quadrangle was converted into a cattle pen.[21] Disruption of scholarly pursuits of all kinds was inevitable and, with his fortune so closely tied to that of his disgraced patron, Pococke's position looked increasingly precarious. Nevertheless, as Toomer has demonstrated, whilst the revolution heralded a series of 'personal difficulties and persecutions' for the Orientalist, these years must also have been a time of great scholarly productivity. In 1642, Pococke had been granted the living of Childrey, Berkshire but was constantly harassed there for his perceived royalism and Laudian associations. In 1644, following the sequestration of Laud's estates, he lost the stipend from his Arabic chair, the payment of which was only restored three years later thanks to the intervention of Selden, Greaves and Langbaine. Oxford fell to Parliamentary troops in 1647 and, following the execution of the king, Pococke, having avoided the mandatory 'engagement' or oath of allegiance, was again threatened with the

---

20 Quoted in G. A. Russell, ed., *The 'Arabick' Interest of the Natural Philosophers in Seventeenth-Century England* (Leiden: E. J. Brill, 1994), p. 9.
21 Frederick John Varley, *The Siege of Oxford: An Account of Oxford During the Civil War, 1642–1646* (Oxford: Oxford University Press, 1932).

loss of his ecclesiastical and academic positions. In the event, Pococke hung on to the Hebrew and Arabic chairs and, in the midst of these vicissitudes, succeeded in publishing his groundbreaking *Specimen historae Arabum* (1650), a densely annotated edition of Abu 'l Faraj's thirteenth-century history, and the culmination of his diligent study of Arabic manuscript sources.

In Cambridge, Wheelocke's studies encountered less disruption but, owing to the lack of the necessary Arabic type, there was to be no equivalent publication there. In the early years of the Protectorate, however, the scholarly energies of both universities were devoted to the great theological and linguistic project of the mid-century – Brian Walton's Polyglot Bible. Both Pococke and Wheelocke were among the host of scholars who collaborated in its four-year production.[22] The first volume of the *Biblia Sacra Polyglotta* appeared in 1654 with a dedication to Cromwell.[23] As the *Calendar of State Papers* records, despite his suspect record,[24] Walton's undertaking received the support of the Council of State in the form of a dispensation to waive the duty on the importation of the paper needed for its production.

> The readiness of the Protector and Council to favour this design of printing the Bible, in the original and other learned languages, encourages the undertakers to beg a warrant for 3,000 reams of paper, custom free, for printing an introduction and guide to the 9 languages, viz., Hebrew, Chaldee, Samaritan, Syriac, Arabic, Persian, Aethiopic, Armenian, and Coptic, without which it will be to most a sealed book. We ask it not for our own interest, but for God's glory, the advancement of religion, and the honour of our nation.[25]

The volume in question appeared in 1655 under the title *Introductio Ad lectionem Lingarum Orientalum* and became a valuable aid, not only to biblical scholars but to those engaged in the study of Arabic and other languages in their own right. Previous polyglots, most notably those produced in Antwerp (1571–80) and Paris (1629–57), laid the foundation for Walton's project but his was unique in its scope, augmenting the standard Hebrew and Greek with the related languages listed above. In this regard, the publication of the monumental London Polyglot constitutes a landmark of English Orientalism and exemplifies the chief motivation for the pursuit of Arabic studies in the period. As the terms of Laud's instruction to the Levant merchants and the university's commendation of 'the wealth of Araby' both indicate, the longstanding

[22] Walton's entry in the *Dictionary of National Biography* lists the correcting committee as consisting of 'Stokes, Wheelock, Thorndike, Pococke, Greaves, Vicars, and Thomas Smith; on the death of Wheelock in 1653, Hyde was substituted for him ...'.
[23] Later editions were modified to include a prefatory dedication to Charles II.
[24] Walton had been deprived of his living at St Martin's Orgar in 1641. Amongst the papers of the Thomason collection is a pamphlet entitled 'The articles and charge proved in parliament against Doctor Walton, Minister of St. Martins Orgars in Cannon Street, wherein his subtile tricks, and popish innovations are discovered. ...' (1641).
[25] *C.S.P.*, 1655, p. 234.

belief that Arabic held the key to ancient stores of knowledge was still current. Whilst the prestige of Arabic texts, particularly in the fields of medicine and astronomy, had been maintained throughout the Renaissance, by the seventeenth century the *language* that had been traditionally credited with the preservation of the knowledge of ancient writers, both Eastern and Western, was deemed to be increasingly obsolete. The real fuel for this resurgence of interest in the Arabic language in the seventeenth century was religious controversy and, in this regard, Civil War and Protectorate England provided fertile soil. Thus, in the name of biblical exegesis, Arabic was appropriated for the service of Christian theology. Somewhat paradoxically perhaps, it was domestic revolution that provided the initial impetus for the intellectual upsurge, a transformation that impinges upon political and dramatic discourses of the period. Outside the aegis of the two universities, there is also evidence for a lively interest in Arabic studies in the 1640s. Preserved in the Thomason Tracts and dated June 1648, a fulsome petition addressed to the Commons, and submitted by 'about 40 Ministers, and 60 Citizens of quality' evokes a picture of academic life in London:

> That in *August* last, in *London House* a Lecture was happily begun for the propagation of piety, and learning, in the discovery of the oriental Languages (to this nation remaining but yet obscure) which hitherto hath been elaborately performed twice a week, since that time neer foure score Lectures in Latine, and highly approved by those of greatest parts and learning that frequent the same: And your Petitioners fearing lest a work of this nature, for the advancing such learning and Languages, should for want of maintenance and countenance from Authority fall to the ground. And forasmuch as an estimate hath been taken of the necessary charge which is requisite for the maintenance of Professors, and Students, as also for the erection of a Presse, for those Languages for the more effectual prosecution of the desired ends. ... Therefore your Petitioners bold to make this humble addresse to your Honours, That if to your wisdomes this kind of learning, on which the clearer knowledge of the sacred Scriptures, and our usefulnesse for the propagation of the Gospel, to such as understand those languages, and their usefulnesse to us so much dependeth, and is therefore in the present age so much esteemed by other reformed Churches, shall also be judged usefull for this kingdome.[26]

The lecture to which the petition refers was given by the German orientalist Christian Ravis (also Ravius) who had recently arrived in London seeking employment in the field of Arabic studies. During the 1640s, Ravis had travelled extensively in the East under the patronage of Archbishop Ussher charged with the collection of manuscripts, and in 1648 published *A Discourse of the Oriental Tongues* in London. During that year, Ravis was sponsored by the

---

26 *To the Hon. the Commons of England ... the humble petition of ministers and other inhabitants in and about London, praying for assistance in the establishment of a lecture in Oriental languages* (London, 1648), A1r.

London Presbyterian clergy of Sion College to lecture at '*London House*' near St Paul's; the nature of those lectures can be surmised from the contents of his *Discourse*. In common with the majority of biblical scholars, Ravis believed that all the so-called semitic languages sprang from a single root, hence the central significance of oriental languages to the accurate formulation of an English Scripture. Moreover, he advocates the study of Arabic as the language of a living culture, as opposed to the Latin and Greek relics of a long dead antiquity. Most innovative of all, however, and notwithstanding the petition's reference to 'neer foure score Lectures in Latine', was Ravis' practice of lecturing, and certainly publishing in English. Indeed, supporters of the establishment of the Oriental lecture in London, with Samuel Hartlib at their fore, were also dedicated to wider religious reforms. Thus, it is in the context of contemporary debates concerning the nature of divine revelation that the work of mid-century Arabists must be properly placed. Clearly for many of those involved, the drive to incorporate the study of '*Oriental Tongues*' into the educational curriculum of the City was ineluctably bound up with a religious revolution that sought to do away with the received wisdom of state-authorised Church and Scripture.

In this highly charged political and religious atmosphere, the first English translation of the Qur'an appeared in 1649, entitled *The Alcoran of Mahomet* and accompanied by a robust defence that acknowledges the potential explosiveness of the text whilst slyly maintaining the innocuousness of its heresies to any right-thinking Christian. The author of this defence was neither a proponent of Islam nor Arabic scholar and, as I shall explore in the next chapter, was not, as has been commonly assumed, directly responsible for the translation that was published along with his attributed defence. Nevertheless, the appearance of an English translation of the Islamic holy text was both symptomatic of an ongoing impulse to address the religion and culture of Islam whilst itself transforming the nature of that engagement; as the following account will show, the ramifications of that transformation were felt throughout English political and cultural life. Although the precise circumstances of the *Alcoran*'s first appearance are unclear, it is possible that the publication of this extraordinary document may well have been facilitated by the more general willingness of Commonwealth authorities to sanction Oriental studies at this time. Whatever the case, this rendition remained the only full translation available to English readers until the publication of George Sale's translation in 1734.

The identity of the translator is uncertain but the self-professed political import of his work is unequivocal – to expose the 'Heresies' of religious nonconformity in England. This is an ironic transposition of one of the motivations frequently cited to justify the study of Arabic in the period: the conversion of Muslims to Christianity. To some extent, the stated goal of the Arabists had always been partly missionary. Earlier in the century, Bedwell's translation of the gospels of St John and his *Mohammedis Imposturae* had been conceived in this vein. The expectation that knowledge of Oriental languages could not only illuminate the true message of the Gospels, but assist in their dissemination, was also written into the institutionalisation of Arabic studies in the 1630s. In May 1636, writing to Adams, the founder of the Arabic chair at Cambridge, the Vice Chancellor of the University outlined the purpose of the lecture:

> The worke itself was conceived to tend not onely to the advancement of good Literature by bringing to light much knowledge which yet is lockt up in that learned tongue; but also to the good service of the King and State in our commerce with those Eastern nations and in God's good time to the enlarging of the borders of the Church, and propagation of Christian religion to them who now sitt in darkeness.[27]

As in the Londoners' petition for an oriental lecture of 1648, which had promised its 'usefulnesse for the propagation of the Gospel', the imagined recipient of this evangelism is only vaguely defined. Despite several well-publicised accounts of specific conversions to Christianity,[28] the reality of Anglo-Ottoman power relations in the period made the conversion of the 'Turks' a more rhetorical than realistic proposition. Although unsuccessful, a notable exception was the series of missions undertaken by the Quakers in the years of the Commonwealth and early Restoration. In 1657, confident in the righteousness of her calling, Mary Fisher set out to convert Sultan Mohammad IV who, by all accounts, received her with much civility but politely declined her exhortations. In 1660, John Perrot published *A Visitation of Love, and Gentle Greeting of the Turk*, again indicative of an earnest desire for the Muslims to convert and take their rightful place in the millenarian schema.[29] Anglicanism too had its own zealous missionary in the shape of Issac Basire, a former chaplain of Charles I at Oxford, who travelled extensively in the East between 1651 and 1661, preaching the gospels and distributing the catechism as he went.[30] For the most part, however, English attempts to bring the 'Christian religion to them who now sitt in darkeness' were a deal more circumspect. Rather than

---

27 Quoted in Russell, *The 'Arabick' Interest*, p. 78.
28 For example, an issue of the newsbook *Mercurius Politicus*, dated 6–13 May 1657, reports the conversion of a Turk to the 'Roman rather than the Reformed' church by the Reverend John Despagne in the French church in Somerset House. For a survey of other conversion narratives, see Matar, *Islam in Britain*, pp. 120–52.
29 For an account of Perrot and Fisher's missionary travels in the context of radical Quaker writings, see Nigel Smith, 'Exporting Enthusiasm: John Perrot and the Quaker Epic', in *Literature and the English Civil War*, eds. Thomas Healy and Jonathan Sawday (Cambridge: Cambridge University Press, 1990), pp. 248–64.
30 In his diary entry for 10 October 1661, John Evelyn records a sermon delivered by Basire soon after his return: 'In the afternoon, preached at the Abbey Dr. Basire, that great traveller, or rather French Apostle, who had been planting the Church of England in divers parts of the Levant and Asia. He showed that the Church of England was, for purity of doctrine, substance, decency, and beauty, the most perfect under Heaven; that England was the very land of Goshen.'

the wholesale conversion of Muslims, attention turned instead to the Arabic-speaking Christians who were resident throughout the Ottoman Empire. In theory at least, there was much common ground between the English and Eastern Churches, particularly, it was often felt, in its Greek Orthodox manifestation. In the course of justifying his Arabic translations of the Scriptures, Bedwell had praised the 'writings of the Arabs' for containing 'nothing about purgatory, about the impious sacrifice of the mass, about the primacy of Peter and his apostles … nothing … that savours of Papism, Pelagianism, Arianism, Epicurianism, Mohammedanism or Judaism – nothing that savours of heresy'.[31] Thus, the 'Arabic' Christians could be depicted as either devotees of an ancient and uncorrupted faith or as victims of religious persecution, depending upon the writer's own ideological convictions. Above all, however, it was their independence from Rome that defined the Eastern denominations. Whilst there were plenty of writers for whom the doctrines of Eastern Christians represented an unconscionable heresy, the belief that there could be a spiritual union between Anglican and Greek churches persisted throughout the century. Perhaps partly motivated by this belief, in 1660 Robert Boyle commissioned Pococke to translate Hugo Grotius' *Veritate Religionis Christianae* into Arabic for distribution in the Levant. Following the Restoration, Pococke became increasingly involved in producing missionary publications of this kind, translating the catechism of the Church of England in 1671 and part of the Anglican Book of Common Prayer four years later.

By the last quarter of the century, however, the intense interest generated in the study of Arabic during the Revolution had faded. At Cambridge, Edmund Castell had succeeded Wheelock as professor of Arabic in 1667. His *magnus opus*, the enormous *Lexicon Heptaglotton*, incorporating Bedwell's own unpublished dictionary, consumed seventeen years of his life and much of his income, but by the time of its publication in 1669 must have seemed an outmoded contribution to the orientalism that had defined biblical scholarship twenty years earlier. At Oxford, however, there was one more significant publication. Pococke had been grooming his eldest son for the chair of Arabic and, in 1671, under the watchful eye of his father, Edward Pococke published a Latin translation of a twelfth-century Arabic philosophical treatise by Ibn Tufayl. Reinscribed as the *Philosophus autodidactus*, it tells the story of a man who, despite being raised in absolute isolation, comes to understand the nature of God and religion through innate reasoning. In the context of ongoing theological controversies, it is not difficult to see why the translation proved so influential,[32] and it did not take long for the text to be appropriated for the

---

31 Hamilton, *William Bedwell*, p. 117.
32 G. A. Russell makes an interesting case for the influence of the Pocockes' translation upon the formulation of John Locke's *Essay Concerning Human Understanding* (1689) whilst all three scholars were at Oxford. Russell, *The 'Arabick' Interest*, pp. 224–65. See also Hans Daiber, 'The Reception of Islamic Philosophy at Oxford in the 17th Century: The Pocock's (Father and Son) Contribution to the Understanding of Islamic Philosophy in Europe', in *The Introduc-*

propagation of a distinctly English religious philosophy; in 1674 George Keith, a prominent Quaker, translated Pococke's version into English and was clearly rapt by the paradigm of spiritual self-sufficiency he found there. In this sense, the *Philosophus autodidactus* is perfectly illustrative of the ways in which the Arabic legacy was received and rechannelled in seventeenth-century England. In whatever guise Islam was invoked, it seemed that the religious and political considerations of the day were rarely far behind. In many cases it remains simply enough to damn through association. In this regard, the sermons of Isaac Barrow, Arabist and Lucasian Professor of Mathematics are an apposite example of how an appreciation of Arabic learning and literature need not preclude a vigorous detestation of 'Mahometanism' itself.

> ... for it hath continued a long time, and hath vastly over-spread the earth: neither is it more formidable in its looks, than peremptory in its words; vaunting it self to be no less than a complete, a general, an ultimate declaration of God's pleasure, cancelling and voiding all others that have gone before. But examining both the substance and circumstances thereof ... the manner of its rise, progress and continuance; as also the matter it teaches or injoins; we shall not find stamped on it the genuine characters of a divine original and authority; but have great reason to deem it a brood of most lewd and impudent cozenage. In times of great disturbance and confusion, when barbarous nations, like torrents, did overflow the world ... in a very blind and obscure corner of the earth, among a crew of wild thieves and runnagates (such have those *Arabians* been always famed and known to be) this *Sect* had its birth and fosterage; among those fierce and savage over-runners of the world it got its growth and stature ... the first Author hereof being a person, according to the description given of him in their own Legends, of no honest or honourable qualities, but having all the marks of an Impostour; rebellious and perfidious, inhumane and cruel, lewd and lascivious, of a base education, of a fraudulent and turbulent disposition, of a vicious life, pretending to enthusiasms, and working of wonders ... and for its propagation it had that great advantage of falling in the way of barbarous people, void of learning and civility. ... Afterward being furnished with such Champions, it diffused it self by rage and terror of arms; convincing mens minds only by the sword, and using no other arguments but blows. Upon the same grounds of ignorance and force, it still subsists.[33]

Barrow became notorious for his lengthy orations, but it is worth quoting this excerpt from his sermons on the Apostles' Creed not for any conspicuous insight afforded, but because it is unexceptional. This approach is an attempt to tackle an ongoing problem that had dogged Christian theologians since at least 1453, namely, how to reconcile the manifest imposture of Islam with the,

tion *of Arabic Philosophy into Europe*, eds. Charles Butterworth and Blake Kessel (Leiden: E. J. Brill, 1994), pp. 65–82.
33   Isaac Barrow, *The Works* (London, 1716); quoted in David A. Pailin, *Attitudes to Other Religions: Comparative Religion in Seventeenth and Eighteenth-century Britain* (Manchester: Manchester University Press, 1984), p. 204.

equally manifest, success of its earthly embodiment in the Ottoman Empire. With its rival claim to sole divine authority, Islam was relentlessly confuted from the pulpit and, in so doing here, Barrow reiterates many of the standard imputations. For example, the same attributions of lasciviousness and of religion maintained 'by the sword' are made in the previous century in the popular sermons of the puritan divine Henry Smith and are themselves promulgations of long-established myths.[34] Interestingly, attacks of this kind often focus upon the history of Islam's foundation and the character of the Prophet himself rather than on specific points of theology, perhaps because the two religions would have seemed uncomfortably close when framed in these terms. Barrow's argument boils down to the assertion that Islam must be false since God would never choose to bestow divine truth upon such a people. Barrow's, then, represents the authorised version of Islam, oft rehearsed before and since.

What had irrevocably changed by mid-century, however, was the very nature of this authority. With the proliferation of nonconformity precipitated by the politico-religious crises of Civil War, English Christians could no longer approach Islam from anything resembling a fixed viewpoint. Throughout the century, the fractures of Church and State that had culminated in the collapse of the old order were never far below the surface. Even from the relative stability of the Restoration, Barrow would have been aware of addressing a very different congregation from that which had formed the national church in pre-revolutionary years. In this heady atmosphere, fraught with internalised religious anxiety, the old constructions of the East and Islam were apt for reinterpretation as never before. In some cases, polemical treatments were more embittered and entrenched than ever. In the myriad religious controversies of the period, the charge of 'Mahometanism' was frequently levelled at heterodoxy of any kind and the overall impression could be contradictory. For example, a commonly drawn parallel, particularly in the latter half of the century, is between the tenets of Islam and Unitarianism or 'Socinianism'. In Elizabeth's reign, the strict monotheism of Islam had been cited in evidence of an ideological rapprochement with English Protestantism; by the 1670s, however, to oppose the Trinitarian doctrine of the Anglican Church was to invite an unfavourable comparison with the 'deluded Mahometan'. In rare cases, religious dissent gave rise to a radically new imaginative engagement with Islam. One example of such is found in the writings of Henry Stubbe whose extraordinary biography of Mohammed I shall later consider in the context of the particular conditions of the 1670s.

---

34 Henry Smith, *Gods Arrow Against Atheists* (London, 1593). In fact, Smith's zealous disapprobation goes somewhat farther than Barrow's: 'yet because the filthinesse of this Prophet may not be concealed, I must utter it: Hee committed buggery with an Asse'.

'TRAFFIQUING WITH THE TURK': TRADE AND DIPLOMACY

As many of the writers cited above demonstrate, the language of trade slips easily into that of religious and intellectual exchange. Contained within the encomium for Laud's 'importing Araby to Oxford', for instance, is acknowledgement of the consanguinity between the merchant-adventurer and Arabic scholar, consummately embodied in the life of Edward Pococke. Whilst academic enthusiasm for Arabic declined, however, the pursuit of the Levant trade with which it had been so closely associated was booming. During the Interregnum and early years of the Restoration, political and economic benefits had sometimes been appended, almost as an afterthought, to the primary epistemological and intellectual motivations for the organised study of Arabic. By 1677, it is important to note that the situation was reversed:

> [there are] proposals for a large lexicon of the Turkish language, containing not only their ordinary language but the learned part thereof, whereby their language and literature will be learned more easily and sooner, and interpreters procured with less charge in their breeding and better able to transact the great and public affairs which pass through their hands. Merchants likewise or others may hereby attain with much less difficulty unto a knowledge of that language.[35]

Trade was a central mechanism of cultural exchange between East and West. Whilst England's scholars and controversialists were occupied in what was, to greater or lesser extent, a theoretical engagement with the East, the great trading cities of the Levant were the site of a cultural encounter that directly impinged on the domestic situation, and was itself modulated by affairs at home. Here, Englishmen were involved in complex and sometimes fraught negotiations, not only with the Ottomans themselves, but also with representatives of the rival trading nations of Europe and, increasingly, each other.

Even before the tribulations of Civil War, relations between the Crown, the Levant Company and its resident officials had not always been entirely cordial. Following the end of Roe's term in 1625 a series of disputes regarding the king's right to appoint the ambassador became increasingly bitter and, as civil war loomed, control of the Company and its assets increasingly imperative. With the appointment of Sir Sackville Crowe in 1638, Charles had attempted to co-opt the so-called 'strangers' consulage', a lucrative duty paid by nonnationals using English ships, and the cash-strapped king was clearly keen to tap into a new source of badly needed revenue. For its part, Parliament seems to have recognised the value of the Levant trade early in the war. In March 1643, Parliament issued an ordinance permitting

> all merchants of the Levant Company to import in English bottoms currants, being the growth of Zante and Cephalonia, into the port of London, or any port

[35] *C.S.P.*, 1677, p. 398.

being within the power of the Parliament … paying 6s. per cent. for every cwt. over and above the customs and excise due for the same.

Moreover, this special duty was to be funnelled directly into the war effort 'for the use of the garrison of Gloucester'.[36] As a leading organ of the City, the Company would find itself unavoidably entangled in the collision of King and Parliament throughout the 1640s.[37]

If the activities of the Levant merchants were directly implicated in the war at home, then the reverberations of that conflict were also felt in Constantinople. The State Papers for this period and the communications of the Company with its ambassador, and the various factors supposedly under his jurisdiction, sketch a fascinating picture of English political and professional rivalries played out on an Ottoman stage. With the outbreak of war, the thorny issue of the rights to the 'strangers' consulage' had once more arisen, with Crowe determined to requisition the frozen assets for the king. In turn, Parliament confiscated Crowe's property in England. Then, in 1646, the ambassador took the extraordinary step of sequestering all the cargo and monies belonging to English merchants in the Levant. Soon afterwards, the Company petitioned the Commons for Crowe's removal. As their petition reveals, the affair embroiled not only English merchants, but the representatives of other European nations resident at the Porte; the Ottoman authorities were called in to referee this little local difficulty:

> That Sir Sackville Crow, being chosen by petitioners to reside at Constantinople and dignified with the title and authority of Ambassador, did in July 1638, by covenant with petitioners, promise to protect their trade, defend their goods and servants from impositions, and would not exact any moneys. … Notwithstanding which Sir Sackvile Crow hath greatly abused the royal authority, contrary to his covenant, under pretence that his Majesty had given to him the duty called Strangers' Consulage, and prohibited all ships to leave Constantinople, which he supported by the capitulations and grants of the Grand Signior. He also accused petitioners of having gotten by false suggestions into their power his lands and debts in England. … The English nation at Constantinople, in this their desperate condition, were necessitated to fly to the protection of Signior Copes, the agent for Holland, by whose means, with the aid of Turkish justice, the English there obtained the release of their persons and goods, but at the cost of 10,000*l.* to the Company. Pray that the Parliament would either move or grant petitioners leave to move his Majesty for a letter for the recall of Sir Sackville

---

[36] *C.S.P.*, 1643–44, p. 59.
[37] At the beginning of the war especially, the attitude of the Levant merchants was not unanimously anti-royalist despite Parliament's influence in the City of London. Brenner writes that, 'the virtually unparalleled support they had received from the Crown throughout most of their companies' existence, the eastward trades naturally tended to assume a highly conservative socio political outlook'. Brenner, *Merchants and Revolution*, p. 283.

Crow, that he may be removed from his employment according to their charter and Ordinance of Parliament.[38]

Despite his imprisonment at Carisbrook, Charles was himself petitioned and reluctantly agreed to the appointment of Sir Thomas Bendish to take Crowe's place at Constantinople. As Dorothy M. Vaughan puts it, however, 'the Civil War and Commonwealth produced the spectacle of two rival envoys at the Porte'.[39]

As the story of the Levant Company in this period testifies, English relations with the Ottomans were inevitably tempered by the diplomatic entanglements and strategic alliances of the other Eastern players. In the previous century, Europe's complex and shifting relations with the Ottomans had been significantly defined by the great ideological confrontation between the forces of Reformation and Counter-Reformation. In its enmity toward the rival Hapsburgs, the Ottoman Empire had long been perceived as the natural ally of Protestantism and the outbreak of the Thirty Years' War only served to heighten the belief that the 'Turks' could be instrumental in establishing the balance of power in Europe. By the mid-seventeenth century, however, Ottoman energies were occupied in fighting a new war against an old trading partner, Venice, and it is against this backdrop that Anglo-Ottoman relations must be fully understood.[40]

The conflict had its origins in an act of piracy. A familiar feature of Mediterranean trade in the period, piracy had long been the subject of concern to English writers, politicians and, not least, to its sailors. Despite the maintenance of cordial relations with the Porte, English shipping was continually plagued by attacks from so-called 'Turkish' corsairs that were more often operating from the so-called Barbary ports of North Africa – primarily Algiers, Tripoli and Tunis. Although technically Ottoman regencies, the Porte could not or did not always concern itself to regulate the activities of its subjects there. A petition to Charles I made by 'his Majesty's subjects in captivity in Algiers', dated 3 October 1640, gives an idea of the scope of the problem and the keen anxiety aroused:

> Here are about 3,000 of your subjects in miserable captivity undergoing most unsufferable labours, as rowing in galleys, drawing in carts, grinding in mills, with divers such unchristianlike works, most lamentable to express and most burdensome to undergo, withal suffering much hunger and many blows on their bare bodies, by which cruelty many not being able to undergo it have been forced to turn Mahometans, so that these burdensome labours will cause many good seamen and others your subjects to perish unless some course by you be taken

---

[38] *C.S.P. Domestic, Charles I, 1646*, p. 469.
[39] Vaughan, *Europe and the Turk*, p. 241.
[40] For an account of the role of Venice in the region, see Setton, *Venice, Austria and the Turks* and Vaughan, *Europe and the Turk*.

for our release, which we ourselves cannot procure by reason of our great losses and the extraordinary ransoms imposed on us. *The names of the shipmasters and the number of their men who have been taken prisoners since May 18, 1639, Total 957.*[41]

By 1640, the predatory attentions of the Barbary fleets were no longer confined to the shipping lanes of the Mediterranean but had become a menace in the English Channel itself. In the State Papers of the early 1640s, news of impending civil strife is continually interpolated with reports of the coastal threat. For example, the 'Deputy-Lieutenants of Cornwall' complain that the recruitment levy imposed on their county is being hampered by

> the mischief lately done on our coast by the Turkish pirates, who have fought with our ships, and taken away divers of our people at Looe, Penzance, and other places, whereof we are unable to certify the numbers. These Turkish miscreants are reported to be at least 60 men-of-war. The fishermen are afraid to put to sea, and we are forced to keep continual watches on all our coasts.[42]

Whilst the cost of sea-defences was used by the king to partly justify the exaction of the notorious ship-money, the merchants of London protested that they were unable to pay precisely because 'their ships and goods have been taken by Turkish and other pirates'.[43]

However, piracy was by no means the sole preserve of the Ottomans and their subject dominions. Throughout the period, Ottoman ships and coastline had fallen prey to the raids of the knightly orders, of Saint Stephen, and particularly of Saint John, operating from Malta. These militant orders, vestiges of the Crusades, were a constant thorn in the side not only of the Ottomans but also of the Christian powers who wished to stabilise relations with their Muslim neighbour, either for reasons of trade or self-preservation or both. In September 1644, not far from Rhodes, a Maltese squadron fell upon a convoy of richly laden ships, flying the Ottoman ensign. After a struggle, during which some of the passengers were killed, the Christian attackers plundered the ships before sailing on to Crete, a strategic port in Venetian hands. Soon after news of the fracas reached the Porte, which had resulted not only in the humiliating loss of a valuable cargo but in the death of a senior official of the harem, Ottoman forces were mobilised to take reprisal. In April of the following year, the navy moved, not against Malta, but Crete on the grounds that it was here that the attackers had found harbour but, more pertinently, from where an occupying power could control entry to the Aegean. After quickly taking Canea and Rettimo, the Turks began their twenty-four-year-long siege of Candia.

Venice did not make its first diplomatic overtures to the new Commonwealth of England until 1653. Cromwell received the ambassador Paulicci and

[41] *C.S.P.*, 1640, p. 134.
[42] *C.S.P.*, 1640, p. 438.
[43] *C.S.P.*, 1640, p. 94.

expressed sympathy for the Venetian cause against the 'Turk' but demurred from offering naval assistance to the Senate on the grounds that English forces were consumed in the current war with Holland and the threat any involvement in the conflict would pose to the activities of the Levant Company. Meanwhile, at least one Englishman was strenuously advocating an opportunistic intervention in the war. Writing to the Admiralty Committee from Leghorn in the same year, Longland reported,

> It is rumoured that the Turkish fleet has gone out of Rhodes into Candia, and there surprised and taken a strong place from the Venetians, who it is supposed will be forced to quit the island. The Venetians are at Milo. If a good English fleet should appear in the midst of this war between the Turks and Venetians before Constantinople, they might obtain what conditions of trade they pleased from the Turk, even to the exclusion of other nations from the trade, and reserve it for ourselves …[44]

In the succeeding months, Longland repeatedly urged the committee to 'spare a squadron for these seas', diligently reporting the rich pickings afforded by French and Dutch trading vessels in the region. Thus, naval action is proposed as a remedy for the loss of trade, even a substitute for it:

> If you intend a fleet for these seas this winter, as soon as they are come into the Straits, let 4 or 5 frigates be sent to ply between Cape Spartavento and the eastern end of Malta, where they cannot fail to meet with all ships from the Levant. They should not speak at any port, or make themselves known, neither should their design be known in England until a month after their departure; for if it be known here, news will be carried to all parts, and your ships prevented of that purchase that otherwise cannot well miss them. All their prizes, as well ships as goods, may be sold here at their full value, and the money lie here to supply the fleet, without putting the state to any charge.[45]

Whilst there is no evidence of state-sponsored piracy on the scale so zealously recommended by Longland, English ships were involved in the war. In a later audience in 1657, the Venetian representative Giavarini complained to Cromwell of an English ship allegedly used in the war against Venice 'in the recent action at the Dardanelles'. Again it seems that the Protector was cautiously open to entreaty and Giavarini was able to report to the Senate that

> beyond question, if they do not obtain favourable answers from Constantinople to their demands for the restitution of the ship and compensation for the goods, active hostilities will be begun against the Tripolitans, as the merchants there desire, who would be glad to see the destruction not only of Tripoli, but of Algiers, Tunis, and other places on the Barbary Coast, if this would not irritate

[44] *C.S.P.*, 1653, pp. 157–8.
[45] *C.S.P.*, 1653, p. 183.

the Grand Turk and break the peace with the Porte, which they wish to be continued and enlarged.[46]

This final caveat is a fair summation of English foreign policy in the Levant; whilst contained action against the Barbary corsairs was feasible, engaging the might of the Ottoman Empire was clearly an entirely different matter. Nevertheless, the robustness of Cromwell's rhetoric does reflect the development of growing English naval confidence in the Mediterranean.

In the summer of 1654 Admiral Blake arrived in the vicinity with his formidable squadrons fresh from their decisive victory over the Dutch at the Battle of Portland in the previous year. Dispatched to harrying French and Spanish shipping, the English fleet also took the opportunity to quash the troublesome Barbary pirates and, in April 1655, Blake bombarded Tunisian vessels at Porto Farina, inflicting significant damage. The attack, it seems, had been instigated on the admiral's own initiative but, judging from the Council's instructions in the following year, they wholeheartedly approved:

> You are to go to Algiers, send for the English consul, ascertain what English prisoners they have, and what prizes have been taken by the Algiers' ships, and demand restitution of all ships and goods taken since – from English subjects, and the liberty of all the captives. You are to say that we wish to agree on articles for a friendly correspondence and mutual commerce, and you are to treat on articles of peace, such as are usual and necessary. If they refuse to do us justice, you are to use the force under your command to compel it, and assault them by land or sea, as you think fit.[47]

In 1646, Parliament had ordered the resumption of the consulship at both Tunis and Algiers, but with little impact upon either the activities of the corsairs or the plight of the captives held and traded from there. Gunboat diplomacy of the kind advocated by Blake did, it seems, meet with some short-term success, but these nominal subjects of the sultan continued to plague Mediterranean merchant shipping well into the next century.

After the Restoration, the English merchants began to steadily recover their dominance of the Levant trade.[48] In 1661, the king renewed the Company's charter and recalled Thomas Bendish who, on this occasion, had no choice but to capitulate. His replacement, Heneage Finch Earl of Winchilsea, oversaw a period of increased centralisation in which the Company sought to reassert its authority over its sometime dissident factors. Whilst competition from Venice had all but disappeared, the Dutch and French trade continued to play

---

[46] *C.S.P. Venetian*, 1657, p. 674.

[47] *C.S.P.*, 1656, p. 49.

[48] 'Except for the disturbance of England's trade during the English civil wars, from which the Dutch drew some profit, the English were the undisputed leaders in the Levant trade between 1620 and 1683.' Bruce McGowan, *Economic Life in Ottoman Europe: Taxation, Trade and the Struggle for Land, 1600–1800* (Cambridge: Cambridge University Press, 1981), p. 21.

second fiddle to that of the English. Reforms within the Ottoman state had also facilitated trade and the resurgence of the Company accorded with that of the Empire. When Mehmed IV had succeeded his executed father, he was only seven years old and the factionalism of the government initially continued in the rivalries of his mother, Turhan and grandmother, Kösem. Following Kösem's murder by her enemies in 1651, effective government lay in the hands of the sultan's mother and her clique of supporters.[49] By 1656, the empire was in crisis once more; the Venetians had countered the occupation of Crete with a devastating attack on the Ottoman ships supplying the army there, and had captured the isles of Tenedos and Lemnos, imposing a crippling blockade in the Dardanelles. Turhan was then forced to relinquish her grip on power and turned to an elder statesman to impose order on an increasingly restless populace. Accordingly Köprülü Mehmed Pasha was appointed grand vizier in September 1656 and famously imposed conditions upon his acceptance: that all his directives should be acted upon without question and that the sultan would brook no criticism of the grand vizier whatsoever. In this autocratic guise, Köprülü ruthlessly purged the government of opposition and crushed the rebellions in Asia Minor that had constantly threatened to overturn the empire. By 1657, Ottoman forces under the Grand Vizier's command had reopened the Dardanelles and averted the Venetian threat to Istanbul.

To match his aggressive domestic policy, Köprülü opened up a second front in 1658 by moving against the disputed province of Transylvania; Europe was once again the object of Turkish expansionism. Köprülü himself died in 1661, leaving the office to his son, Fazil Ahmed, who maintained Turkish pressure on the western provinces. In 1663, the grand vizier led his army through Buda and seized Neuhäusel. The Turkish advance on Vienna was stopped, however, at St Gothard on the Raab, although the subsequent treaty of Vasvar with its territorial concessions in Hungary represented a partial victory for the invaders. In 1669, Candia finally fell after a renewed assault and, in 1672 a series of campaigns began against Poland that would ultimately lead to Ottoman dominion over parts of the Ukraine. The empire, it seemed, was at its most puissant and its territories reached further than at any point in its history.

English trade at the Porte continued to flourish. In 1675 Winchilsea secured the renewal of the time-honoured capitulations for the final time, winning further concessions for the English factors. As well as adding clauses standardising the payment of duties, the agreement also safeguarded against the larcenies of renegade Englishmen who could no longer simply defect to Islam in order to escape legal redress for the Company. This updated trade agreement was published by Paul Rycaut as *The Capitulations and Articles of peace betweene the Majestie of the King of England, Scotland, France and Ireland &c. And the Sultan of the Ottoman Empire* in 1679. Rycaut had first arrived in

---

[49] See Leslie P. Pierce, *The Imperial Harem: Women and Sovereignty in the Ottoman Empire* (Oxford: Oxford University Press, 1993), pp. 248–59.

Constantinople as secretary to Finch and, through diligent diplomacy, attained the position of consul to the English factory at Smyrna. Most famous for his continuation of Knolles' *General Historie of the Turkes*, Rycaut was a keen observer of Ottoman society and policy, and I shall later return to his crucial contribution to English perceptions of Islam in the Restoration. Most striking in his preface to the *Capitulations* is the deference still observed in relation to dealings with the Porte. As Rycaut observes there, they are 'of an other nature & forme, then articles of peace are usuall to bee betweene two nations; for hee requires no counterpart from his Majestie'. Such unilateralism is indicative of the enduring authority of the sultan in Anglo-Ottoman interactions well into the last quarter of the seventeenth-century.

A MOOR IN HYDE PARK:
STAGING THE EMBASSY OF THE MOROCCAN AMBASSADOR

As Rycaut's accounts suggest, the language and practice of diplomacy provides a revealing, if densely coded picture of power relations between East and West in the period. Not least because, by their very nature, the majority of Anglo-Ottoman encounters took place in territories within the Porte's jurisdiction, the conduct of trade served to reinforce the sultan's authority in English eyes. Quite simply, it was the European trader and not the Ottoman host who constituted the cultural 'outsider'. In this sense, diplomatic relations between the two were never wholly reciprocal and there would be no resident Turkish ambassador to Britain until the end of the next century.[50] Charles II did, however, formally receive a representative of a Muslim state. In 1682, the celebrated visit of the Moroccan ambassador, Kaid Mohammed ben Hadu, marks the early stages of English interest in North Africa. The foreign visitor seems to have made a deep impression upon London society and reports of his stay are extremely suggestive of the nature of representations of Islam in the last years of Caroline monarchy.

Charles II was not the first English monarch to receive a Moroccan envoy. Between August 1600 and February 1601, the court had played host to a sixteen-strong embassy, dispatched to discuss with the English queen the possibility of an alliance against Spain.[51] By 1682, however, English entanglements in North Africa were of a rather different order, and the ambassador's visit was a valuable opportunity to assert the nation's interests in the region. A strategic and trade alliance with Morocco might provide a counterforce to the problem of the Barbary pirates who continued to harass English shipping in the Mediterranean. Whilst the regions dominated by the ports of Tunis and Algiers were

---

[50] The appointment of Yusuf Agah Efendi by the Ottomans as ambassador to London in 1793 marks the establishment of mutual diplomatic relations.
[51] This visit is often mooted as an immediate context for *Othello*.

nominally subject to Ottoman suzerainty, Morocco had maintained its independence and, under the kingship of Moulay Ismael (1672–1727), had begun to heal its civil divisions. More thorny, though, was the issue of Tangiers. In 1661 the Portuguese had ceded the fortified port of Tangiers as part of the dowry of Catherine of Braganza, and twenty years on the latest occupiers were still struggling to establish their troublesome outpost. Upon ben Hadu's departure, Charles made a present of six hundred muskets to the Emperor of Fez, with the implicit assurance that they would be used to suppress the Moorish tribes that continually assaulted the English garrison at Tangiers. Nevertheless, various attempts to stave off its hostile neighbours proved both futile and costly, and the garrison was finally evacuated in 1684. During that time, Tangiers remained the only English toehold on Muslim territory.[52]

For the most part, however, detailed negotiations were left to the respective attachés, leaving the king and the flamboyant ambassador free to indulge in displays of extravagant diplomacy. On 21 January, ben Hadu 'presented his Majesty 24 ostriches' and, for his part, the king introduced his visitor to London where, the 'Morocco ambassador went to see the building of St. Paul's, where he gave 15 guineas to the workmen'. The State Papers also report that,

> The Morocco Ambassador has made several visits to most of the great persons about Court, the King's coach and footmen constantly attending him. He was so well pleased with what he saw at the King's Chapel on Thursday, where the King himself offered, that he said, we have been told the Christians worship a god made of wood or stone, which they may throw into the fire and see consumed and this we have believed, but I have this day, I thank God (of whom he always speaks with a great deal of reverence) seen the contrary. I believe the English nation the best people in Europe …[53]

The urbane diplomat certainly knew how to flatter his hosts. What is striking about the description though is the extent to which religious difference is acknowledged, even respected in the context of courtly compliment. Although inevitably shaped by the mandatory protocol, the kind of refutation often provoked by previous encounters with Islam is nowhere to be found in accounts of the embassy. Instead, in a reversal of the standard strategies of religious representation, the Christian assembly are presented with a startling image of themselves, seen as it were through the eyes of another culture. In the telling, the fact that the Moroccan's preconceptions of Anglicanism prove as apparently fantastical as certain English renditions of Islam curiously does not expose the visitor to ridicule but puts him on an equivalent footing with his Christian hosts. Moreover, that the 'English nation' is vindicated not by

[52] See E. M. G. Routh, *Tangier, England's Lost Atlantic Outpost, 1661–1684* (London: John Murray, 1912), pp. 220–31.
[53] *C.S.P.*, 1682, p. 61.

any self-sufficient sense of its own superiority but by the approbation of the ambassador belies any straightforward cultural hierarchism at work.

The ambassador was even granted admittance to the universities where the king decreed that a ceremony conferring 'such degrees as you shall think fit on any persons of quality' would be performed for his entertainment. Writing to Secretary Jenkins, a Dr Timothy Halton of Queen's College Oxford communicated his colleagues' resistance to the proposed visit, 'alleging that it never had been practised here and that such a precedent might be of very ill consequence', to which the King replied with a simple edict to the vice-chancellor: 'Whereas the Morocco ambassador has a desire to visit the University, our will and pleasure is that on his arrival you receive him with all the civility and respect due to his quality'.[54] For Charles and his court at least, this innate nobility or 'quality' is the measure of intractable similitude and not of difference. Signifying his ready acceptance by the establishment, the ambassador's visit was commemorated by the court painter Godfrey Kneller whose sitters would include a multitude of prominent society figures, including both Stuart monarchs and their Dutch successor (see Fig. 3). In an early example of Kneller's baroque style, the ambassador is pictured astride his rearing stallion, lance in hand. Attired in rich Eastern dress complete with turban, Kneller's portrait displays the acceptable face of Islam, familiarly exotic and, reading between the strokes, reassuringly assimilable. In many ways such a reading projects a specifically post-Enlightenment construction of Islam upon the painting, but the incipient marks of the imperialistic stratagem later characterised by Said as Orientalism are already faintly discernible. Of course, the figure of the chivalrous Oriental was a well-established facet of constructions long before Kneller's painting. What is new is the setting, comfortably containing the Muslim horseman in the environs of Hyde Park.

In his diary entries recording the embassy of 1682, John Evelyn evinces a comparable privileging of cultural assimilation over religious difference in ways that encapsulate many aspects of Islamic representations throughout the period:

> To Lond: Saw the *Audience* of the *Morocco Ambassador*: his retinue not numerous, was receivd in the Banqueting-house both their Majesties present: he came up to the Throne without making any sort of Reverence, bowing so much as his head or body: he spake by a *Renegado English* man, for whose safe returne there was a promise: They were all Clad in the *Moorish* habite Cassocks of Colourd Cloth or silk … but with lether socks like the Turks, rich Symeters, large Calico sleev'd shirts etc: The Ambassador had a string of Pearls oddly woven in his Turbant; I fancy the old Roman habite was little different as to the Mantle and naked limbs: The Ambassador was an handsom person, well featur'd, & of a wise looke, subtile, and extreamely Civile: Their Presents were *Lions & Estridges* etc: Their Errant, about a Peace at Tangire etc: But the Concourse and Tumult of the

---

54 *C.S.P.*, 1682, pp. 117, 178, 222.

Figure 3. Portrait of the Moroccan Ambassador in Hyde Park by Godfrey Kneller, Chiswick House, London. Reproduced by Permission of English Heritage.

People was intolerable, so as the Officers could keepe no order; which they were astonish'd at at first; There being nothing so regular exact & perform'd with such silence etc, as in all these publique occasions of their Country, and indeede over all the Turkish dominions.[55]

Evelyn's admiration for the richness of the visitors' dress betrays a well-established fascination with the exoticism of the East, presenting an opportunity for spectacle and display that was quickly seized upon by Restoration dramatists. Crucially, however, this is not yet the undifferentiated exoticism of later authors. Evelyn carefully distinguishes the Moroccan from the Turkish mode of dress but, most significantly, speculates upon its resemblance to 'the old Roman habite' investing its wearers with an implied lineage and a classical decorum that underpins many characterisations of noble 'Moors' on stage. Equally telling is the anxiety engendered by the 'Tumult of the People', a portrait of domestic and civic unruliness invoked in direct contrast to the enviable regulation exercised 'over all the Turkish dominions' by what was commonly supposed to be a strong centralised authority. Here too is that ever-present reminder of the threat of apostasy embodied in the figure of the '*Renegado English* man', although now rehabilitated from degenerate backslider to an authorised go-between for the two cultivated parties. The same tendency to construct a version of Islamic culture through a series of parallels and contrasts with its English equivalent is even more evident in Evelyn's subsequent description of 'the Entertainment of the *Morocco*',

> at the Dut: of *Portsmouths* glorious Appartment at W.hall, where was a greate banquet of *Sweetemeates*, & *Musique* &c but at which both the *Ambassador & Retinue* behaved themselves with extraordinary Moderation & modestie, though placed about a long Table a Lady betweene two Moores: viz: a Moore, then a Woman, then a Moore etc: and most of these were the Kings natural Children … they drank a little Milk & Water, but not a drop of Wine, also they drank of a sorbet and Jacolatte: did not look about nor stare on the Ladys, or express the least of surprise, but with a Courtly negligence in pace, Countenance, & whole behaviour, answering onely to such questions as were asked, with a greate deale of Wit and Gallantrie. … In this manner was this Slave (for he was no more at home) entertained by most of the Nobility in Towne; & went often to *Hide-Park* on *horse back* where he and his retinue shewed their extraordinary activity in Horsmanship and the flinging & Catching their launces at full speede. … He also went to our *Theaters*, whereupon any foolish or fantastical action he could not forbeare laughing, he endeavoured to hide it with extraordinary modesty and gravity: In a word, the *Russian Ambassadour* still at Court behaved himself like a Clowne, compar'd to this civil *Heathen*.[56]

---

[55] John Evelyn, 'Diary entry for January 11, 1682', *Diary*, ed. E. S. de Beer, 6 vols. (Oxford: The Clarendon Press, 1955), vol. 4, pp. 267–8.

[56] Evelyn, 'Diary entry for January 24, 1682', *Diary*, ed. E. S. de Beer, vol. 4, p. 269.

This account, a puzzling composite of expectation and experience, is notable for the ways in which it shapes both English and Moroccan figures alike to fit the author's immediate purpose. By giving the lie to their stereotypical lasciviousness, the Moors are cast as ideal courtiers, apparently the perfect amalgam of cavalier 'Wit' and puritan 'modestie'. In Evelyn's rendition, the clear implication, of course, is of the decadence of Charles' court, his 'natural Children' so conspicuously interspersed between the model visitors as living proof of the king's own failure to set the correct moral example to his court and the nation as a whole. Thus, the accomplishments of this 'civil *Heathen*' are held as a mirror up to Christian monarchy, deploying a comparative strategy that unconsciously echoes many dramatic renditions of the same kind and depends upon an assumed reciprocity between 'elite representatives ... of two highly stratified societies, whose different protocols are brought into relation without great difficulty'.[57] Most intriguing of all, however, is the suggestion that the ambassador even knows how to conduct himself in a public theatre, which is in Evelyn's view, with a seemly dignity notwithstanding the absurdity of the play. Soon after his arrival, ben Hadu and his retinue were introduced to the theatre 'at the King's playhouse with a play that has relation to that country, viz., Caius Martius' and, later at the Duke's theatre, 'a play named Circe'.[58] The former reference is most likely to Nahum Tate's adaptation of *Coriolanus* first performed in 1681 and fully entitled, *The Ingratitude of a Commonwealth: Or, the fall of Caius Martius Coriolanus*. Precisely what the Moroccan visitors made of the performance and its 'relation to that country' is not recorded, but it is plausible to imagine that Tate's version, with its emphasis upon the perils of the popular will, may have been intended as a salutary example to the ambassador. Even more extraordinary to contemplate are the feelings of the company performing before this audience of Moroccan dignitaries who were due to stage *The Heir of Morocco*, the sequel to Settle's popular spectacular *The Empress of Morocco* that very season. As a series of carefully staged events, the Moroccan embassy was itself an elaborate spectacle designed to impress both visitors and public alike. With its implicit confusion of audience with characters, domestic with foreign settings and contexts, fictional construct with empirical fact, the ambassador's visit provided a fitting corollary to the drama's staging of Orient.

In Europe, however, Ottoman territorial ambitions were about to reach their climactic resolution. Following the death of Fazil Ahmed in 1676, Kara Mustafa Pasha had succeeded as grand vizier, under whose sway the empire would attempt to recapture the glories of Suleiman's reign. In 1682 the treaty of Vasvar expired and, when irreconcilable claims over Hungarian terri-

---

57 Orr, *Empire on the English Stage 1660–1714* (Cambridge: Cambridge University Press, 2001), p. 16. Orr also finds in Evelyn's account evidence for something approaching cultural parity between the two parties and makes the crucial point that skin colour is nowhere mentioned as a marker of difference.

58 *C.S.P.*, 1682, pp. 28, 35.

tory led to a breakdown of negotiations, hostilities with the Austrians were resumed. The Hapsburgs, and perhaps even the sultan himself, believed that two Austrian-held fortresses in Hungarian territory were the Vizier's immediate goal. Instead, Kara Mustafa led the army across the Raab and marched westwards, arriving at the gates of Vienna on 12 July 1683. The prolonged siege that followed almost broke the city's defences but, in September the allied forces of Poland and Bavaria finally arrived under the command of John Sobieski. Unprepared for their arrival, the Ottoman army faced a concerted attack from both Viennese defenders and the Christian relief forces and was routed on 12 September. The war would continue sporadically for the next sixteen years, but the might of the Ottoman Empire, which had overshadowed Western Europe since 1453, was spent. In the following years, Hungary was finally lost to the Hapsburgs and the Venetians opportunistically occupied the Morea and Dalmatia. In 1699, the treaty of Carlovitz, mediated by the English ambassador Lord Paget and his Dutch counterpart, marked the beginning of the end of imperial expansion in the West.[59]

In November 1687, following the catastrophic defeat at Mohacs, Mehmet IV was exiled, having been accused of paying more attention to the hunt than to affairs of state. A year later in England, the series of events known as the Glorious Revolution would also depose a monarch. The parallel, it seems, did not pass entirely unnoticed in the Porte: when the French ambassador urged the new grand vizier to refuse recognition to William's government, he is reported to have 'rejected such a course, reasonably insisting that it was not for the Ottomans, who had so often dethroned their sovereigns, to contest the right of the English to dethrone theirs'.[60] As the Ottoman Empire approached its fifth century, that of the British began to coalesce and assert its position in the new world order. The nation that emerged from the 'bloodless Revolution', its constitution, religion and armed forces, had all been forged in the extraordinary years since the calling of the Long Parliament. This much is well documented. What is often hidden from view is the extent to which Islam, its peoples and histories participated at some times implicitly, at others directly, in that transformation. More than any other medium, it was theatre in all its various guises that provided the principal means for English writers to trace the contours of their evolving history in direct correlation to the Islamic East.

---

[59] See Coles, *The Ottoman Impact on Europe*, pp. 173–83.
[60] Kinross, *The Ottoman Centuries*, p. 351.

Chapter 2

FRAMING 'AN ENGLISH ALCHORAN': *THE FAMOUS TRAGEDIE OF CHARLES I* AND THE FIRST ENGLISH TRANSLATION OF THE QUR'AN

WRITTEN IN THE WAKE of the execution of King Charles I, *The Famous Tragedie* reconstructs the events of the Second Civil War, from the death throes of royalist military resistance at the Siege of Colchester (June–August 1648), up until the moment of regicide. The publisher and bookseller George Thomason, also an assiduous collector of contemporary publications, added the pamphlet play to his collection on 26 May 1649, barely four months after the king's death, allowing the date of publication to be pinpointed with relative accuracy. The topicality of the action points to the dual status of *The Famous Tragedie*, partially informed by the conventions of printed dramatic texts, but also clearly participatory in the propaganda wars waged in print, munitioned by the salvos of newsbooks, broadsides, sermons and tracts that poured from the presses in the 1640s. The generic ambivalence of the text further arises from the particular conditions of authorship in which the anonymous playwright-pamphleteer operates. As recent studies of the literature of the English Civil War have emphasised, following the closure of the playhouses in 1642, the drama was not simply strangled out of existence, but driven underground, adapted and reformulated.[1] Deprived of legitimate arenas of performance, the dramatic form increasingly found expression in the pamphlet literature, harnessing the currency and vitality of a newly liberated print culture in order to reach its audience. Temporarily emancipated from the control of the Stationers' Company following the abolition of Star Chamber in July 1641, the press enjoyed a short period of untrammelled activity that would permanently transform the nature and pervasiveness of printed texts in relation to the political and literary expression of English society. Despite prompt and repeated attempts by Parliament to reassert state control over the production

---

[1] As well as Smith, *Literature and Revolution*, see Susan Wiseman, *Drama and Politics in the English Civil War* (Cambridge: Cambridge University Press, 1998).

and dissemination of the printed word, unauthorised and seditious publications played a prominent part in the battle for public opinion, waged alongside the military conflict of the 1640s.[2]

The Famous Tragedie, then, represents one way in which pre-war drama evolved in order to survive the hostile conditions of religious censure and government censorship. In the immediate months following the king's execution, the barrage of material discharged by the royalist press alarmed the authorities, prompting a renewed assault on dissident publications. As the report of one royalist newsbook, *Mercurius Aulicus*, for the week of 14 to 21 August suggests, the publication of *The Famous Tragedie* was a prominent source of Parliamentary consternation in the summer of 1649 and probably contributed directly to the official anxiety precipitating the draconian Printing Act of September.[3] Shielded and liberated by his anonymity the author taunts the latest attempt at censorship:

> By your leave Journey-men of the Juncto, for what if I shall scarce appear, neverthelesse I hope you that have so long pretended for a general Liberty, will give my conscience Liberty to speak home to your Consciences without danger of being snapt in your new *Treason Trap*, or if I must continue a mute, I hope your Masters the Coxcombs of State, will command you the Supreme Conventicklers to padlock up my ink bottle with a peculiar Act for that purpose, least that I should commit iniquity and sinne against the sence of the times, and so be brought before the Members judgment seat, to give an account of my actions, which indeed may soon be, since there are so many State Intelligencers and tell-tales, to convey all to *Westminster*, but what need I care, cause I am one of them, I wonder at, and admire at the Grandees and their actions, as much as any Independent of them all ...

More galling for those instructed to close down the opposition news industry, the author appears to have access to some privileged information concerning the business of the House:

> And in but little better case are those who write or print anything contrary to the sense of the supreme Conventicle, as appears by their debates the other day; where a motion was started by *Sir Whimsey Mildmay* and some other of the godly gang, that *Newmarket Fair*, *The Tragedy of King Charles the First*, and other

---

2 Subsequent attempts to regulate the press met with varying degrees of success. In March 1642, a resolution was passed outlawing the publication of unlicensed 'diurnals', and in June of the following year, an 'Ordinance for the Regulation of Printing' ordered that pamphlets and newsbooks were to be brought once more under the licensing authority of the Stationers' Company. However, the available evidence suggests that it was not until the stringent Printing Act of September 1649 that any consistently effective suppression of opposition views in print was achieved. See Frederick Seaton Siebert, *Freeedom of the Press in England 1476–1776: The Rise and Decline of Government Control* (Urbana: University of Illinois Press, 1965), chs. 10 and 11.

3 This legislation, enforced until the Restoration, required all printers to post a bond of £300 and prohibited the production of seditious material.

(by them stiled) scandalous Pamphlets, might be examined, and the Authors and Printers receives some corporal punishment, or be converted to Bullion for the use of the State; which motion was no sooner started, then approved of, and carried on with a full cry by the whole kennel (Alderman *Atkins* squirting out *Amen* to every sillable) and was presently past in the Affirmative, and a Committee appointed to see it done accordingly.[4]

Distinguished as the first royalist newspaper, *Mercurius Aulicus* had been revived in 1649, but would itself fall victim to the 'Supreme Conventicklers', surviving for only two more numbers in its reincarnated form. By the end of the year, all licensed newsbooks had been suppressed and the few surviving underground publications would be closed down by the following year.[5] Pamphlet plays like those cited in the leaked Parliamentary report participated in the last wave of concerted protest mustered before the consolidation of Cromwell's authority at the head of the Council of State.

If the increasing assiduity with which the prevailing authorities sought to suppress the activities of the presses may be taken as an indication of the perceived virulence of printed sedition, so a survey of legislation to control the theatres provides an insight into the state of theatrical activity in the Interregnum. As both Wiseman and Randall have observed, the initial and most notorious ordinance of September 1642 did not represent the most repressive attack to be levelled at the theatres in the period, and some theatrical activity seems to have survived this 'Order for Stage-plays to cease', not only in the new royalist 'capital' at Oxford, but in the London playhouses themselves.[6] Instead, the series of ordinances, beginning with that of July 1647 and culminating in 'An Ordinance for the utter suppression and abolishing of all Stage-Plays and Interludes' (February 1648) signalled the determination of the new regime to abolish public playing once and for all. In this climate, it is hardly surprising, then, that the *The Famous Tragedie* is shrouded in anonymity. In his prefatory address 'To the Author', the mysterious 'E.D.' has clearly experienced the play in printed form, having 'perus'd' the 'well writ Tragedie' and 'hastned, to the latter page'. The shift from playhouse to print house, however, need not have precluded the possibilities of performance. In the author's own 'Prologue to

---

4   *Mercurius Aulicus (For King Charles II), Communicating Intelligence from all parts, touching all Affaires, Designes, Humours and Conditions throughout the Kingdom. Especially from* Westminster *and the Head Quarters, From Tuesday August the 14. to Tuesday August 21. 1649*, pp. 1–2.

5   Joseph Frank, *The Beginnings of the English Newspaper 1620–1660* (Cambridge, MA: Harvard University Press, 1961), pp. 197–8. A new generation of officially sanctioned newsbooks came to replace those excised in 1649–50 and opposition opinion did reach the press in the 1650s although, according to Frank, 'the early newspaper never regained that smell of health it had briefly acquired in the later 1640s', p. 198.

6   Dale B. J. Randall, *Winter Fruit: English Drama 1642–1660* (Lexington: University Press of Kentucky, 1995), ch. 3; Wiseman, *Drama and Politics*, intro.

the Gentry', a tangible audience is more readily imaginable.[7] Although there are no known records of the play's performance, it is not inconceivable that this prologue was composed, not for an unidentifiably nebulous readership, but for a carefully selected coterie of royalist sympathisers. Certainly, the private houses of members of the nobility did function as venues for performance throughout the period of official closure. Whether aimed at spectators or readers, however, the prologue articulates the overtly politicised nature of both theatre-going and play-acting in the social context of 1649, a reciprocity that is enacted in the main body of the play. Beginning with an evocation of the canon of pre-war drama, the prologue deploys a strategy that is both eulogistic and appropriative:

> Though Johnson, Shakespeare, Goffe, and Devenant,
> Brave Sucklin, Beaumont, Fletcher Shurley want
> The life of action, and their learned lines
> Are loathed by the Monsters of the times;
> Yet your refined Soules, can penetrate
> Their depth of merit, and excuse their Fate:[8]

Thus, the old political order is nostalgically affiliated with the halcyon days of theatre, whilst the current regime, 'Monsters of their times', are charged with its philistine repression, depriving the personified drama of the 'life of action' (i.e. performance). An appreciation the theatre and its 'depth of merit' is thereby mooted as a badge of political even class allegiance 'vile, and beastly Ignorance' of its, and by implication, the audience's enemies. Such polarisations are a commonplace of contemporary discussions of the literary scene, but serve to highlight the particular assumptions and preoccupations of this royalist author. Having invoked the legitimising force of history, and in particular *staged* history, the prologue alludes to the current status of the theatre as political battleground – 'Their bloudy Myrmidons, o'th' Table round/ Project, to raze, our [*sic*] Theaters to the ground'. The latest Parliamentary attack upon 'Stage-Plays' had stipulated the demolition of London theatres and, in March 1649, the Fortune, Cockpit and Salisbury Court had indeed been pulled down.[9] As current as any newsbook report, the prologue then turns to a recurrent

---

7   In his study of newbooks, Joad Raymond is sceptical of the possibilities of actual performance. Writing of the pamphlet play *The Second Part of the Tragi-Comedy called New-Market Fayre* (1649), Raymond argues that theatrical references are metaphorical: 'This creates a textual stage, embracing a performance of language and political satire rather than proxemics and embodied speech.' Joad Raymond, *The Invention of the Newspaper: English Newsbooks 1641–1649* (Oxford: Oxford University Press, 1996), p. 208.

8   *The Famous Tragedie of King Charles I* (London, 1649), A4r. This and subsequent references are to the copy of the play held in the Thomason Collection of the British Library.

9   Leslie Hotson, *The Commonwealth and Restoration Stage* (New York: Russell and Russell, 1962), pp. 39–42.

fixation of *The Famous Tragedie*: the subsequent interpretation of this 'Story' and the judgement of posterity.

> No marvell they lap bloud as milke and glory
> To be recorded, villaines, upon Story.
> "For having kill'd their King, where will they stay
> "That thorow God, and Majestie, make way,
> "Throwing the Nobles, and the Gentry downe
> "Levelling, all distinctions, to the Crowne.

Encapsulated in the reported speech of succeeding generations are the familiarly indignant tones of the authorial voice, suitably outraged by the sheer iconoclastic presumption of it all. Combined with such characteristic righteousness, however, is a deftly calculated appeal to the self-interest of his imagined audience/readership. Having defied 'God, and Majestie' in their disruption of divinely ordained hierarchy, may not those 'villaines' now set about 'Levelling' the nobility? As well as containing a punning allusion to the radical political movement of the day, the final line also hints at the bloody fate that may lie in store for the gentry, after the King's example, who has been literally severed from his 'Crowne'.

For all its vigorously defiant rhetoric, the prologue inaugurates the vein of self-doubt that, I wish to argue, riddles the play as a whole. Most evidently, this uncertainty stems from the precarious nature of the royalist position by 1649. In its attempt to lay claim to past, present and, in particular, future representations of history, the prologue betrays an awareness of the political futility of the royalist cause. In the context of the crushing blow of the regicide, the parting shot of the prologue, 'But Joves all potent thunder shall divide/ Their plots, and sinke them, in their height of pride', reads less like an act of faith and more the last resort of an abject ideology. Although hope for a resurrection of the Stuart cause was not yet dead – the Battle of Worcester was still two years away – the author is clearly struggling to square the topical subject matter with his ideological remit. This tension is evident from the outset. Although the title page of *The Famous Tragedie of King Charles I* promises to *include* such marginalia as 'The several Combinations and machinations that brought that incomparable Prince to the Block', the reverse description would be more accurate. From the opening scene in which the stage-villain Cromwell, in dialogue with his preacher accomplice Hugh Peters, revels in the ingenuity of his evil design, the action evinces a fascination with the machinator that all but eclipses the supposed tragic hero of the piece. Verbal echoes within the play, its paratexts, even the title all intimate the dramatic character of the regicidal *act*, and yet the 'deed' (p. 40) itself is only parenthetically present, reported in a letter to Cromwell at the end of the play. In lieu of directly embodying the king himself, the play represents a contingent of prominent royalists, heroically defending the besieged royalist stronghold at Colchester and intensely loyal to his cause.

In the second act the action turns to the siege itself and introduces the besiegers Thomas Fairfax, Henry Ireton and Thomas Rainborough, apparently fresh from their subjugation of the south-west. Confident in the hopelessness of their enemy's plight, they call a parley for the town's surrender and its noble defenders, Sir Charles Lucas, Sir George Lisle, Lord Capel and Lord Goring, appear 'as upon the Walls'. The subsequent exchange is characteristic of the play's deeply ambivalent representation of the heroic ideal. Having unleashed an impressive volley of invective against the 'Mechanick Slave' Rainsborough, from the battlements of Colchester, Lord Capel shifts from prose to rhyming couplet and, in so doing, sententiously countermands the force of the preceding rejoinder: 'Our comfort is, though we be left i'th' lurch, / We Martyrs, fall, for God, the King, and Church.' (p. 11). Thus royalist rhetoric is constantly undermined from within, destabilised by an apparent prescience of the ultimate outcome. In the same way, having broached the possibility of Scottish and Welsh reinforcements, to 'breake in pieces Fairfax his guilty Forces', Lisle's confidence abruptly vanishes adding, 'But should all faile (by force of Destinie)/ Our comfort is, we (when we list) can die' (p. 14).

Lisle's submissive obsequence to the 'force of Destinie' at this point, is one example of the strand of fatalism that pervades the royalist discourse of the play. In the face of apparently overwhelming parliamentarian successes, the royalist contingent within the play and, by implication, the playwright and his, presumably partisan, reader are forced to take solace in the notoriously capricious dealings of the 'Fates'. When, having been informed of Charles' execution in the final scene of the play, Cromwell deems himself to be 'above the reach of fate' (p. 41), the suggestion is undoubtedly of the kind of hubristic justice familiar from the tragic mode. Crucially, however, this *Famous Tragedie* is encumbered by the political realities of the regicide and any hoped for vengeance must remain putative at best. It is perhaps this same impulse that prompts Sir Lucas' extraordinary explanation for the ascendancy of the Cromwellian forces:

> For, by the same rule Ottaman may boast.
> The partiall Deities favour him the most. (p. 10)

By this analogy, Cromwell is both morally invidious and militarily successful. Both attributes are, paradoxically, self-evident and utterly confounding to the royalist representatives of the play. Like the imperial might of the infidel 'Turk', the irrefutable prevalence of anti-monarchical (and by implication anti-Christian) forces poses a difficult question for an author desperately seeking an ideological schema in which to contain the experience of defeat. One solution posited here, and in keeping with the play's attempt to impose a providential rule of history on its unruly subject matter, is to identify Cromwell as both devil and scourge. Turk-like, he can be made to corroborate a redemptive as well as an apocalyptic eschatological narrative. Conflations of this kind abound in the polemic of the period and, characteristically unstable, become increasingly contested in the drama of the Interregnum. Here, the 'Ottaman' is one amongst myriad precedents enlisted in the denunciation of republicanism but is, I wish to argue, uniquely fraught and central to an understanding of *The Famous Tragedie*.

As this suggests, the play often appears to be speaking with several, frequently dissonant, voices. Of course, this is what it may literally be doing – the intensive print conditions of the 1640s encouraged a degree of literary borrowing that regularly occludes the identification of a single authorial intent. Moreover, given the vicissitudes of publication and the fact that unlicensed production was prone to disruption by the imprisonment of authors, or the confiscation of presses, a single text might conceivably pass through many hands before reaching the streets. Equally, the inconsistencies of tone and characterisation touched upon thus far are the result of the diverse discourses that feed directly into the text – the *Famous Tragedie* is largely a derivative and indiscriminate composite of both its newsbook source material and certain mainstays of the popular stage. Such polysemy, as I have argued with regard to the Cavalier voice in the play, often undermines the overall polemical scheme. If *The Famous Tragedie* may be regarded as representative of a broader royalist aesthetic, the instability of its rhetorical strategy would seem to indicate the fragility of the ideological framework it attempts to impose upon the 'Story of this unnaturall, uncivill Warre' (p. 13). Such issues crystallise around the central figure of the play, the dynamic villain of the piece who, despite valiant attempts to promote royalist fortitude in the face of republican perfidy, comes to steal the show. As well as providing a focus for the play's self-reflexive preoccupation with the political significance of language and theatre, a closer examination of the play's often puzzling characterisation of Cromwell also serves to highlight the significance of the Islamic allusion within the play and suggests ways in which such representations may help to unravel the rhetorical schema, or at least account for the contradictions that pervade the text.

In keeping with the play's unremitting allusiveness, Cromwell is made to assume a bewildering array of identities, including Richard III (with Peters as Buckingham), Faustus (with Mephistopheles) and Machiavelli.[10] Whilst these stock identities, cursorily surveyed in recent criticism of Interregnum drama,

---

10 In her fleeting acknowledgement of the play, Lois Potter mentions the anonymous playwright's indebtedness to Shakespeare, drawing 'on the relationship of Richard and Buckingham for the dialogue of Cromwell and Hugh Peters', a comparison that is explicitly made by the chaplain within the play, saying in soliloquy, 'This fellow (sure) was born (as the Third Richard,/ who once rul'd this Land) with his mouth full of teeth' (p. 7). Lois Potter, *Secret Rites and Secret Writing: Royalist Literature, 1641–1660* (Cambridge: Cambridge University Press, 1989), p. 118. Conversely, Nigel Smith notes a comparison 'between Cromwell and Peters, and Faustus and Mephistophilis' in verbal echoes of Marlowe's play. Smith, *Literature and Revolution*, p. 81. Susan Wiseman foregrounds Cromwell's function as 'a focus for consideration of the complexities of Machiavellian thought'. Wiseman, *Drama and Politics*, p. 69.

are undoubtedly ascribed to the chief rebel, there is a fourth and crucial role in which Cromwell is cast. In bombastic praise of his 'better Genius' (p. 3) Hugh Peters, Cromwell declares,

> Thou art that Load-stone, which shall draw/ my sense to any part of policy I'the Machiavilian world,/ we two (like Mahomet and his pliant Monke) will frame/ an English Alchoran, which shall be written with the/ self-same pensil great Draco grav'd his Lawes. (p. 4)

On the face of it, a reference to the founding father of Islam would seem an odd comparison to draw at this point. Most evidently, the playwright intends to tap into the rich seam of pejorative characteristics conventionally ascribed to 'the Turk', many of which overlap with the stock identities already cited; like the Machiavel he expounds political expediency over honour, the heresy of his faith is tantamount to the atheism of Faustus and, as Richard III, he is archetypally cruel and ruthless in his dealings with enemies and kin alike. However, the specific context of the reference implies a more complex appraisal of the relevance of the Islamic tradition to the new English republic. Crucially, the play's anxiety centres upon the role of language and textual interpretation in the constantly shifting terms of contemporary political debate. Cromwell's pledge to 'frame/ an English Alchoran' suggests not only the heinous apostasy of the new government but also its power, invested with the authority of an, albeit heretical, sacred text. Significantly, Cromwell's image also draws upon the permanence of the written word, 'grav'd' upon the English constitution. Elsewhere in the play, comparable images of the inexorable authority of the printed word combine with the recurrent fate motif to underscore the differences between the two factions. As a mouthpiece for the particular brand of stoic heroism espoused by the royalists of the play, Lucas can only submit to this greater power: 'let it hap ... if it be written in the/ Booke of Fate the Rebels shall dissolve the English Monarchy'. By stark contrast, however, Peters, a prominent Independent here portrayed as the archetypal sophistical cleric, seeks to actively wrest the pen from fate, erasing all that has gone before in order to inscribe a republican version of history:

> Let the fam'd Villaines of all/ former times have their dire deeds razed out of Fames/ black Booke as triviall accidents and neglected dreams,/ that these may take up all the roome on Record for the/ most glorious Miscreants e're Rebell'd;
> (p. 8)

As this suggests, and as *The Famous Tragedie* is acutely aware, in the aftermath of the regicide, the war has become, more than ever, a conflict of language and competing authorships.[11] As Cromwell's rhetorician, Peters' task is the

---

11 The most prominent battle for interpretation was fought over *Eikon Basilike*, a collection of prayers and meditations purportedly compiled by the king and published soon after his death. Immensely popular, thirty-five English editions were produced in 1649 alone. Like *The*

manipulation of language in order 'both at Presse and Pulpit, to/ render Kingly Government obnoxious and incompatible/ with the Peoples Rights' (pp. 4–5), an internalised reference to the discursive milieu in which the pamphlet play itself operates. However, as the play is anxious to point out, even Peters, the Commonwealth's arch 'Similist' (p. 6), is subject to the vagaries of an ultimately ineffable destiny: 'but what strange/ fancy lurks within my braine ... what vile sinister fate governs my life?' (p. 8). The hope that lies behind this dogmatic fatalism, of course, is that the same 'sinister fate' that raised Cromwell will crush him just as arbitrarily. In fact, Cromwell emerges from *The Famous Tragedie* as more the embodiment than the servant of destiny, an aspect of his characterisation that resurfaces elsewhere in the literature of the period. Writing one year later, Marvell famously identifies Cromwell's 'active star' as the reason for his meteoric rise, 'Though Justice against Fate complain/ And plead the antient Rites in vain'.[12] Lacking the poise of Marvell's studied ambivalence, however, the author of *The Famous Tragedie* resorts to fatalism in order to reconcile ideology with subject – the depiction of an immoral, yet undeniably successful tyrant. In his search for a suitable analogue to treat these themes, the author seems to have been influenced by the spate of dramatic treatments of Ottoman and Persian history that reached the stage in the opening decades of the seventeenth century.

In his dedicatory address to the exiled Charles II, the playwright makes a desperate appeal for foreign intervention in civil affairs, counselling the mobilisation of an unholy alliance of fantastic proportions to restore the English monarchy:

> Summon all Nations, to thy speedy aide,
> Search from the *Orient* to the *Occident*,
> The *Gets*, and *Parthians*, *Switzers*, (who are swaid
> By fierce *Camillas* second) *Tartars* bent
> To bloud and horrour, those whose God is said
> To hang twixt Heaven and Earth, the *Truculent*;
> *Fastidious Moore*, take all, except 'gainst none,
> For many hands, must lead Thee to Thy Throne.[13]

Thus, historic enemies of Western Europe are notionally enlisted as mercenaries for the exiled king. Not only does the proposal, a great deal more

---

Famous Tragedie, *Eikon Basilike* is heavily invested in the construction of martyr mythology, a strategy strenuously contested by Milton in his *Eikonoklastes*. In February 1649, Milton also published his *Tenure of Kings and Magistrates* and as the Commonwealth's appointed apologist his role in the propaganda war is clearly implicated in the play's portrayal of the sophistical Peters. For a discussion of the controversy over *Eikon Basilike*, see Lois Potter, *Secret Rites and Secret Writing*, pp. 170–6; Zwicker, *Lines of Authority*, pp. 37–47.

12 Andrew Marvell, 'An Horatian Ode upon Cromwell's Return from Ireland', ll. 37–8 in *The Complete Poems*, ed. E. S. Donno (Harmondsworth: Penguin, 1996), p. 56.

13 *The Famous Tragedie*, A3r.

rhetorical than realistic, demonstrate the degree to which old foreign enmities had been supplanted by a new 'other' within, it is also indicative of appropriative strategies within the play, evoking the gamut of national difference from '*Orient* to the *Occident*' in order to demonstrate the justness of the king's cause in its transcendence of conventional ideologies. What the dedication ambitiously advocates in political and military terms, the play attempts in rhetorical terms, searching beyond the confines of the national borders in order to recruit confederate paradigms for the political predicament at home. Characteristically, however, such recruits may prove unruly and apt to mutiny.

The inherent contradiction of Cromwell's characterisation is evident from his first appearance. Having been introduced as Cromwell's 'fine facetious Devil', Hugh Peters responds in mock-heroic terms:

> Most valiant, and invincible Commander,/ whose Name's as terrible to the *Royallists* as e're was/ *Huniades* to the *Turkes*, or *Talbot* to the *French*; thy/ Nose, like a bright Beacon, sparkling still (the *Ætna*,/ that doth fame our English world) hangs like a Comet/ o're thy, dreadfull face, denouncing death & vengeance;/ the Ancients fam'd *Alcides* for his Acts, thou hast not/ slaine, but tane the Kingly *Lyon*, and like great *Tamberlaine*/ with his *Bajazet*, canst render him within an Iron-Cage/ a spectacle of mirth, when e're thou pleasest (p. 2)

Superficially, Cromwell is crudely satirized, his celebrated nose 'like a bright Beacon'. Underlying this rather uneasy derision, however, is a grudging acknowledgement of the force of Cromwell's ascendancy. His nose 'hangs like a Comet', not only for its luminescence but perhaps also its auspiciousness. Following a litany of heroic precedents, interestingly, it is Charles and not the 'invincible Commander' Cromwell who is here compared to the Turk. Such an inconsistency may simply indicate the relatively non-specific way in which the history and imagery of Islam feed into the play text. However, given any audience's familiarity with the details of the Bajazet legend, not least from Marlowe's play, the allusion may further signify the play's, presumably unwitting, ambivalence towards the meaning of Cromwell's success and the demise of the 'Kingly *Lyon*' that surfaces throughout. In the popular version of the story, reenacted in *Tamburlaine, Part I* and elsewhere, the vanquished 'Baizeth' is encaged and processed through the streets by Tamburlaine before committing suicide by braining himself against the bars (V.ii).[14] Certainly, such an image sits somewhat uncomfortably beside that of the martyred monarch. Whilst the death of the 'emperor of the Turks' is undeniably heroic, it is nevertheless suicide induced by humiliation; Bajazet was himself synonymous with an overweening pride tamed. Could a similar judgement upon Charles lie submerged in the play's more conventional rhetoric? If so, this deployment of

---

[14] For a survey of contemporary treatments of the Bajazet story, see Chew, *The Crescent and the Rose*, pp. 469–72.

a perilously loaded historical analogue merely exposes the problems the play encounters in its attempts to reconcile its idealism with political reality.

This unstable tension, between contempt for and fascination with the epic figure of Cromwell, pervades this tonally elusive play. He is both the object of the satire, but also, strangely, its orchestrator. In one of the most incongruous moments of the play, Cromwell's providential transcendency finds expression in his sexual potency. Having cuckolded his general Lambert, with the help of Hugh Peters' 'most sugred eloquence', Cromwell awakes to hear the news of the king's execution. The implication is clear: like Mrs Lambert, the kingdom has been cozened, seduced and dishonoured by Cromwell with the abetment of his pander-preacher Hugh Peters. Again, returning to the keynote of irresistible 'Fate', Mrs Lambert speaks in terms of an involuntary attraction:

> Sir, you have robb'd me both of honour,/ and my heart at once;
> so strange a Fate doth/ sway me, that whatsoe're you judge to be
> convenient, I/ must not contradict. (p. 41)

The interrogation of notions of fate and honour here, in the context of political and sexual intrigue, again suggests the influence of earlier 'Turkish' drama. Unlike the many lecherous sultans who have tried the honour of Christian women before him, however, Cromwell's desire is not thwarted.[15]

Cromwell's conquest of Mrs Lambert, and by analogy the English state, is sealed with a masque comprising 'ambition, treason, lust, revenge, perjury, sacrilege' followed by a song celebrating these qualities. In terms of the rhetorical patterning of the play, this expression of gleeful anarchism finds its mirror image in the royalist drinking scene of Act II. In this curious digression, Lucas and Lisle, two of the besieged Cavaliers, resolve to 'frollick one halfe houre' and toast 'Him whom fame of all/ the European Kings doth call the best' (p. 16). Then, in a singularly bathetic moment, the two generals strike up in a song praising 'Plump cheek'd Bacchus' and the restorative powers of 'Canary'. Ostensibly, this is an act of defiant bonhomie in the face of certain defeat. Nevertheless, in contrast to the exuberant malevolence of Cromwell's ritual 'perform'd as I would wish' (p. 36), the royalist version, which, according to Lisle was also 'well perform'd' (p. 17), seems particularly ineffectual. This emphasis upon performance draws attention to the play's attempts to address the political meaning of action within and beyond the parameters of the theatre. Through the insistently cautious admonitions of Lucas ('This doctrine … is dangerous', 'we play with lightning too securely'), the play intimates the impotence of

---

[15] The infatuation of an Oriental/Barbary despot for a captive Christian princess was a familiar dramatic situation by 1649. In Thomas Heywood's *The Fair Maid of the West* (1631), the Moorish King Mullisheg is captivated by the English heroine Bess Bridges. Perhaps the most popular analogue of this kind was the story of Irene, the Greek maiden betrothed to and betrayed by the sultan, recounted in Knolles' *Generall Historie of the Turkes*. See Chew, *The Crescent and the Rose*, pp. 479–90 and Chapter 6, below.

the cavalier ritual, hinting that, like the drinking bout, the royalist ethos is misguided, even escapist. Elsewhere in the play, royalist performances are infused with the language and imagery of death. In its reluctance, or perhaps inability, to directly represent the regicide itself, *The Famous Tragedie* relies upon the execution of Lucas and Lisle to mimetically anticipate the royalist *coup de théâtre*. Having been introduced to his 'Executioners', Sir Charles' inflated valediction is couched in the bromidic idioms of the *theatrum mundi* tradition:

> SIR CHARLES.   You are our welcomest friends; who is/ allotted to
> make his exit first?
> 1 SOULD.   Your selfe must lead the dance of death.
> SIR CHARLES.   Here then I bid farewell, unto this Stage/ of misery,
> my life hath been but one continued Scene,/ woven
> with peturbations and anxieties – (p. 27)

Interwoven with this well-worn rhetoric, however, is a significant polarisation of the two opposing ideologies in terms of their theatrical function, which must have seemed entirely current in the summer of 1649. With his final 'loyall breath' (drawn some forty lines later), Sir Charles exhorts Jove to 'Take vengeance on the *Authors*' of his death, underlining the pivotal juxtaposition in the play between the nature of parliamentarian *author*ity and the passivity of royalist performance.

Interestingly, however, *The Famous Tragedie* incorporates two protagonists whose characterisation challenges this polarisation of royalist subject versus republican other. Like the presence of the anti-heroic Cromwell, these figures serve to disrupt and undermine those rhetorical patterns that purport to signify allegiances within the text. Firstly, Lord Fairfax is ascribed the kind of moral stasis that ordinarily afflicts the royalist contingent of the play when, during a Machiavellian aside, Cromwell contemns him as that 'silly Foole' who 'sits like a Statue' (p. 20). Similarly, in the execution scene of Act III, the playwright permits Fairfax a claim on the notionally loaded virtues of honour and nobility conventionally held as a royalist prerogative by loyalist writers of the period. Whilst Rainsborough and Ireton conform to the expected type of the bloodthirsty Myrmidon, Fairfax appeals for clemency to be shown to the defeated generals of the royalist garrison at Colchester, arguing that 'The Law of Armes' (p. 24) proscribes their execution. Secondly, the play also sporadically features a convert to the royalist trinity of 'God, the King, and Church' (p. 11). Having been inspired by the noble performance of their deaths, one of the nameless executioners of the two cavaliers repents his 'former crimes' and pledges to requite 'the bloud of/ noble Lucas and brave Lisle'. The now-identified 'Blackburne' reemerges at the end of Act IV, to murder Rainsborough, only to abruptly disappear once more in self-imposed exile: 'Beyond the Seas, for safety I will flie./ Till England once more be a Monarchie' (p. 39). Indeed, it is tempting to discern a cipher for the playwright himself in the marginal figure of Blackburne. Like the soldier-convert of his play, an initially unnamed individual emerges to actively resist the parliamentarian ascendancy before taking refuge abroad. Certainly, it is conceivable that the play was imported from abroad to be printed and distributed on the streets of London and many writers did leave England as Cromwell's victory seemed assured – for example Davenant was in retreat in Paris during 1649 in order to compose his epic poem *Gondibert*.

Clearly, the kind of ideological overlap depicted in such figures as Fairfax and the intriguing Blackburne, is designed to emphasise the justness of the royalist cause. In the context of existing theatre, and in particular the strand of Turkish and Persian drama I have posited as an underpinning element in the formulation of *The Famous Tragedie*, these two apparent anomalies of characterisation find multiple analogues. As an honourable infidel, Fairfax conforms to the type of the noble Moor, exemplified, for instance, by the bashaw Joffer in Thomas Heywood's *The Faire Maid of the West*. Having witnessed the valiant 'prowesse' of the Englishman Spencer, the 'noble Bashaw' Joffer, like Fairfax, is moved to argue for mercy to be shown to the prisoner. Similarly, there are copious precedents for renegades such as Blackburne in a genre preoccupied with fears of conversion and apostasy. For example, in their gratuitous manipulation of the historical facts, both Robert Daborne's *A Christian turn'd Turk* (1612) and Philip Massinger's *Renegado* (1624) may provide interesting dramatic models for a play that attempts to appropriate history in order to resist the prevailing current of political realities.

In a broader sense, the allusions to Islam that infiltrate the text of *The Famous Tragedie* are indicative of the ongoing political currency of the Ottoman Empire in the mid-seventeenth century. As religious anxiety mounted in England, so did the rhetorical appropriation of Ottoman history and religion by proponents of all factions. To return to Cromwell's compelling image of an 'English Alchoran', the Islamic model was both ideologically ambivalent, longstanding and, above all, invested with the authority of its imperial might. Moreover, the remarkable currency of the Qur'anic allusion can be traced even more directly to the pamphlet marketplace of early 1649. On 7 May, Thomason added another tract to his collection. As cited in the previous chapter, *The Alcoran of Mahomet*, translated from a recent French rendition, was the first full translation of the Qur'an in English and, despite its scholarly shortcomings, represents a landmark in the development of Arabic studies in England. Routinely ascribed to Alexander Ross, this extraordinary document sandwiches its French source text between an opening address 'The Translator to the Christian Reader' along with 'A needful Caveat or Admonition for them who desire to know what use may be made of, or if there be any danger in reading the *Alcoran*', appended to the translation.[16] Apparently intended for dedication to Charles, the translation was not ready until after the king's execution. Unsur-

---

[16] The prevailing assumption of Ross' authorship has been questioned in the recent study by

prisingly, the authorities were not immediately disposed to countenance such a controversial work. For 19 March 1649, the *Journal of the House of Commons* records 'The humble Petition of Colonel *Anthony Welden*, touching the *Turkish Alcoran*, informing the same to be now in the Press.'[17] Parliament issued a warrant 'for the serjeant-at-arms and an officer of the guard … to search for the press where the Turkish Alcoran is being printed, and to seize the same, and the papers; also to apprehend the printer and take him before the Council of State'. Two days later, the House was informed that the printer had indeed been apprehended and copies of the book seized. On 29 March, a committee was formed 'for examining the business as to printing the Turkish Alcoran', consisting of 'Sir Jas. Harrington, Alderman Wilson, and Mr.Robinson'. Two further days later, the *Calendar of State Papers* reports, the suspected author was himself called to give evidence: 'Thos. Ross to be summoned to give an account for the printing of the Alcoran.'[18] Evident here is anxiety about the subversive potential of a rival holy text. Extraordinarily enough, however, it seems that the licensing committee approved *The Alcoran of Mahomet* as publication went ahead in 1649, the translation appearing barely four months after the regicide and virtually concurrently with *The Famous Tragedie*. Indeed, it seems highly plausible that controversy surrounding the translation was directly responsible for the play's evocation of an 'English Alchoran', a hybrid script like the play itself, half English, half Muslim. In his introduction, the translator scathingly and rather daringly alludes to this state intervention:

> Therefore (Christian Reader) though some, conscious of their own instability in Religion, and of theirs (too like the Turks in this) whose prosperity and opinions they follow, were unwilling this should see the Presse, yet am I confident, if thou hast been so true a votary to orthodox Religion, as to keep thy self untainted of their follies: this shall not hurt thee: And as for those of that Batch, having once abandoned the Sun of the Gospel, I believe they will wander far into utter darknesse, by following strange lights, as by this Ignis Fatuus of the Alcoran.[19]

Making the political connotations of the translation overt, the preface turns censorious objection on its head in order to attack the new political establishment. A direct knowledge of the contents of the Qur'an does not preclude a typical disparagement of its teachings and culture. Clearly, however, such censures are secondary to the true target of the writer's opprobrium, the heresy of those following the 'Ignis Fatuus' of a growing non-conformity in English religion. In a similar vein, the preface preempts conventional objections to the unveiling of a profane scripture with a frontal attack on the prevailing heterodoxy:

Alexander Hamilton and Francis Richard, *Andre du Ryer and Oriental Studies in Seventeenth-Century France* (Oxford: Oxford University Press, 2004).
[17] *Journal of the House of Commons*, vol. 6, p. 168.
[18] *C.S.P.*, 1649–50, pp. 42, 45, 59, 63.
[19] 'The Translator to the Christian Reader', A3r–A4v.

There being so many Sects and Heresies banded together against the Truth, finding that of *Mahomet* wanting to the Muster, I thought good to bring it to their Colours, that so viewing thine enemies in their full body, thou mayst the better prepare to encounter, and I hope overcome them. It may happily startle thee, to finde him so to speak *English*, as if he had made some Conquest of the Nation, but thou wilt soon reject that fear, if thou consider that this is his *Alcoran* (the Ground-work of the *Turkish* Religion) hath been already translated into almost all Languages in Christendom ... yet never gained any Proselyte where the Sword, its most forcible, and strongest argument hath not prevailed ...[20]

Evident here is the still embryonic nature of formal Islamic studies in England compared to its prevalence in European thought (the Qur'an having been 'already translated into almost all Languages in Christendom') as well as the commonplace assumption that Islam was the exclusive domain of 'the *Turkish* Religion'. Pursuant to this, is the idea that the translation might result in a linguistic 'Conquest of the Nation', in the same way that the seemingly unstoppable momentum of Ottoman imperialism had threatened to do since the time of the Crusades. Most striking of all, however, is the writer's scornful contention that '*Mahomet*' and his religion are merely the latest in a long line of 'Sects and Heresies' that have already invaded the nation, the clear implication being that the new political and religious order of 1649, like its invidious 'Turkish' counterpart, is maintained not by right, but by the 'Sword'. Such unambiguous contempt for the Commonwealth authorities clearly suggests that following objections in the House, publication had gone ahead without the licensing committee's approval of the final text. Given the availability and prominence of *The Alcoran of Mahomet* as evinced by Thomason and the unmistakable allusion of *The Famous Tragedie*, what is harder to explain is the apparent failure of the Council of State to pursue the seditious author, generally misidentified as Alexander Ross. In comparable cases, the Council had shown itself prepared to act decisively in order to combat the destabilising influence of seditious opposition in print. For example, in 1649 the royalist propagandist Samuel Sheppard was imprisoned and his papers confiscated.[21] Ross, by contrast, remained free to complete work on his mammoth *The Marrow of Historie* (1650), an account of events from 'the Creation to the end of the last Macedonian War'.

Whilst the views of the prefatory address are most likely consistent with those of the contraversialist and former chaplain to King Charles, it is important to note that the name of Alexander Ross appears only in relation to the 'Needful caveat', a treatise defending the study of the Qur'an appended to the translation. Like the translator's preface 'To the Christian Reader', the separate caveat has clearly been written after the publication's brush with the law and is specifically addressed to those 'who desire to know what use may be made of,

[20] 'The Translator', A2r.
[21] See Potter, *Secret Rites*, p. 122.

or if there be any danger in reading the *Alcoran* in answer to a series of inferred charges. Nevertheless, the two are markedly different. In contrast to the defiant tone of the preface, Ross strikes a scholarly rather than doctrinaire attitude, explicitly referring to a discrete 'Translator' in the course of his defence:

> I suppose this piece is exposed by the Translator to the publick view, no otherwise than some Monster brought out of Africa, for people to gaze, not to dote upon, and as the sight of a Monster or misshapen creature should induce the beholder to praise God, who hath not made him such, so should the reading of this Alcoran excite us both to bless Gods goodness towards us in this Land, who enjoy the glorious light of the Gospel, and behold the truth in the beauty of holiness. ... I know the publishing of the Alchoran may be to some dangerous and scandalous, dangerous to the Reader, scandalous to the higher powers, who notwithstanding have cleared themselves by disliking the publishing and questioning the publishers thereof; but for the danger, I will deliver in these ensuing Propositions my opinion, yet with submission to wiser judgements.[22]

The seventeen propositions that follow offer standard refutations of the Qur'an as self-evidently erroneous[23], alongside more thought-provoking justifications for its investigation. Why, for example, should the study of 'Mahomet's Heresies' be any more dangerous than the reading of 'those errors which are recorded in Scripture ... the damnable errors and abominations of the Egyptians, Canaanites, Hittites, Sidonians, and other Gentiles, and of the Hebrews themselves'? Similarly, how does the fallacy of 'Mahometanism' compare with the doctrinal errors of the ancients 'Tertulian, Ireneus, Epiphanius, Austin, and other Fathers'? Provocative comparisons of this kind are consonant with Ross' theological writings elsewhere. Despite a deep-seated philosophical scholasticism, typified in the schoolmaster's attack on Browne and Digby in his *Medicus Medicatus* (1645), Ross' interest in comparative religion reflects a new, albeit highly sceptical engagement with Islamic doctrine culminating in his grandiose Πανσεβεια; *or, a View of all Religions in the world* (1653).[24] In the chapter

22 'A needful Caveat or Admonition for them who desire to know what use may be made of, or if there be any danger in reading the *Alcoran*', E1r.
23 The following description is typical of one commonplace attitude towards the Qur'an throughout the period although the certainty with which Islam might be dismissed in this way was under constant erosion, not least by the appearance of the 1649 translation itself: 'If there were any loveliness, beauty, excellency, or anything else in the Alchoran that might win the minde, and draw the affection after it, I should hold the reading of it dangerous, but whereas it is such a mishapened deformed piece, I think the reading of it will confirm us in the truth, and cause us love the Scripture so much the more: for as a beautiful body is never more lovely than when she is placed neer a Black-More, neither is truth more amiable than when it is beset with Errors.'
24 '*Religio Medici*, claimed Ross, showed its author to have been dangerously attracted to the Arabic commentaries through which many Europeans had interpreted ancient Greek doctrines ... on the burning question of the immortality of the soul, Browne had been far too feeble in his attempts to distinguish original Greek wisdom from erroneous, essentially Islamic doctrine.' David Allen, '"An Ancient Sage Philosopher": Alexander Ross and the

devoted to 'the two prevalent Religions this day in Europe', Ross asserts that the '*Alcoran,* was much altered after his ['Mahumet's'] death' and refers his reader back to the earlier 'Caveat'.[25]

By 1649, Ross had been ejected from his living at Carisbrooke, having been forced to move to the isolated parish in 1642 from his original post at Southampton.[26] Now lodging with his friend Sir Andrew Henley at Bramshill in Hampshire, Ross was clearly no supporter of the Commonwealth but was politic enough to defer to 'wiser judgements' in his openly attributed defence of the translation. Although Ross may not have been directly responsible for the translation, however, he was clearly intimately involved with its production and seems to have been instrumental in justifying its appearance to the Council of State.

Nevertheless, like the author of *The Famous Tragedie,* Ross is engaged in an act of cultural mediation, negotiating the point at which established and revolutionary worlds collide. Unlike the outspoken Ross, however, the author of *The Famous Tragedie* takes refuge in an anonymity that not only suggests the increasingly hostile conditions in which the dissenting author must operate, but accords with desperate attempts, within the play, to come to terms with the radically changing meanings of authorship in the new post-regicidal order of 1649. Ironically enough, although a staunchly royalist supporter may have been responsible for introducing the Qur'an to England, its connotations were most commonly deemed to be republican. For the ardent devotee of Charles and his divine right, it must have seemed that the ultimate heresy had been perpetrated – that 'Mohamet' and his 'Alchoran' had truly come to England.

Defence of Philosophy', *The Seventeenth Century* 16, no. 1 (2001), p. 76. In common with other modern commentators, Allen assumes Ross to have been solely responsible for the 1649 translation and cites it only as evidence of Ross' 'versatility' (n. 4, p. 86).

25 Alexander Ross, Πανσεβεια; *or, a View of all Religions in the world* (London, 1653), p. 145. In his preface, the author provides a list of his works to date occasioned by 'the desire of some Friends'. Included is 'A Caveat for reading the *Alcoran*' but, crucially, not the translation itself.

26 Allen, 'Alexander Ross', p. 72.

Chapter 3

ORIENTING THE MONARCH:
TYRANNY AND TRAGEDY IN ROBERT BARON'S
MIRZA AND JOHN DENHAM'S *THE SOPHY*

H ISTORICAL TYRANTS HAD long been stock villains of English drama, and a particular fascination with Oriental tyrants of one kind or another may be traced back to Marlowe's *Tamburlaine* and beyond.[1] As Rebecca Bushnell has noted, the early seventeenth century witnessed a spate of tyrant plays that points to contemporary anxiety at the projection of James' absolutist prerogative:

> In representing tyranny, tragedy thus more often confuses rather than supports the antithesis between king and tyrant. On one level, tyrant tragedy brings out the contradictions at the heart of the Humanist formulation of the tyrant's theatricality. In his acting the tyrant is paradoxically powerful and vulnerable …[2]

This formulation and the identification of an inherently fissured form of tragedy provides a suggestive context for another strand of historical precedent customarily deemed to be outside the humanist tradition. Alongside classical European sources, episodes in Islamic and particularly Ottoman history emerge as increasingly prominent analogues for dramatic treatments of sovereignty.[3] Moreover, as we might expect, as dissatisfaction at Charles' personal rule grew in the 1630s, so interest in the nature and history of tyranny intensifies both within and outside the drama. In his study of the period immediately preceding the Civil War, *Theatre and Crisis 1632–1642*, Martin Butler makes a compelling

---

[1] The fact that at least one Persian tyrant was so familiar to playgoers of the 1590s as to be a figure of fun is attested by Falstaff's declaration that he will play the part of Henry 'in King Cambyses' vein' (*1 Henry IV* II.v.352).

[2] Rebecca W. Bushnell, *Tragedies of Tyrants: Political Thought and Theater in the English Renaissance* (Ithaca, NY: Cornell University Press, 1990), pp. 264–5.

[3] For example, Thomas Goffe's two sorties into Turkish history, *The Raging Turk* (1613) and *The Couragious Turke* (1619), dramatise the reigns of Bajazet II and Amurath respectively. A later example is Lodovick Carlell's *Osmond the Great Turk* (1637). Many of these plays recall in some way the Turk as the familiar embodiment of cruelty, lasciviousness and, above all, an untrammelled despotism.

case for the increasing politicisation and dissidence of theatre in the last decade of pre-war Caroline theatre up until the point when 'parliament went to war on the king in 1642, the stage fell with the monarchy and remained inhibited until the court's return eighteen years later'.[4] Citing a court play as early as 1620, which staged the 'basic motifs of tyrannical kingship, misplaced trust and misused power' as evidence of the ways in which 'cavalier' drama was able to critique monarchical authority, Butler identifies an impulse of the drama that can be usefully projected beyond the conventional watershed of 1642. As *The Famous Tragedie* evinces, Parliament's closure of the public theatres, in conjunction with a vitally transformed print culture in the 1640s, only served to heighten the political import of the surviving drama. Deprived of legitimate arenas of performance, dramatic writings of the 1640s and 1650s become increasingly fascinated with metaphors of subversive and political playing. In this sense, the two plays under consideration offer a revealing comparison. Published on the eve of the Civil War, *The Sophy* was among the last plays to be acted by the King's Company 'at the Private House in Black Friars', whilst *Mirza*, a lengthy closet drama, was published in 1655 and clearly intended to be read rather than performed. Dramatising the same episode in Persian history, variations in the two treatments highlight crucial differences between the political and dramatic arenas in which the two texts operate; located at either end of a political and dramatic revolution in England, the contrasting responses of these 'royalist' authors to their oriental source material suggests ways in which dramatic representations of the East were transformed in direct response to the conditions of performance and politics radically altered in the intervening fourteen years.

'ACTIONS O' TH' LAST AGE ARE LIKE ALMANACKS O' TH' LAST YEARE': TOPICAL ORIENTS AND DANGEROUS HISTORIES

The Sophy and *Mirza* are highly specific dramatic responses to their own discursive conditions although both adapt a familiar theatrical strategy: the staging of a narrative ostensibly concerned with events that are geographically distant in order to describe situations that are politically close to home. Their immediate source is Sir Thomas Herbert's *A relation of Some Yeares Travaile, Begunne Anno 1626* (1634), which relates the diplomatic visit of Sir Dodmore Cotton to the Persian court of King Abbas in 1626. Included in the party was one of the most well-known English visitors to Persia, the intrepid if now somewhat older Sir Robert Sherley, one of the celebrated Sherley brothers whose exploits had been publicised in Anthony Nixon's pamphlet of 1607 and positively eulogised on stage in the same year in *The Travels of the Three English*

---

4   Martin Butler, *Theatre and Crisis 1632–1642* (Cambridge: Cambridge University Press, 1984), p. 3.

Brothers, a play attributed to Rowley, Day and Wilkins by its most recent editor. In his introduction to the play, Anthony Parr gives the following account of the place of Persia in the early modern imagination:

> Traditionally, a land of wealth and luxury, with a glorious imperial past, [Persia] was for Western writers a genuinely exotic country, not a malign and unknowable neighbour but a fabulous resource. Like India or Japan, it was not so much Europe's Other as its opposite or foil; and while the fascination with the glamorous east was later to become a disabling orientalism, arguably it was during the early modern period a positive alternative to views of Asia either as the home of barbarian hordes or of the hellish doctrine of Islam. [5]

Whilst this is a useful starting point for understanding English constructions of Persia in the early part of the century, the identification of a straightforward binary of a proximate Ottoman Empire in tension with a distant, relatively benign Safavid civilisation is less tenable by the 1640s. This is not to argue that English writers did not continue to be fascinated by perceived religious and political differences between the two greatest exponents of Islam; throughout the sixteenth century, the Persian Empire had often been seen as a potential bulwark against Ottoman military expansion. However, the focus of that interest had shifted and sharpened in response both to ongoing Anglo-Persian encounters in trade and diplomacy as well as the altered terms of the political and religious debate in England. By 1616 the East India Company had reached an agreement with the Safavids to trade English cloth for Persian silk and, in 1622, the English helped Abbas to retake Hurmuz from the Portuguese. [6] In 1623, Abbas had reclaimed Baghdad and his military successes against the Ottomans were closely followed in the West. By the time of the English Civil War, therefore, contemporary Persia was in Parr's phraseology, increasingly 'knowable'. In depicting the recent history of the reign of King Abbas as they found it in Herbert, far from taking refuge in the safety of an exotic fantasy, both Denham and Baron are self-consciously engaging with source material that is both topical and ideologically active.

The precise month in which *The Sophy* received its first audience is unclear, although the play is steeped in the controversies of the early 1640s and acutely aware of its own political currency. [7] In his prologue, the playwright punningly

---

5   Anthony Parr, ed., *Three Renaissance Travel Plays* (Manchester: Manchester University Press, 1995), p. 11.
6   For an account of Anglo-Persian relations in this period, see Roger Savory, *Iran under the Safavids* (Cambridge: Cambridge University Press, 1980).
7   Of Denham's success with *The Sophy*, Edmund Waller is said to have remarked, 'that he broke out like the Irish rebellion, three-score thousand strong, when nobody was aware, or in the least suspected it'. Samuel Johnson, 'The Life of John Denham', *The Works of the English Poets, from Chaucer to Cowper*, 21 vols, vol. 7 (London: J. Johnson et al., 1810), p. 223. News of the Irish rebellion reached London in November 1641 and it is possible that the play was conceived and certainly received with the Irish situation in mind.

alludes to the struggle between Parliament and the King and, in his role as censured (although not yet censored) playwright, playfully aligns himself with the beleaguered monarch:

> Hither yee come, dislike, and so undo
> The Players, and disgrace the Poet too;
> But he protests against your votes, and sweares
> Hee'll not be try'd by any, but his Peeres;
> He claimes his priviledge, and sayes 'tis fit,
> Nothing should be the Judge of wit, but Wit.[8]

If a performance date late in 1641 is entertained then it is possible that these lines refer to the Grand Remonstrance, brought before the Commons on 8 November and presented to the king on 1 December (and rejected three weeks later). Containing the summarised grievances of the country and setting forth Parliament's specific criticisms of Charles' government since 1620, including the influence of 'evil counsellors', the terms of the Remonstrance overlap with the play action in suggestive ways. Undoubtedly, the constitutional crisis sparked by Parliament's formalised objections to the conduct of Charles' government would have been paramount to the ways in which the play was *read* in 1642. In the context of a 1641 performance, however, the figure of a peer protesting his 'priviledge' against the calumny of an audience's 'votes' is an unmistakable evocation of the impeachment and trial of the Earl of Strafford in March 1641. On 10 May, Charles gave his assent to the Bill of Attainder against Strafford, who was executed two days later, as a direct result of public pressure.[9] In the play proper, it is Haly, the King's favourite, who becomes the focus for the denunciation of self-serving counsellors. Potent paralleling of this kind suggests the degree to which pre-war drama, conventionally ascribed to a cavalier sensibility, might question the actions of its monarch and most influential patron.[10] Moreover, the irrefutable topicality of Denham's representation of Persian polity underlines the powerful valency of the Islamic model on the eve of Civil War.

The play opens with the ominous threat of war and an allusion that must have seemed somewhat audacious in the environs of the Blackfriar's theatre. Discussing the strength of the approaching Ottoman army, two loyal courtiers deliberate the need to impress upon the Persian monarch the military and financial dangers that beset his proposed campaign. Having been informed that his 'Treasures/ Are quite exhausted, the Exchequer's empty' (p. 3), the

---

8   John Denham, *The Sophy* (London, 1642), A2r. All subsequent references to the play are to the first London edition dated 1642.

9   Derek Hirst, *England in Conflict 1603–1660: Kingdom, Community, Commonwealth* (London: Arnold, 1999), p. 168.

10   In public life, Denham's royalist credentials are well documented – at the beginning of the Civil Wars Denham was high sheriff of Surrey, and took up arms for the king. In 1642 he was forced to surrender Farnham Castle, of which he was governor.

Sophy retorts, 'Talke not to me of Treasures, or Exchequers,/ Send for five hundred of the wealthiest Burgers,/ Their shops and ships are my Exchequer' – a conspicuous reference to Charles' disastrous decision to levy new taxes on the kingdom in order to finance his war against Scotland. It is Haly who identifies the fatal flaw of absolute monarchy, who identifies the fatal flaw of absolute monarchy, '… where Subjects want the priviledge/ To speake; there Kings may have the priviledge/ To live in ignorance' (p. 13). Moreover, Denham introduces a new character, that of the Caliph, in order to emphasise the degree to which religion may be made to conspire with sedition, since the people 'must be pray'd, and preach'd into a tumult' (p. 49). Conversely, state-endorsed religion may be equally dangerous since, in the words of one courtier,

> … they, whose sacred office 'tis to bring
> Kings to obey their God, and men their King,
> By these mysterious linkes to fixe and tye
> Them to the foot-stoole of the Deity:
> Even by these men, Religion, that should be
> The curbe, is made the spurre to tyrannie;
> They with their double key of conscience binde
> The Subjects soules, and leave Kings unconfin'd; (p. 26)

As Martin Butler has pointed out, the play's representation of the Caliph and his 'sacred office' is a fair reflection of popular resentment towards Archbishop Laud,[11] who had enforced religious conformity throughout the realm since 1634 and who was widely perceived as the conduit through which popish factions influenced the king.[12] By the end of 1641, Laud too had been impeached for treason and imprisoned in the Tower.

Whilst such pointed references distinguish *The Sophy* as a remarkably unflinching critique of contemporary events, however, Denham effects a number of significant changes to his source that mitigate the tragic impact of the original narrative. Robert Baron's *Mirza*, as the author is anxious to bring to his reader's attention, is a more faithful rendering of Herbert's account. Comparing his own treatment with that of *The Sophy*, Baron assures his reader that he 'had finished three compleat Acts of this Tragedy before I saw that, nor was I then discouraged from proceeding, seeing the most ingenious Author of that has made his seem quite another story from this'. In terms of plot, *Mirza* is chiefly distinguished by the fact that Abbas survives the conspiracy to depose him and that the prince carries through his resolve to murder Fatyma, a moment that Baron crucially identifies 'as the compleatest Conquest that ever Revenge obtained over Vertue' and the crux of his tragedy. In dispensing with these two problematic elements of the story, as they derive from Herbert's

---

11 Butler, *Theatre and Crisis*, p. 80.
12 'The Church in England 1642–1649', in Morrill, *The Nature of the English Revolution*, pp. 148–75.

Relation, Denham circumvents the potentially unsettling images of a prince who destroys his own line and a tyrant who remains on stage and in power at the end of the play.

Where Denham had seen fit to exercise a degree of licence, Baron is repeatedly compelled to protest the veracity of his story. From the outset, *Mirza* trumpets its authenticity, the subtitle to the play, 'A Tragedie, Really acted in Persia, in the last Age' not only specifying a generic designation but also laying claim to an all-important historical truth. As an instruction in how to read the narrative, the subtitle suggests that events may be 'Really acted' in the same way that a play text portrays those events, in other words, that the boundary between real and imagined performance is shifting and inherently uncertain. That the same language may be applied equally to the internal world of the play and the external world of domestic politics is central to the play's rationale. In making a glancing allusion to the current status of the dramatic form in England in the 1650s, one of the approbatory verses that introduce the play picks up on this central preoccupation of *Mirza*:

> When I read yours (dear friend) I seem'd to see
> In Persia acted this sad Tragedie,
> But might we see it acted on the Stage
> ABBAS in his, and MIRZA in his rage …
> Persia would then seem but in theories
> To Personate what you to life have drawn …[13]

As we might anticipate from the prohibitive conditions of 1655, Baron's 'audience' have not experienced the play acted out on stage, but have 'read' the text of 'this sad Tragedie'. Certainly, there is plenty of internal evidence to suggest that Baron fully intended *Mirza* to be read and carefully digested, not least the inclusion of over a hundred pages of annotation at the end of what is, by the standards of its day, an exceptionally long and elaborate play.[14] More significant, however, is the notion that real and fictive arenas can be readily interchanged, that 'theories' may come to mimic 'life' and vice-versa. As this writer goes on to argue, such a confusion of representations constitutes an expedient strategy, legitimising and empowering the play fiction in order that the audience might 'resent with such a Sympathy/ As might extract a deluge from their eyes'. In many ways, however, the play itself is at odds with this, convention-

---

13 Robert Baron, *Mirza: A Tragedie, Really Acted in Persia, in the last Age* (London, 1655), A5r. Subsequent references are to the copy of the play held in the Thomason Collection of the British Library.

14 In his address 'To the Reader', Baron adapts the conventional disclaimer; if any 'exceptest against the length of the Play' it is enough to say '— Neque, me ut miretur turba, laboro:/ Contentus paucis Lectoribus' (and take no pains to make the multitude admire you, content with a few [judicious] *readers*). Horace, *Satires,* I.10.73–4. Significantly in view of Baron's veneration of Jonson, the same quotation appears in the front matter of *Sejanus his fall* (1616).

ally cavalier, account of drama's function. *Mirza* does not subscribe to such an unconditional sanctioning of play-acting any more than it succumbs to an unequivocally royalist version of history. Indeed, Baron's play repeatedly emphasises the moral imperative of distinguishing between reality and its mimetic representation. In the context of the status of theatre by 1655, *Mirza* emerges as a more problematic and ambivalent critique of royalist ideology than has been hitherto suggested.[15] Far from being the straightforward rendition of royalist suffering at the hands of malevolent factionalism, the play's adherence to its Persian subject matter repeatedly undermines its ostensible loyalism. Before turning to specific ways in which the text thwarts such expectations, it may be useful to provide a brief summary of Baron's version of this 'story sad and sublime'.

The tragedy opens with the ghost of Emir-Hamze-Mirza's, the murdered brother of the present King Abbas, who calls for revenge in a scene that self-consciously echoes Jonson's *Catiline*.[16] With the connivance of Floradella, the king's concubine, Ally-Beg incites the king's jealousy of his son's popularity and convinces him that the prince and his 'faction' intend a rebellion. Abbas summons Mirza from the battlefield where he has been laying siege to a nameless Turkish town, and lures him to court where he is set upon by seven 'Mutes with bow-strings'. Having valiantly killed three of his assailants, Mirza is finally overcome but Abbas relents and intervenes before the sentence can be carried out, ordering instead that 'a flaming steel be drawn before/ His eyes, to take away his sight' (p. 60), a detail faithfully transposed from Herbert's account. The blind prince is imprisoned and, descending into madness, believes himself transported to a classical underworld. Tormented by a desire to take revenge upon his father, Mirza resolves to murder his own daughter Fatyma, who has become a favourite companion to her grandfather Abbas, breaking her neck and declaring that 'The world's too little to satiate my revenge' (p. 110). Meanwhile, the exiled Duke Emangoly, who has remained loyal to Abbas, learns of Ally-Beg's treachery thanks to the injudicious gossiping of Floradella's maidservant. The conspirators are discovered and condemned to suitably exotic punishments – Ally-Beg is to have his eyes bored out and is to be imprisoned until Abbas' own funeral day when he shall be burnt on the funeral pyre, whilst Floradella is to have her brains beaten out and her limbs burned with 'Cats

---

15 Randall, for example, identifies Prince Mirza as 'an all-virtuous and long-suffering soldier and family man, much beloved by his followers and yet inevitably brought down – in other words, a reasonable Charles figure', but sidesteps the inherently problematic nature of such an allegorical reading in the play. Randall, *Winter Fruit*, p. 67.

16 Baron's indebtedness to Jonson's play is carefully acknowledged in the annotation that accompanies the scene, describing the convention of the vengeful ghost as being 'not without the example of the matchles Johnson, who, in his Catiline (which miraculous *Poem* I propose as my pattern) makes Sylla's Ghost perswade Catiline to do what *Hannibal* could not wish'. Jesse Franklin Bradley, 'Robert Baron's Tragedy of Mirza', *Modern Language Notes* 34 (1919), pp. 402–8, gives a detailed account of the precise textual parallels.

dung' (p. 146). The king is finally convinced of Mirza's innocence but arrives too late to prevent the prince taking a draught of poison. Mirza dies and the play ends with the king's decree making Soffie (Mirza's son) heir to the Persian throne and 'the Empire's hope' (p. 158).

Insofar as the play dramatises the conspiracy of Mahomet Ally-Beg to overthrow the Persian monarchy and seize the crown for himself, it is not difficult to see why this, and Denham's version of the story, have been construed as comments upon the domestic situation. The commendatory verses that preface the play offer an indication of how the play was first received, albeit couched in the formularised rhetoric of eulogy. Those represented include a selection of Baron's contemporaries at Cambridge[17], as well as at least one notable royalist, John Quarles, who signs himself 'Fell. Of Pet. House Camb' and who had served as a captain in the king's army until its disbandment.[18] For Quarles, at least, Baron's tale of Persian insurrection invites the reader to make a comparison with recent events a lot closer to home. Having entreated 'Great Mirza' to advance, in order to 'let the base world see/ Vertue is Vertue though in misery', Quarles concludes his address with an overt allegorisation:

> We mourn thy loss, admire thy worth, and grieve
> Our Isle a Mirz' and Allybeg can give.
> Thus Text and Time doe sute, and whilst you tell
> Your tale, wee'l easily find a Parallel.

The Mirza of this analogy is, presumably, the martyred Charles or, more broadly, the embodiment of 'Vertue ... in misery' and representative of the royalist predicament in 1655, whilst the perfidious Ally-Beg performs Cromwell's role. Thus the 'Text' is made to mirror the political situation of the 'Time', although, as I shall argue, the play itself resists such a straightforward deciphering of its action. This is not to detract from the political currency of Baron's material that, in his own words 'To the Reader', constitutes 'the Triumph of Revenge, Tyranny, Jealousie, and Hate, in a story sad and sublime, however handled'. Such themes are clearly applicable to a particularly royalist version of recent history, although the meaning of this complex and ambivalent play is not so 'easily' untangled. As a closer look at the events of Baron's play indicates, the degree to which Mirza's demise can be made consistently analogous with that of his English counterpart is problematic. Who, for example, is the Cromwell figure of the play – the treacherous favourite Ally-Beg or the corrupt tyrant Abbas? Similarly, how are we to read a scene in which the enraged Mirza, implicitly compared to the fallen Charles elsewhere in the play, breaks the neck

---

17 Kenneth C. Slagle, 'Robert Baron, Cavalier Poet', *Notes and Queries*, no. 169 (12 October 1935), pp. 254–6: 'We know that Baron was baptized July 22 1630, educated at Caius College Cambridge where he spent one year; that he was admitted to Gray's Inn, London in 1646; and that he died in Norwich in 1658', p. 254.

18 Slagle, 'Robert Baron', p. 255.

of his daughter in order to exact revenge upon his father? Such anomalies are, to some extent, intrinsic to the source material but are examples of the ways in which Baron exploits the dualistic nature of the Persian model to interrogate the prevailing trope of the royalist aesthetic post-1649, that of the martyred monarch.

In the play's opening address 'TO HIS MAJESTIE' it is telling that Baron avoids making the kind of direct allegorisation evident elsewhere in the prefatory material and opts, instead, to emphasise a broader concern of the story.

> To wait on YOU, the Persian Mirza's come
> From the fair shades of his Elizium:
> > ... for he hopes now
> Not onely to delight, but profit YOU,
> In warning to eschew what spoild his Right,
> The Flatterer, and too powerfull Favourite.[19]

In the author's own judgement, Mirza's ghost has been invoked not merely to entertain but to instruct and, contrary to Quarles' emphasis upon the Mirza/Ally-Beg binary, the inherent ambiguity of the story of 'spoild ... Right' is retained. However, the precise identity of the intended recipient of Baron's admonition has been a source of confusion and has precipitated a related disagreement over the dating of the play text. Clearly, given the overt topicality of the action, the issue of dating has a fundamental bearing upon interpretation of the play. Several early accounts of the play mistake Baron's dedication to be intended for Charles I and consequently misdate the play by seven years. For example, having asserted that the author 'claims distinction as one of the most successful of plagiarists', Baron's entry in *The Dictionary of National Biography* goes on to say that *Mirza* is 'without date, but is dedicated to the king, whence probably it was not later than 1648'. Reiterating a similarly erroneous dating in a different cause, that of attempting to secure Baron's reputation as a legitimate member of the 'Cavalier group', Kenneth Slagle urges that,

> We must not forget that 'Mirza', Baron's second work, 1647, is dedicated to the King at a time when His Majesty's cause was admittedly all but lost and King Charles himself was a prisoner in Carisbrook Castle. ... It is ... probable that, with King Charles executed, Cromwell firmly in the saddle, and the elder Baron dead, the poet returned to live quietly in Norwich and to pray privately for better times.[20]

That the printed *Mirza* properly belongs to the post-regicidal era is confirmed by the playwright's allusion to 'our late King Charles' in his annotations. Moreover, the copy of the play held in the Thomason Collection of the British Library has been hand-dated by the bookseller 5 May 1655. Admittedly, these

---

[19] 'To His Majestie', A2r.
[20] Slagle, 'Robert Baron', pp. 254–6.

facts need not preclude an earlier composition date; indeed, the intricacy of the play and the comprehensiveness of the accompanying scholarly apparatus point to an extended period of preparation, if not composition, as does Baron's claim to have supplemented Herbert's account of Cotton's embassy with 'a Manuscript of which Embassadours Letter, to a friend of his in Cambridge' (presumably first discovered when the author was himself in Cambridge in the late 1640s). Nevertheless, several internal references in the annotations and prefatory matter underscore the fact that the text as we now have it belongs irrevocably to the Protectorate and was specifically prepared and formulated for its publication in May 1655. In a more recent account of the play, although acknowledging the existence of two posited dates, Linda McJannet offers the following explanation for Baron's dedication:

> Apparently in Baron's view the suggestion that this episode in contemporary Persian history might hold a moral for a Christian king was not impertinent or risky. Of course, if this preface was written after the king's execution and the octavo didn't appear until 1655, it is ironic and posthumous advice at best. But if, as Baron claims in his preface to the reader, he had already written three acts of his play before John Denham's *The Sophy* appeared, he may have meant these words for the king's eyes, and the work might even have been published and read by Charles or other members of the court before his defeat in 1646 and his death in 1649.[21]

Baron's claim to have completed three acts of his play before 'seeing' Denham's play clearly cannot refer to the first appearance of *The Sophy*, given the fact that Baron was aged only eleven at the time. Such misinterpretations are indicative of a reluctance to divorce the play from its supposedly courtly inception and, more generally, point to the deliberate ambiguity of Baron's dedication, poised between commendation and salutary caution. Similarly, whilst Slagle's extrapolation is clearly based on a false supposition, it does, ironically, draw attention to the fact that the playwright did *not* simply withdraw from public life after his early forays into poetry.[22] Rather, Baron's play, all the more remarkable for its later dating, represents an extremely audacious intervention in the political discourse of the day, imbuing the play with a meaning that is not merely politically current, but irrefutably forward looking, a proleptic warning from history not to repeat the mistakes of the Persian king and, by implication, those of his own father.

---

[21] Linda McJannet, 'Bringing in a Persian', *Medieval and Renaissance Drama in England* 12 (1999), pp. 236–67.

[22] Baron published *The Cyprian Academy* in 1647, dated 'from my chambers in Gray's Inn, 1, April, 1647'. Two further books of poetry, *Apologie for Paris* and *Pocula Castalia* appeared in 1649 and 1650 respectively.

'SLEEPING THOUGHTS':
IMAGINING PERFORMANCE IN *MIRZA* AND *THE SOPHY*

Like *Mirza*, Denham's play is suffused with metaphors of performance and authorship, which are repeatedly applied to malevolent forces within the play. Having inherited the Persian throne from his dead (in Denham's rendering) father, the young Soffy equates the 'performance' of the late king's funeral rites with the conspirators' *act* of rebellion: 'then all that were/ Actors, or Authors of so black a deed,/ Be sacrific'd as Victims to his ghost' (p. 53). Crucially, however, Denham's play suggests that redemption remains a possibility, that it is not too late to re-appropriate authorship in the cause of virtue, once 'justice' (p. 53) has been served. In the final analysis, Denham's martyred prince emerges untainted, having heroically resisted the temptation to take revenge upon his daughter and defied the 'tyranny of Fate' (p. 44). The sacrificial 'bloud' of the 'holy Devill', Caliph (Laud), and 'th'abuser of' the 'Princes ear', Haly (Strafford) will be enough to cleanse the body politic.

By 1655, however, the prince appears less the model of martyred virtue and more the embodiment of an all pervasive crisis of morality. With his dying breath, Mirza imagines his own dramatic resurrection, reflexively prefiguring the play's own rendition of the story: 'I shall again live—and on some sad Stage/ Be mourn'd.—Great wrongs reach further then one Age.—/ O—O./ [Dies.' (p. 156). Of course, that 'Stage' did not yet exist when Baron composed his play – the prince's prophecy incorporates a vision of the future beyond the scope of 1655, suggesting that the tyrant's legacy cannot be simply erased in the cathartic act of Mirza's death. Indeed, throughout, *Mirza* insistently renounces the redemptive force of tragedy, which authorised the resolution to Denham's play, and is at pains to demonstrate the moral danger inherent in fictive representations. Toward the end of the first act, the play introduces the youngest generation of the Persian monarchy, Soffie and Fatyma, 'Looking upon a Picture' that depicts the story of Medea.[23] The royal party, it transpires, intend a visit to see the story 'play'd at Madam OMAYS', a lady of the court. They are interrupted, however, by the arrival of Floradella, the king's concubine and Ally-Beg's co-conspirator, who probes Nymphadora, Mirza's wife, and tries to tempt her to treason by wishing her husband king. Remaining staunchly oblivious to Floradella's Machiavellian stratagem (scrupulously explained to the audience in her 'secret' asides), Nymphadora decrees that the discovery of 'trai'trous plots' (p. 21) against the king can wait until after the performance. The full significance of this curious and digressive scene does not become apparent until the play's dénouement. Having been warned of Ally-

---

[23] As Iffida, the maidservant, explains to the royal siblings, 'That fierece Lady MEDEA resolv'd to fly/ With her new servant JASON from her Father;/ To hinder his pursuit she tore in pieces/ Her brother ABSYRTUS, and bestrewd ith'way/ His limbs …' (p. 17). The story of unnatural cruelty exacted upon kindred family members is obviously an anticipation of events later in the play.

Beg's treachery, the king at first mistakes truth for fantasy – 'What Pageant's this!' (p. 123) – before finally agreeing to hear out the allegations of the loyal Duke Emangoly, who tells him that the conspirators are holding their 'black counsell' at that very moment again, tellingly, at Madam Omay's, the venue for the earlier performance of Medea. Meanwhile, Ally-Beg stages his final *coup de théâtre*, in which the credulous courtiers are persuaded that armed insurrection is necessary to rescue the prince, and restore the Persian monarchy.

> Yet the old King's so fast in his dead sleep,
> So lost in his strong Lethargy, he feels,
> Nor sees, at least regards, nothing of this ...
> Nor think't at all unjust; "That War is just
> "That's necessary, and those arms religious,
> "When there's no hope left otherwise but in them.
> The Prince restor'd, the King once shewn his error,
> SOFFIE return'd to safety, how will all
> Applaud the Actors! (p. 131)

Inveigled by Ally-Beg's virtuoso performance of patriotic ardour, the nobility are lured into the false security of the show and made unwitting actors in his conspiracy. Also significant here is a reproach of the king's negligent government described in terms of a 'dead sleep' or a 'strong Lethargy'. Elsewhere in the play, sleep, like wanton play-going, is equated with a pernicious moral laxity: in the act of devolving power to Ally-Beg, his newly appointed 'second in glory', Abbas hopes that 'conceit/ Of sword, or Treason' will no longer disturb his 'troubled slumbers' (p. 45) and signs Ally-Beg's commission for a personal guard, before hurrying away to attend a 'Masque' (p. 105). Manifest here are many of the criticisms that had dogged the last years of Charles' administration, namely that the king was oblivious to the plight of his kingdom and embroiled in pleasures at court, a disregard exemplified not least in the commission of frequent masques and other frivolous entertainments at great expense to the nation. The play's underlying implication is that Charles, like Abbas, had courted his own demise, that he was guilty not only of 'tyranny but of abdication'.[24] However, it is in its portrait of Mirza's madness that the play fully expands this metaphor for dissolute government. Having been lured from the (ironic) safety of the battlefield, and symbolically divested himself of his 'Scimitar ... glutted/ With Ottoman blood' (p. 56), the

---

[24] John Morrill gives a suggestive account of Parliament's initial defiance of the king that strikes a chord with Baron's portrayal of Persian negligence: '... men like John Pym were genuinely convinced both of the reality of the plot and of the need to take up arms to defend the nation from it. In their account of the plot, the radicals around Pym saw Charles as a man whose mind had been so poisoned by the lies and deceptions of the papists and their fellow-travellers that he was no longer capable of defending his office or his realm. He was guilty not of tyranny but of abdication, not of over-mightiness but of supineness.' *The Nature of the English Revolution*, p. 297.

soporific effect of the court induces the prince fatefully to decide that 'a nap shall settle' his 'toss'd braine' (p. 56). Of course, Mirza is then taken unawares by seven mute executioners, 'deaf in soul and body', and his lack of foresight is punished with blindness. In the scene immediately following, Fatyma tells how she has dreamed that she has seen 'an eagle pick his chickens eyes out' (p. 62). Nymphadora's sententious response resonates with a multiplicity of meanings, sustaining the twin themes of sleep and play-acting and combining them in a metaphor that seems to encapsulate Baron's view of the function of his own piece of drama.

> ... our sleeping thoughts are oft
> Idle and imperfect, but most commonly
> They're either Histories of something past,
> Or dark presages of what is to come. (p. 62)

As both 'Histories of something past' and 'dark presages of what is to come', drama (in both the senses of staged representations and the parallel ceremonies of absolute monarchy they mimetically reproduce) becomes invested with not only the power but also, as several voices in the play insist, the dangerous prescience of dreams. When Iffida, the princess' maidservant, entreats her mistress to seek an interpreter for her dreams – 'let some Magus read them to you' – Nymphadora reproves her, warning that 'The heavenly powers are to be reverenced,/ Not searcht into'.[25] Moreover, in the context of the play's conflation of moral and dramatic discourses, the princess' exhortation also articulates the tenet of divine right and is closely echoed by Farraban's belief that 'Kings great intents are to be serv'd, not searcht' (p. 55); according to this strand of opinion, monarchs, like dreams derive their authority from an ineffable 'heavenly power'. Clearly, however, the play as a whole does not, indeed cannot, unconditionally endorse such an assessment of royal prerogative – Mirza is itself collusive in the very acts of representation and interpretation it appears to condemn.

At the heart of the play, therefore, is a conflicting impulse. Whilst, on one hand, Baron's dedication 'TO HIS MAJESTIE' confidently contends drama's ability to 'profit' its participants, the play proper is fraught with the suspicion that the dramatic form itself has been rendered irredeemably corrupt by political events and vice-versa. Constantly undermining its own mode of

---

25 A tacit borrowing from the first book of Sidney's *Arcadia*. Basilius, the Prince of Arcadia, proposing a trip to Delphos, entrusts the 'government of the country' to his friend Philanax, who counsels him that 'the heavenly powers to be reverenced and not searched into, and their mercy rather by prayers to be sought than their hidden counsels by curiosity'. Sir Philip Sidney, *The Old Arcadia*, ed. Katherine Duncan Jones (Oxford: Oxford University Press, 1985), p. 6. In the context of the play, it is telling that auguring is connected with neglectful government. Sidney's epic was intensely politicised following the king's defeat and commonly appropriated by royalist writers (most notoriously in the *Eikon Basilike*'s inclusion of Pamela's prayer). See Potter, *Secret Rites*, pp. 93–4.

expression, it is this tension, between the salutary capacity of fiction and the morally debilitating potential of illusion, that erupts in the scene of the prince's madness.

> I'm in the Torrid Zone, right O right under
> The vehement Line — Water-O-Water quickly. —
> What Devill has in my sleep thrown me to Affrick? (p. 22)

Mirza's hallucination represents a version *in extremis* of the confusion of fantasy with reality that, more generally, infects the courtly life of the play. Moreover, the prince's madness transports him to a distant land in the same way that the play fiction purports to dramatically transport its reader to Persia. Thus, Mirza the man, as much as *Mirza* the play, seethe with self-contradiction. When the prince believes himself in Hades, casting those around him in the various roles of denizens of a classical underworld, Nymphadora, who has been forced to play Prosperine, declares, 'I cannot flatter his wild frenzy' but Soffie urges her to 'seem to be what he conceits you' (p. 89). Like the playwright, those attending the prince seem uncertain of how to contain his ravings and, are similarly torn between an impulse to shelter behind the protective mask of analogy, and a desire to confront reality. In this sense, the 'sleeping thoughts' of Nymphadora's earlier 'conceit' also come to signify the barely latent contradictions that riddle the rationale of the play action.

As much of this suggests, *Mirza* is far from being the consistent expression of a single, identifiable political credo. Instead, there is the mounting sense that an inherent explosiveness in the source material itself constantly causes the action to spill over its ideological parameters. The choric interludes that intersperse the play are perhaps one way in which the play attempts to harness this tendency. Having depicted the initial manoeuvres of Ally-Beg in sowing the seeds of the king's jealousy, the first act ends with an exposition of the moral thus far: 'those ear-wiggs to a King' are

> As Ivy seems the blooming spray
> T'adorn but sucks his heart away:
> So do they rob their Prince of's heart,
> In making him his duty 'invert
> And the best Government Monarchy,
> Degenerate into Tyranny; (p. 24)

Here, it would seem, is the voice of the playwright, maintaining an essentially royalist reading of the collapse of Persian, and we must surely infer, Caroline monarchical authority. In the scene that directly follows, Mirza soliloquises on the inconstancy of 'Fortune' and offers an aphoristic rendition of ideal kingship:

> 'Tis not enough to be
> But born a Prince our greatest Royaltie
> Lies in our Acts ... (p. 25)

Perhaps punning on 'Acts' as legal ordinances, theatrical performances, as well as literal deeds, these lines pick up on the reference to monarchical 'duty' made in the chorus and suggest the bond of mutual obligation between the king and his people that moderates in Parliament had continued to emphasise in the years leading up to the Civil War. Judging from the tone of these opening sorties, it is easy to imagine that the author was not entirely unsympathetic to such calls for reform in order to avert the constitutional crisis of 1642. However, Mirza, it is important to remember, singularly fails to live up to the ideal espoused by his soliloquy and becomes possessed with the spirit of vengeful madness which, quite literally, haunts the Persian court.

As I have sought to suggest, therefore, much of the play's ambivalent treatment of what purports to be 'the best Government Monarchy' is coterminous with the deep misgivings towards courtly culture that pervade the text. Those we may loosely term the 'noble' characters of the play variously sleep, dream and attend plays whilst Ally-Beg, suggestively described in 'The Argument' as 'a person raised to that height from so obscure a descent, that he knew no further then his Father',[26] is able to exploit this vacuum in political authority in order to authorise his own 'black Tragedie' (p. 61). In a scene extrapolated from Herbert's account, Baron depicts the clash of courtly and martial spheres in a particularly suggestive way. Having come from his 'Merchants', the courtier Farraban is followed back to court by two thieves who overhear him locking his money in a trunk –

> Thus are we but Gaolers of our wealth,
> Which although most men make their God, is but
> The Poets slave and mine — And but for use — (p. 15)

In the context of the central image of incarceration within the play, Farraban's comparison is a parodic version of Mirza's imprisonment by his father in Act III, and perhaps a submerged allusion to Charles' infamous imprisonment in Carisbrook Castle. As such, the metaphor invites the suggestion that royal virtue, like money, is an abstract beloved of 'Poets' and similarly, a commodity 'for use' in cynically representing and justifying the divine right to rule. The thieves offer to liberate this 'rich prisoner' but are captured and, two acts later, tried by Abbas. They are, it transpires, deserters from the army who 'Ran from their colours hither' and 'rob'd ith'Court it selfe' (p. 46). Farraban's emphasis upon the violation of the court is, paradoxically, used to draw attention to the degree to which courtly values have infected the military sphere. For instance, when the king supplants Mirza with his own man Beltazar, Emangoly complains that 'There's not a Captains place now to be given/ But some Court-Madam must dispose it, to/ Perhaps some little leg'd Gentleman-Usher' (p. 39).

---

[26] This description echoes the charge of ignoble birth frequently levelled at Cromwell by his royalist opponents.

As we learn elsewhere in the play, the soldiers have been driven to thievery by necessity – 'Our Regiments and companies are thin,/ ... thus hard duty comes/ Oftner to the same men. ... But which is worse,/ A masse of Treasure daily is consum'd/ On idle officers, Parchment Colonells/ And titular Captains' (p. 29). Abbas' sentence is characteristically cruel (in accordance with Herbert's account) but indicative of the court's preoccupation with appearances, being more concerned with the crime of 'prophaning/ Our Court, with such base rags' than the spreading corruption of the army – 'Give them new Coats, then dragg'd out of the Town,/ Impale them high on stakes, thrust through their bodies'.

However, the first interruption of the outside world into the courtly sphere is made by Floradella, the king's concubine, who brings news of the prince's growing fame:

> Alas! My Lord, the peoples common theam
> Still grates mine ears; no other voice is heard
> But MIRZA's praises: the Gods hear no vowes,
> No prayers, but for MIRZA's safety: ...
> (As if all were Historiographers)
> And for each blow he dealt return a statue? (p. 4)

The reference here to the people as 'Historiographers' is a peculiarly self-reflexive glance to the literary–political conditions in which the play itself operates. In his 'Preface to the Reader', Baron is anxious to distinguish his play from that 'Tragedy abroad of this subject, intituled The SOPHY' by emphasising the authenticity of his own story, deriving from the 'Authority' of Thomas Herbert's *Travels*. It is also clear from the copious annotations that accompany the play that Baron had more than a cursory interest in Islamic history and had conscientiously mined the available information in order to research his topic. For example, both George Sandys' *A Relation of a Journey Begun* (1615) and Richard Knolles' *Generall Historie of the Turkes* (1603) are among the studies frequently cited by Baron, both popular accounts of Eastern culture and history in the period. The playwright is, therefore, himself engaged in a self-consciously historiographical exercise, although of a rather different kind than that described by Floradella. Indeed, Baron's professed purpose in treating history is the opposite of the people's unconditional adulation of Mirza's virtues and, as this scene explores, 'popular' shows of this kind are no less dangerous than the indulgence of courtly spectacles censured elsewhere in the play. As Floradella's indignation at 'the peoples common theam' indicates, once history is placed in the hands of the people, the consequences are liable to be explosive. Characteristically aware of the power of illusive representation, Ally-Beg's description of one piece of public spectacle is carefully designed to fan the flames of the king's fearful jealousy:

> We met i'th way a stop, a giddy stream
> Of people, with broad eyes, and right-up ears,

Powring themselves from all parts to the Buzzarr
The novelty made us too mixe among them,
What then made all this concourse, but to hear
A Panegyrick, sung by hired Eunuchs,
In adulation of the valiant Mirza? (p. 5)

Hampered by a fatal inability to distinguish between reality and illusion, the king mistakes public theatre for mob rule and is prompted to precipitously condemn the object of its 'Panegyrick'. Also latent within this portrait of Persian public life is, perhaps, a derogatory analogue for the self-indulgent pageantry of pre-war court drama, 'sung by hired Eunuchs' in praise of the English monarch. In a more transparent evocation of the contemporary news-book trade, Beltazar, another of the king's favourites, relates how the prince's 'green valour conquers all example./ So, said the flattering pamphlet ...' (p. 6). Like *Mirza* itself, such imagined examples of Persian political literature evince a fascination with historical precedent and are anxious to secure the tribute of posterity, symbolically represented by the 'statue' of Floradella's metaphor.

As the embodiment of the most pejorative aspects of courtly and feminine attributes, Floradella is, next to Ally-Beg, the most engaging figure in the play. Unlike Ally-Beg, however, she is not derived from Herbert but the pure invention of the playwright and, as such, the vehicle for much of the play's moralising. Throughout *Mirza*, deception is conceived of as a particularly feminine characteristic. Having duped the king into relinquishing his personal guard, Ally-Beg exults in the ingenuity of his machinations with the characteristic gusto of the Machiavellian villain:

Who will not say, I cunning Master am,
That can deceive, and that in their own game,
Greatest deceivers when they me shall know
Out-cheat a woman, and a strumpet too. (p. 105)

Described in 'The Argument' as one of Ally-Beg's 'Instruments to besot the King', Floradella is portrayed as the archetypal figure of feminine guile and, for the play's first readers, may have called to mind the similar invective aimed at Henrietta-Maria by Charles' political opponents in the previous decade: 'so dangerous Serpents are they in the bosomes of Princes' ('The Argument'). It is, however, Floradella's vanity that makes her susceptible to the manipulations of Ally-Beg, who has promised to make her 'name the subject of all Poetry' (p. 14) in yet another act of authorial appropriation. In Act III, we overhear Floradella and her maidservant Cloe discussing the deceptive art of cosmetics, and contraception ('sirrup of Savin') as well as Ally-Beg's meteoric rise – 'now the only Sun/ Next to the King' (p. 49). Alongside this fairly standard satire on the morally dubious nature of feminine enhancement, colourfully evoked in their conversation of 'Purruck', 'Pomatum' and 'fucus', is the distinct implication that the political situation at court, like the 'sweets and graces' of Floradella's toilet, masks its corruption with an illusive 'lustre'. Similarly, in Act IV, the ladies of the court discuss their part in financing the conspiracy and play-fully hypothesise upon participating in government – 'sha'nt we improve the debt, the State/ Owes us, by injoyning offices, and sitting/ In councell with the men!' (p. 82). In the context of the play, the suggestion is, of course, intention-ally absurd. Nevertheless, it highlights the broader theme of the dangerous connection between social reform and political chaos – as the play's argu-ment expounds, 'So essential a beginning of all rebellions, is a smooth and fair pretence either of Reformation or safety'. Again, an aptitude for political 'Rhetorick' is perceived as being peculiarly consonant with a feminine sensi-bility:

> True vertu's not oblig'd to live with beards
> Alone, she may chuse the smoother edifice.
> But the rough part of vertue, skill in armes
> I am content to let the men ingrosse...
> And to become Counsellors would become us well.
> Our Witts are sharpest, and we fittest made
> For Embassies, as having smoothest tongues. (p. 83)

Here too, the play attempts to confront the knotty problem of what constitutes 'True vertu' in terms of an antithesis of courtly and martial values. 'Counsel-lors', like the treacherous women in the play, are not only endowed with the 'smoothest tongues' but must also rely on deceptive appearances to mask their true intent.

FALSE FIRES: *MIRZA* AND THE TOLERATION
OF AN ENGLISH ALCORAN

It is significant that, as the marginalised concubine, Floradella is made the mouthpiece for the play's most explicit and sustained piece of political allegory. At this central moment, half way though the third act, Floradella congratu-lates Ally-Beg on his manipulation of the various factions of Persian society, in terms that must have seemed particularly resonant to a reader of the 1650s. She enthuses,

> T'were good you won the Muftie to your purpose;
> And some o'th'Abdalls, that at publique meetings,
> And market Lectures, may expound the Text
> O th'Alchoran, according to your Comment. (p. 53)

As in Denham's play, the subversion of religious doctrine in order to provoke a split between Church and State is deemed an essential constituent of political sedition. Religion, like the earlier examples of 'Panegyrick' spectacle, is made all the more dangerous by its popular appeal, expounded 'at publique meetings,/ And market Lectures'. Continuing the play's depiction of rebellion as a conflict of competing authorships and rival interpretations, this reference to the Islamic holy text invokes the tumultuous debate incited by state attempts to regulate public worship and Scripture in England throughout the century and which, at the time of Baron's play, was still raging. As a rival sacred text, the 'Alchoran' had long been perceived as the expression of a depraved heresy and was frequently invoked by English writers anxious to denounce a threatening apostasy perceived in the military and cultural successes of the Ottoman and Persian empires. By 1655, however, the Qur'an was associated with a nexus of images and ideas that were increasingly translated in political, as well as religious and moral terms. At the epicentre of this re-imagining of the familiar diametric between Islam and Christendom is, as we might expect, an act of translation.

Six years before the appearance of *Mirza*, the first full English translation of the Qur'an had been published. As discussed earlier, the text makes an overtly political stance in the aftershock of regicide. The translator-cum-commentator takes the opportunity to impugn not only the teachings of Islam but the directly analogous heresies of a growing non-conformity in English 'orthodox Religion'. In its broadest terms, this attack on the schismatic nature of religion was nothing new. In a short treatise of 1641, entitled *A Discovery of 29 Sects here in London, all of which, except the first, are most Divelish and Damnable*, the, self-evidently Protestant, writer claims to have identified a whole subculture of dissident creeds harboured by the capital. Eighth on the list, after 'Puritans', 'Papists' and the 'Family of Love' are the 'Mahometans', who are vaguely described as being 'led along with a certaine foolish beliefe of Mahomet, which professed himselfe to be a Prophet'; it retells the old myth that 'He taught a pigeon to pecke a pease from forth his eare, bearing the ignorant in hand that the Holy Ghost brought him newes from Heaven.'[27] Whilst to some extent *The Alcoran of Mahomet* draws upon a similarly dismissive tradition of representing Islamic doctrine, the 1649 translation does represent a far more comprehensive appraisal of its teachings and, in the process, makes an intervention in mid-century political discourse in a way that both reflected and further enflamed the politicisation of the Oriental tradition.

The prevalence of material relating to the Qur'an and the life of the Prophet, which was available in the decade following the 1649 translation, is evident in the expansive annotation that glosses Baron's reference to 'th'Alchoran' in Act III:

(16) *The Alcoran*]   The Book of the *Mahumetan* Law, In Arabic the word imports, *a gathering together of precepts*, or *Alfurcan*, which is *Redemption*. ...
But the glossers of the *Alcoran*, and their Book *Azar* (which is a History of

---

[27]   *A Discovery of 29 Sects here in London, all of which, except the first, are most Divelish and Damnable* (1641), p. 4.

Mahomet, authentique among the *Moores,* as the Gospel among us Christians) say, that those that helped *Mahomet* in compiling his *Alcoran,* were two Sword-Cutlers (Christian slaves unto one of *Mecca*) who knew much confusedly of the new Testament, and out of their imperfect informations, he gleaned what served his turn, not looking for antecedents, subsequents, or coherence any where. So observes *Joannes Andreas Maurus* (who was once an *Alfaqui* (or Bishop) among the *Moores* ...) ... To speak a word of the chief author *Mahomet* ... *Bonfinus* writes that he permitted adultery and Sodomy and lay himselfe with beasts; and Mr *Smith* (in his Confutation of *Mahumetism*) arraigns him of Blasphemy, Pride, lyes, Sodomy, Blood, Fraud, Robbery, (for he was a common Thief, usually robbing the Caravans of Merchants as they travelled) as entitles him Heir apparent unto *Lucifer,* no lesse then 12000 falshoods being contained in his fabulous *Alcoran* ...[28]

Authorised by his purportedly scholarly motive ('for to such chiefly I wrote this Tragedy'), Baron recounts the litany of imputations traditionally heaped on Mahomet, whilst maintaining the mask of historical authenticity he is so anxious to promote. Manifest here, I wish to suggest, is a version of the bivalency that had long characterised English treatments of the Islamic other, torn between a self-righteous impulse to condemn what was clearly perceived as a self-evidently profane system of beliefs and a grudging admiration for its military and political organisation, the dangers of the former being clearly intensified by the latter. Published in 1656, for instance, Francis Osborne's *Politicall Reflections upon the Government of the Turks,* extensively explored the ways in which the old anathema of the Turkish state might suggest a model for English government. Eschewing such radicalism, Baron's play is nevertheless representative of the beginning of a transformation in the old ways of representing Islam. It is surely significant that the authorial interventions that frame the play text lack much of the vituperative rhetoric familiar from other contemporary treatments of Islam – *Mirza's* anti-Islamic dogma is, as it were, safely contained in the quotation marks of its multiple textual allusions.

One of the authors cited by Baron, serves as an example of this kind of ideological ambivalence, fuelled by an ever-increasing uncertainty about the domestic situation. The observations of '*Joannes Andreas Maurus*' would seem to be a reference to the confutation of the Qur'an made by the Spanish convert and itself translated into English in 1652 by Joshua Nostock.[29] Like Ross, Nostock is at pains to dismiss Islam as an insubstantial chimera, and yet such bluff confidence belies the threat such writers obviously felt was posed by this rival, and increasingly ubiquitous, ideology. Again, Baron's annotations suggest the degree to which various translations, commentaries and confutations of the Qur'an had permeated the English literary consciousness by 1655. Alluding to the 1649 translation almost as an afterthought, Baron bombards

28 Baron, *Mirza,* pp. 197–9.
29 Johannes Andreas, *The Confusion of Muhamed's Sect, or a Confutation of the Turkish Alcoran, translated into English, by I. N. (Joshua Nostock)* (London, 1652).

us with an array of contemporary writings on the Qur'an, referring the reader 'that would know more of the *Alcoran*' to,

> Cardinall *Nicolas de Cusa*, his examination of the *Alcoran*. *Lod Vives. L. 4. De veritat. Relig. Christ. Ricoldus* in his computation of the Lawes of *Mahomet*. *Barthol. Hungarius. Johannes Andreas Maurus* his confutation of Mahomet's sect, and the *Alcoran* itself, translated out of the *Arabic* into *Latin* by *Theod. Bibliander*, for the late published *English* translation I cannot commend its faithfulnesse. I had almost forgotten, (though quoted above) *Baudier* his *History de la Religion des Turcs, &c.*[30]

Interesting here, is the playwright's disparaging appraisal of the 1649 translation for its dubious 'faithfulnesse'. Whether motivated by a desire to lay claim once again to an unimpeachable authenticity (the 'faithfulnesse' of his own act of dramatic translation), or simply by intellectual snobbery, it is symptomatic that Baron wishes to imply a knowledge of the Qur'an in its original language, as well as a thoroughgoing familiarity with its attendant literature. Moreover, as writers of the period became embroiled in a more sustained engagement with patterns of rhetoric and imagery derived, with varying degrees of poetic licence, from Islamic history, so they found it harder to simply dismiss the culture from which they were drawn as being safely contained without the borders of Christendom. For those opposed to the Protectorate regime, the long-threatened invasion had finally come, the kingdom overrun, not by the Ottoman hordes but insidiously, by the Cromwellian faction within.

Such a recognition of an analogous spiritual menace both at home and abroad is specifically dramatised in *Mirza*. Having rejoiced in Ally-Beg's appropriation of the 'Alchoran', Floradella goes on to promote precisely this kind of anarchic apostasy:

> Bid them inveigh against the Tyranny
> They now groan under: promise silken Yoaks,
> And easie burdens in your Government.
> Pretend a Reformation of the Law,
> To take down all illegal Courts and Taxes … (p. 54)

Here is a condensed history of the Civil War and subsequent collapse of monarchical government, a mirror image of that frequently recounted by Anglican royalists in the literature of the period. In the last years of his reign, the charge of tyranny had frequently been made against Charles' government, either directly in seditious pamphlets[31] or more obliquely, as I have discussed, in plays like John Denham's *The Sophy*. Such portraits were often, at least partially, informed by the conventional figure of the Turkish tyrant who had

---

[30] Baron, *Mirza*, p. 207.
[31] For instance, the anonymous treatise, *A Briefe Discourse upon Tyrants and Tyranny*, published in 1642.

stalked the Elizabethan and Jacobean stage. Lurking behind King Abbas are Turkish counterparts, archetypes of cruelty and lasciviousness who, although politically inimical in the narrative, are clearly imaginatively related in the drama.

By the time of Baron's play, however, tyranny was no longer the sole prerogative of monarchs. Even before the regicide, Cromwell and his faction were already being cast in the same mould. The anonymous *Tyranny of Tyrannies*, written in December 1648, declares 'to all free-born English men, that the new Turkish *Tyrants, Cromwel and Ireton, at a Councel of War*, have already privately condemned to death Sir WILLIAM WALLER and Major General BROWNE'.[32] A similar analogy had been made at the very beginning of the conflict in relation to the outbreak of the Irish rebellion in 1641, although in an opposite cause. One of the pamphlets designed to outrage English Protestant opinion, *The Rebels Turkish Tyranny* (1641), described in lurid detail the atrocities and exotic torments inflicted on the innocent population by the infidel Catholics in their midst. That 'Turkish' tyranny had become such a current and politically interchangeable term further suggests the degree to which the ideological ambivalence of Baron's play is directly connected with the inherently protean character of its Eastern subject. The effect of Charles' execution, however, was to polarise the debate still further. From a republican standpoint, the definition of tyranny is a crucial predicate for establishing illegitimacy since, as Hobbes frames it in his *Leviathan* 'they say not regicide, that is, killing of a king, but tyrannicide, that is, killing of a tyrant, is lawful'. The most vociferous advocate for this interpretation of events is Milton, writing in his regicidal tracts. In his hands, the sense of tyranny shifts from a generally cruel despotism to a more strictly defined legal and constitutional transgression and hence, the regicide as an act of open justice legitimised by classical and biblical precedent. By the time of *Mirza*, however, Cromwell was himself looking increasingly vulnerable to a similar charge, particularly after 'The Instrument of Government' drafted in 1653. If tyranny was simply ruling without the consent of Parliament then the Republic had already betrayed its own ideals. Via Floradella, Baron intervenes directly in terms that emphasise the slippery signification of 'Tyranny' in the Protectorate, substituting the dominant model of precursive historiography rooted in Western classicism for its Oriental equivalent. If Milton's regicidal tracts had firmly appropriated the use of Roman and Greek history and rhetoric in the name of the Republic, Baron's play stakes its claim to an authoritative alternative in Persia.

> Floradella's final incitement is to,
> Promise a Toleration of all
> Religions, to ease tender Consciences,
> Or Jew or Christian, but yet persecute
> The Christian still; it is a spreading Sect … (p. 54)

---

[32] *The Tyranny of Tyrannies* (London, 1648).

In the context of the extended analogy Baron, like Ross in his caveat to the 1649 Qur'an translation, implies the malignancy of a 'spreading' sectarianism in English religious life, satirising the heresy that disguises itself as 'a Toleration of all/ Religions'. Whilst the belief that the Islamic empires of the East practised a pragmatic religious toleration towards their subjects had often proved a source of fascination and debate for English writers, the association of Islam with a spreading non-conformity in religion was clearly invested with a new currency in the polemical literature of the Civil War.

Dated 11 July 1648, the anonymous *Liberty of Conscience* provides a fascinating and complex refutation of what it sees as a heinous precedent for religious syncretism, imagined specifically in terms of a Muslim–Christian polarity, and prefigures several aspects of *Mirza* itself – indeed, given the breadth of reading demonstrated in the play's annotations, it is not inconceivable that Baron had at some time come across this treatise.[33] Presented in the form of a 'Discourse betwixt a Turke and a Christian', the text claims to have been inspired by a 'a Peere of this Realme' who remains tantalisingly unnamed.

> My Lord: I could no way avoyd the danger of aparergie, should I heer rehearse any of those invincible arguments, which your Lordship … was pleased yesterday to oppose to that grand Error of this our Factious age; *That a plurality of Religions conduces to the peace and tranquillity of a Commonwealth*; which your Lordship discovered to be nothing but the delusion of ignorant zeal, the *ignis fatuus* that betrays its followers into faction, rebellion, bloud and desolation, and Atheisme cunningly disguised under the specious vizard of *Liberty of Conscience*. Wherefore, I shall now only take up that hint, which your Lordship dropt, concerning the blacke, but comely policy of the *Ottoman Empire*; which seeming to tolerate the exercise of all, or most Religions, does yet lie in the armes of a florishing Civil peace … (p. 1)

Here, one year before the translation of the 'Alcoran', is evidence that at least one politician of the day, presumably royalist and Anglican, had been inspired to invoke the example of the '*Ottoman Empire*' in order to address political discord in England. Here too, is a curious prefiguring of the 1649 translator's disdain for those who 'having once abandoned the Sun of the Gospel … will wander far into utter darknesse, by following strange lights, as by this Ignis Fatuus of the Alcoran'. The false fires of Qur'anic doctrine and justifications for religious dissent in England are clearly perceived as being equivalently 'specious'. In contrast to this ebullient voice, however, this writer demonstrates a striking desire to distance himself from the, undoubtedly provocative, nature of the material. Not only does this 'Discourse' take place under the auspices of the nameless 'Peere', but the dialogue between a (French) Christian and the female personification of the '*Grand Signiors Empire*' will be enacted, according

---

[33] *Liberty of Conscience: Confuted by Reasons of Argument and Policie. Delivered In a Discourse betwixt a Turke and a Christian. Occasioned by a Letter written to a Peere of this Realme* (1648).

to the author, by one 'Trojano Boccolini ... the Itallian in his *Raggualio*, in the person of a Turke'. Having performed this dazzling, and somewhat puzzling, refraction of authorial identity, *Liberty of Conscience* arraigns an 'infamous' Christian for his atheism (since, 'whosoever admits more Religions than one, at the same time introduces more *Gods* than one; and who concedes more *Gods* than one, inclusively denyes any *God* at all ...') and, quite literally, puts the entire Ottoman Empire in the dock for its bad example. The Christian in question is Jean Bodin (1529/30–1596),[34] the French political philosopher and author of the influential *Six Books of the Commonwealth*, published in 1576, for which, according to our author, he was 'deservedly cast into a Dungeon ... for that impious opinion he had publisht ... *That the best meanes to conserve a Common wealth in quiet and peace, was to allow every man the Liberty of his Conscience*' (p. 5). Bodin is then charged as 'a seducer of the people' and, appropriately enough, for one misled by false fires and the 'incendiary of seditious humors', is sentenced to be 'burnt'. Recanting his blasphemy, in mitigation, Bodin pleads that he has been misled by 'the example of the *Turkish Empire* which admits and tollerates all Religions in its Dominions with great and admirable tranquility of the State', which further 'impiety' only serves to '*exasperate*' the court.

> However the Court descended to so much mercy as to examine the truth of his excuse by understanding from the *Ottoman Empire*, how she managed her State in this particular, determining that if it were so, to make her copartner aswell in the punishment, as she had beene in the crime, and condemn her to the same death ... (p. 9)

Clearly taken with the notion of consigning the entire empire to the flames, the author of *Liberty of Conscience* goes on to relate the Ottoman's refutation of the Frenchman's testimony, since 'no Religion was tolerated, taught, or beleeved by the Turkish Musselman, but only *Mahometane*' (p.11). Bodin accuses the '*Ottoman Monarchy*' of falsely attesting a 'unity of Religion' since 'in her Dominions ... you may finde ... Nestorians, Iacobites, Iewes, Christians of the Catholique, Protestant and Greeke Fayth, and Heretiques of all sorts ...' (p. 12). Ottoman's response echoes Floradella's advice to 'persecute/ The Christian still' (*Mirza*, p. 54) and becomes increasingly pointed towards the internal divisions of English religious and political culture:

---

34 The link between Bodin and the Ottoman state was perhaps, on some level, suggested to the author by a mutual translator. Richard Knolles, best known for his *Generall Historie of the Turks* (1603), also published a translation of Bodin's work, *The Six Bookes of a Common-Weale* (1606). In his introduction, Knolles describes how he had occasion to translate Bodin, whilst 'gathering information to continue the lives of the Turkish Emperours'. Bodin's syncretism was engendered by the extreme violence he perceived in his native France between the Catholic and Calvinist factions.

I have rather faln upon the *Persian Heretique*, then enterprised a war with the *Christian Princes*; who being firmely cemented together by union of Fayth, to different *e diametro*, contrary to mine, are not of so much danger to my *Religion*, as is the *Persian Heresie*; it being a far different case to allow in a State a contrary *Religion*, then to tollerate an Heresie in the same *Religion*, which like a nimble Gangraen soon transmits its coruption to the whole body politique … (p. 22)

The difference between the Ottoman and Persian faiths, broadly speaking, between Sunni and Shiite versions of Islam, had frequently been invoked as a reflection of the schismatic upheavals that had wracked Christendom throughout the Reformation. Indeed, it was not unknown for inter-religious alliances to be proposed that crossed the normally fixed, if permeable, frontier between East and West. Earlier in the century, the Sherley brothers had famously advocated an Anglo-Persian alliance against the 'Turk', a delicate piece of diplomacy dramatised in Rowley, Day and Wilkins' *The Travels of the Three English Brothers* (1607).[35] The ongoing wars between the Ottoman Empire and Persia also provide the backdrop for Baron's play, although no 'Turkish' characters actually appear.[36] Nevertheless, *Mirza*'s Persian setting is not entirely incidental to its dramatic stratagem – the clear parallels that are made within the play between the Persian and English monarchies are informed by an established tradition of perceived ideological reciprocity. In his annotations, Baron describes the Turkish–Persian enmity in terms characteristically analogous. Of 'the Turk', he writes,

His Religion is *Mahumetan*, of which sect he is the chiefe patron, and more then slights the Persian, for being lesse zealous than himselfe, so that in balancing the state of *Christianity* and *Mahumetism*; I have heard these two Princes compared to the two Kings of *France*, and *Spain*, the *French* to the *Persian*, the *Spaniard* to the *Turk*.[37]

However, as the tract *Liberty of Conscience* emphatically avers, and *Mirza* represents, the heretic within, 'like a nimble Gangraen', is all the more dangerous for being consanguineous. Like Floradella, the feminised Ottoman state is also aware of the inherently subversive potential of translations:

And to this purpose my *Alcoran* being originally written in the *Arabique* tongue, I have with singular judgement and extream severity prohibited the Translation of it into the vulgar *Turkish* language, having prudently learnt by the miseries of divers *Christian States* what incurable mischiefes accrew to them by the Translating their *Bible* into their mother tongues … (p. 23)

---

[35] Also discussed in the introduction to Parr, ed., *Three Renaissance Travel Plays*, pp. 7–20.

[36] Denham, on the other hand, includes two 'Bashawes' and three Turkish captains who are captured and inspired by Mirza's princely virtues to effect his release.

[37] Baron, *Mirza*, p. 164.

As the opposition of Commonwealth licensors to the 1649 translation testifies, questions of political and social authority were deemed to be inextricably
bound up with notions of sovereignty over language and, in particular, sacred
language. Once religious control is devolved to 'vulgar' hands, the argument
continues, princes should expect to see, 'their swords wrested out of their
hands by rebellion, and their crownes trampled on by the basest of their licentious Vassals …' (p. 24). Finally, the Ottoman sums up with an invocation of
the divine right of an absolute monarchy, God's 'immediate *Lieutenants and
Vicegerents* on earth' (p. 25) and the hapless Bodin is burnt at the stake without
further ado: 'Thus the Court of Parliament with great prudence and justice,
condemned him to the *flames*, that intended such a wild *combustion* in the
world' (p. 27).

In terms of its multiple voices, as well the specific ways in which the author
correlates syncretism, political sedition and translation, *Liberty of Conscience*
feeds directly into the discursive conditions that give rise to the polysemy of
Baron's play. In this context, it is particularly apt that Mirza, the simultaneous
embodiment of both princely virtue and tyranny and the crux of the play's
ambivalence, should resort, like the 1649 translator and the anonymous author
of *Liberty of Conscience*, to an image of false fire. Imprisoned and alone, the
prince rails,

> What have I left me, but to curse my starrs?
> Starrs! Ignes fatu! Glittering Meteors!
> That made a show of greatnesse, and in snuff
> Now loose their glimmering false light, and stink! (p. 106)

In their illusive 'show of greatnesse', the 'Ignes fatu' of fate have led the blind
prince, like the foolish 'Batch' of the translator's metaphor, 'into utter darknesse' and to his tragically inevitable demise. In dramatising the death of a
Persian prince and, from the vantage point of 1655, also thereby representing
the collapse of royalist ideology in England, *Mirza* combines the tragic form
with the irrepressibly current, if constantly shifting paradigm of Islamic history
and culture. As Lois Potter has explicated, following the regicide, the very
form of tragedy was invested with a political power that often overwhelmed
attempts to harness its dramatic power. Just as *The Famous Tragedie* had in fact
offered tragicomedy, Potter argues, so 'the closet drama of the interregnum
shows itself unable to deal directly with the act of regicide', adding that 'fantasies of revenge are rare'.[38] Baron's *Mirza* is neither of these exactly but is, I
wish to argue, an attempt to re-appropriate tragedy in the cause of monarchy,
albeit inhibited and in exile. In the republican cause, Milton had undertaken to
purge tragedy of its royalist connotations, advocating a return to a purer form
of classical and, particularly Senecan drama, with its inbuilt justification for
king-killing as tyrannicide. Taking Jonson as his model, Baron also has Seneca

[38] Potter, *Secret Rites and Secret Writing*, p. 101.

close at hand and, although the play does not attempt to directly represent regicide, it is certainly not squeamish in its relish for revenge. As many of the annotations to the play text testify, although set in the Safavid period, Baron is equally drawn to the pre-Islamic, classical heritage of ancient Persia. To answer a question posed at the opening of this chapter, then, Baron's setting serves a dual purpose. With its long-standing equivalence to the classical worlds of Rome and Greece, Persia offers a suitably weighty authority whilst, as a political paradigm, the Islamic model remained equally available to both royalist and republican thinkers.

The appeal of Mirza's story as an alternative exemplar was also clearly evident to John Denham in 1641. In terms of the impact of Islamic source material upon an identifiably English tragic narrative, one character in *The Sophy* sums up the new geopolitical boundaries:

> ... 'Tis in worldly accidents
> As in the world it selfe, where things most distant
> Meet one another: Thus the East, and West,
> Upon the Globe, a Mathematick point
> Onely divides; Thus happinesse, and miserie,
> And all extreames are still contiguous. (p. 26)

An ever-increasing awareness of this contiguity, variously expressed in acts of translation, refutation and imputation, underpins a significant section of the literary–political expression of the Civil War period. Confronted with their own civil 'miserie', writers of the 1640s and 1650s were compelled to re-orient the longstanding division between East and West in terms of a new, internalised set of political and religious 'extreames'. Both in terms of its political sympathies and its dramatic status, *Mirza* is situated in the darkest hour before the dawn – one year later, a new form of legitimate theatre would emerge in the licensed operatic dramas of William Davenant, and one of the first characters to appear on the new stage would be a 'Turk'.

Chapter 4

TURNING TO THE TURK: COLLABORATION AND CONVERSION IN WILLIAM DAVENANT'S *THE SIEGE OF RHODES*

WHETHER MEDIATED ON STAGE, from the pulpit or via the polemical press, one of the most abiding preoccupations of English treatments of Islam in the period was conversion. From the sixteenth century onwards, stories of Englishmen who had 'turned Turk' abounded, fuelled by the growing depredations of the Barbary corsairs in the Mediterranean where English shipping plied the routes of the burgeoning Levant trade. Long-held misgivings about the threat of further Ottoman encroachment in Europe were overlaid with what was, from an English point of view, the more immediate and tangible peril of piracy and potential captivity. Moreover, from the early part of the seventeenth century, Barbary ships had ventured as far as the Channel, and the coastal regions of England and Ireland were themselves subject to raids. More alarming to many commentators than the suffering of those captives sold or ransomed as booty was the possibility that Christians might succumb to the religion of their captors, seduced by the material or even spiritual allure of this rival doctrine; according to one prevalent reading of the geopolitical situation, Islam and Christianity were in direct competition for souls and, where the two collided, it seemed that the infidel was winning. As the work of Nabil Matar has shown, a spate of dramatic texts respond directly to the anxieties aroused by the figure of the renegade by constructing a fantasy of Christian vindication whereby the renegade repents his apostasy or else suffers divine retribution.[1] Outside the drama, an equivalent concern is evident in the number of sermons and theological tracts that seize upon alleged conversions from Islam to Christianity.[2] Unsurprisingly, in most cases, the particular denomination

---

[1] See Matar, *Islam in Britain*, ch. 4. Perhaps the most flagrant distortion of reality in the service of Christian representation in this regard is the depiction of John Ward's life in Robert Daborne's *A Christian turn'd Turke* (1612). At the end of the play the notorious English pirate is 'torn to pieces and thrown in the sea. In fact he was flourishing in the opulence of Tunis at the very time the play was being performed on the London stage.'

[2] These are discernible throughout the century, but are particularly evident in the religious turmoil following the fragmentation of the English Church. For example, three separate accounts of baptised Turks were published in 1658. As well as Jean d'Espagne's *The Joyfull*

of Christianity embraced – 'Roman' or 'Reformed' – was deemed at least as meaningful as the conversion itself. By the same token, rhetorical strategies used to combat the perceived threat of Islamic conversions were readily transferable to other discourses of religious difference, most notably those representing inter-Christian divisions. Offering a persuasive contextualisation of *Othello*, Daniel Vitkus observes that,

> Post-Reformation anxiety about conversion produced a discourse about 'renegadoes' and 'convertites' which applied to those who converted to Catholicism as well as those who turned Turk, with the interest in Christian Muslim conversions clearly related to contemporaneous polemical writings about Protestants and Roman Catholics who renounced one brand of Christianity for the other.[3]

However, a third and critical meaning emerges in the approach to English constitutional breakdown. To 'turn Turk' in the context of the 1640s did not only encompass literal and figurative defections to the Anti-Christian forces of Pope or Prophet, but came to include political and ideological tergiversation within the emerging domestic conflict. From an English perspective, these were clearly related definitions. The image of the renegade had always carried connotations of the enemy within and, as religious anxiety concerning the influence of unseen Popish influences mounted, the intensity with which political enemies might be condemned as Turk-like traitors could only increase. Furthermore, by 1640 the original problem of the English captives had itself escalated to crisis proportions, an issue which, according to Nabil Matar, was a significant contributory factor in the outbreak of the Civil War.[4] Certainly, the frequency with which the notorious 'ship money' was linked with Barbary piracy along with the number of petitions addressed to both King and Parliament for the redemption of the captives attests to the prominence of this issue in 1642 and subsequently. Indeed, it was not until the arrival of Blake's fleet in the Mediterranean in 1654 that England could contemplate direct naval action against the activities of the Barbary ports. Nevertheless there was still political capital to be made from the captives. In a clear echo of Charles' *Letter to the Great Turk* (1642), Cromwell's interventionist ambitions in the region were

---

convert: *represented in a short, but elegant sermon, preached at the baptizing of a Turke, who ... was baptized in the French Church May 2. 1658* (in fact 1657, see Chapter 1 above), Thomas Warmstry, the Dean of Worcester Cathedral, authored *The baptized Turk, or a narrative of the happy conversion of Rigep Dandulo, the onely son of a Silk Merchant in the isle of Tzio, from the delusions of that great impostor Mahomet, unto the Christian Religion*, and Thomas White introduced *A True Relation of the Conversion and Baptism of Isuf the Turkish Chaous, named Richard Christophilus*.

3 Daniel J. Vitkus, 'Turning Turk in Othello: the Conversion and Damnation of the Moor', *Shakespeare Quarterly* 48, no. 2 (Summer 1997), p. 152.
4 'When Charles I succeeded to the throne in 1625, there were hundreds of these captives among the Barbary corsairs; by 1640, there were thousands.' Nabil Matar, 'The Barbary Corsairs, King Charles I and the Civil War', *Seventeenth Century* 16, no. 2 (2002), p. 239.

publicised in *A Message sent from His Highness the Lord Protector, to the Great Turk with His Demands and Proposals; and the releasing of the English Captives* (1654). Having reported Cromwell's decision to 'graciously … send an Expres to the Governor of Argier', the declaration boasts,

> As touching the influence of the Lord Protector hath gained by his Message to the Turks, 'tis a thing wonderfully to be admired; and indeed, it causeth no little admiration throughout all Christendome; for, true it is, the Argier men of War are become Associates with the English, and will not permit any man of our Nation to be carried captive into thraldome … and brings them into Gen Blake who at this very instant, rides triumphant in the Levant Ocean.

In fact, attempts to curtail the rogue states of Algeria, Tunisia, and Tripoli, both directly and through diplomatic negotiation with the Porte, met with only partial and temporary success. What is more telling in the context of Protectorate relations with the Ottoman regencies is the notion that the traditional enemy might now be counted 'Associates with the English', a dislocation of the commonplace binary that, I shall argue, feeds directly into 'Turkish' texts of this period.

Throughout the period under consideration, then, the possibility that Englishmen might literally be turning Turk was an ever-present concern. Meanwhile, in the crisis of allegiance provoked by Civil War, this trope was accorded a newly powerful and complex significance, a set of meanings that had been unimaginable before Parliament waged war against its sovereign. Of course, just who was the apostate and who the true believer in this scenario was not a matter of consensus. Depending upon one's point of view, the monarch had himself turned, betraying the religious and constitutional ideals of his Protestant people. More commonly expressed after the defeat and execution of the king, however, was the belief that the nation had been overrun with 'renegadoes', traitors who had turned Turk and betrayed England to Cromwell's tyranny. Writing in August 1650, for example, John Cleiveland condemned the official Commonwealth journalist Marchmont Nedham as having 'reproached our whole nation … a three piled apostate, a renegade more notorious than any in Sally or Algier', adding that 'there is no such torment to a Christian as to be tyrannized over by a Renegade'.[5] The subsequent reformulation of traditional notions of Turkish treachery is central to William Davenant's *The Siege*

---

5 John Cleiveland, *Character of Mercurius Politicus* (1650). The career of the mercurial Nedham is a good example of the degree to which the tenor of the times transformed public loyalties. Beginning with scurrilous attacks on the king in 1645 as writer for *Mercurius Britanicus*, he was sent to prison the following year. Upon his release he took over the editorship of the royalist journal *Mercurius Pragmaticus* until imprisoned once again in June 1649. Nedham emerged as a converted republican, in June 1650 inaugurating the official journal of the Commonwealth *Mercurius Politicus*. See Joseph Frank, *Cromwell's Press Agent: a Critical Biography of Marchamont Nedham, 1620–1678* (Lanham, MD: University Press of America, 1980).

of Rhodes and illuminates both the play's mediation of apostasy and innovative treatment of Islamic history.

A 'UNIVERSAL APOSTASY IN THE WHOLE NATION': NEGOTIATING WITH THE INFIDEL IN THE FIRST PART OF *THE SIEGE OF RHODES*

> [Davenant] exercised the office of Master of the Revells to Oliuer the Tyrant, and wrote the First and Second parte of Peru, acted at the Cockpitt in Oliuers tyme, and soly in his fauour; wherein hee sett of[f] the justice of Oliuers actinges by comparison with the Spaniards, and endeavoured thereby to make Oliuers crueltyes appear mercyes, in respect of the Spanish crueltyes, but the mercyes of the wicked are cruell.[6]

So alleged the playwright's old adversary, Sir Henry Herbert, recently reinstated as Master of the Revels following the restoration of Charles II to the English throne. Herbert's lawsuit, brought in indignant opposition to the proposed introduction of a theatrical monopoly was, however, unsuccessful and the king proceeded to grant both Davenant and Killigrew licence to establish two new companies of players. Whilst plainly motivated as much by professional jealousy as righteous fealty to the crown, Herbert's indictment, that Davenant 'exercised the office of Master of the Revells to Oliuer the Tyrant', gives an indication both of the playwright's somewhat precarious position in the aftermath of republican collapse and his seemingly limitless capacity to reinvent himself in response to the ever-changing political conditions in which his drama might be successfully performed. Of course, Davenant never held any such position, at least not in an official capacity. He was, however, responsible for a series of quasi-dramatic entertainments, staged in the final phase of the Protectorate, and takes his place in history as the only dramatist officially sanctioned by Cromwell's regime to write for the public stage.[7]

Herbert's querulous accusation refers to *The Cruelty of the Spaniards in Peru*, which was performed in 1658. This was, however, only one of four plays staged by Davenant in the Interregnum period. As Herbert protests, *Peru*, like *The History of Sir Francis Drake* that followed it (entered on the Stationer's

---

6   *Dramatic Records of Sir Henry Herbert*, ed. J. Q. Adams (Yale Press, 1917), pp. 122–3; Alfred Harbage, *Sir William Davenant Poet Venturer 1606–1668* (Philadelphia, University of Pennsylvania Press, 1935), p. 140.
7   Shirley's masque, *Cupid and Death*, was performed before the Portuguese ambassador in 1653. Although this was clearly a different proposition from Davenant's later public productions, the occasion of the masque's presentation is perhaps indicative of an important difference between Cromwell's own attitude towards drama and the staunchly anti-theatrical convictions of more austere elements of his following – 'the sumptuousness of the scenery and costumes, as well as the court associations of the genre, was definitely anti-Puritan'. Arthur H. Nethercot, *Sir William D'Avenant: Poet Laureate and Playwright-Manager* (New York: Russell & Russell, 1938), p. 299.

Register on 20 January 1659), were enacted, according to the title pages, 'daily at the Cockpit in Drury-Lane, At Three after noone punctually'. The venue for his first tentative production, however, was Davenant's own residence, Rutland House in Aldersgate Street near Charterhouse Square. Introduced on 23 May 1656 and fully entitled *The First Dayes Entertainment at Rutland-House, by Declamations and Musick after the manner of the Ancients*, the piece comprised a series of speeches interspersed with musical interludes. In the first half, Diogenes and Aristophanes dispute the propriety of public performances in a clear reenactment of contemporary controversy surrounding the theatre. Having tactfully repudiated conventionally puritan objections to the drama (expostulated by the cynic Diogenes) and thus established the moral credentials of his own 'Entertainment', Davenant ends with a light-hearted debate between a Parisian and a Londoner as to the relative merits of their respective cities.[8] Naturally, the Londoner emerges the victor, just as Aristophanes had triumphantly demonstrated the morally beneficial effects of public declamations. As the title suggests, the playwright was scrupulous in his avoidance of the potentially inflammatory language of a morally bankrupt pre-war theatre. Indeed, Davenant was acutely aware of the experimental and unrefined nature of his first offering, apologising for the narrowness of the 'cup-board scene' in his prologue. Nevertheless, as the final flourish to the prologue emphatically declaims, *The First Dayes Entertainment* was unambiguously intended as a manifesto for a new, reformed drama that would naturally require a new name: 'Think this your passage, and the narrow way/ To our Elyzian field, the *Opera*'. Davenant's intentions were unmistakable and would prove seminal in the development of the English stage, yet he clearly succeeded in negotiating 'the narrow way' between exciting public interest in the possibilities of a restored drama and inciting official disapprobation for resurrecting one of the trappings of a corrupt and discredited Caroline court. On the face of it, the sparse dialogism of *The First Dayes Entertainment* is evidently far removed from the dramatic genre most closely associated with monarchy, the courtly masque, and with good reason. Sponsored by and tailored for the Stuart court, the masque was a prime target for puritan censure of theatrical decadence in general, and the moral degeneracy of the court in particular.[9] In 1640, Davenant had himself been commissioned to write *Salmacida Spolia*, the last court masque to be staged before the war and a typically spectacular production in which both king and queen participated. For the venture at Rutland House to

---

[8] The play text must have continued to circulate after the Restoration; Samuel Pepys, in his diary entry for 7 February 1664, reports that to relieve his wife's illness he 'with great mirth read Sir W Davenant's two speeches in dispraise of London and Paris'. Pepys, *Diary*, vol. v, p. 40.

[9] However, not all opponents of monarchy were automatically inimical to the theatre. For an important qualification of this dominant assumption, see Margot Heinemann, *Puritanism and Theatre: Thomas Middleton and Opposition Drama under the Early Stuarts* (Cambridge: Cambridge University Press, 1980).

succeed it was clearly essential for the playwright to disassociate this from the most notorious manifestation of monarchical self-validation.[10]

Among the spectators of the first day's performance was a government representative charged with the task of reporting on the conduct of this potentially seditious public gathering. The occasion was, however, clearly deemed innocuous enough and the official observer even reports that 'At the end were songs relating to the Victor (the Protector)'.[11] This apparent corroboration of Herbert's charges of collaboration, levelled at the playwright after the Restoration, indicates the tentative nature of this initial foray into public theatre – Davenant was all too aware of the delicacy of the situation, what he was later to describe in a letter to his unofficial ally in the government, Bulstrode Whitelocke, as 'the nicety of the Times'.[12] For all its placatory diplomacy, however, *The First Dayes Entertainment* issues a direct challenge to its audience that momentarily forgets the niceties of terminology and contains an unequivocal declaration of intent: these are 'your Plays, but get them if you can'. What followed was certainly more akin to the 'Plays' that had been performed up until the closure of the theatres, fourteen years earlier, and portrayed one of the mainstays of the pre-war drama, the 'Turk'.

---

10 The puritan allegation that the courtly masques were in some way symptomatic of Stuart rule (or misrule) finds its analogue in modern accounts of the genre. For example, in his groundbreaking study Stephen Orgel describes the Jacobean masque as an 'expression of the monarch's will, the mirror of his mind', *The Illusion of Power: Political Theater in the English Renaissance* (Berkeley: University of California Press, 1975), p. 45. A similar reading of the political function of masque is posited in Roy Strong, *Splendour at Court: Renaissance Spectacle and the Theatre of Power* (London: Weidenfeld & Nicolson, 1973). More recent accounts have, however, challenged the assumption that the genre was straightforwardly complicit in the authorisation of monarchical power. For Davenant's role in this regard, see Martin Butler, 'Politics and the Masque: Salmacida Spolia', in *Literature and the English Civil War*, eds. Healy and Sawday, pp. 59–74. That the masque might be *both* deeply invested in the political self-fashioning of its patron and potentially subversive is the conclusion of *The Politics of the Stuart Court Masque*, eds. David Bevington and Peter Holbrook (Cambridge: Cambridge University Press, 1998). The conviction that ostensibly neutral or conformist drama not only reflects but intervenes in contemporary political discourse is clearly equally applicable to Davenant's drama after the collapse of the court and underpins the reading of *The Siege of Rhodes* that follows.

11 Interestingly, these 'songs' have not survived and were perhaps only included for this first performance (we may speculate for the sole benefit of the Protectorate's watchful minion) or else thoroughly expunged from the subsequently printed versions of *The First Dayes Entertainment*.

12 Davenant knew Whitelocke from his days at the Inns of Court during the 1620s, and there is some suggestion that Whitelocke, now Lord Commissioner of the Treasury, used his influence to secure Davenant's release from the Tower in 1652. Davenant wrote to Whitelocke in September 1656, enclosing a copy of his new play, *The Siege of Rhodes*, in what appears to be a pre-emptive appeal for official protection: 'My Lord, When I consider the nicety of the Times, I fear it may draw a Curtain between your Lordship and our Opera; therefore I have presumed to send your Lordship, hot from the Press, what we mean to represent ....'. See Harbage, *Davenant*, p. 124.

The Siege of Rhodes was entered on the Stationer's Register on 27 August 1656 and it seems likely that the play's first performance took place soon afterwards.[13] Again, the venue was Davenant's own Rutland House although the audience were charged an entrance fee as in a public theatre. Also, like *The First Dayes Entertainment,* the title page implicitly declares its moral and political neutrality, designating itself 'a Representation by the Art of Prospective in Scenes, And the Story sung in *Recitative* Musick'. In keeping with this diversionary strategy, the play replaces the conventional divisions of act and scene with various 'entries', each preceded by a section of 'Instrumental Musick' and rounded off with a chorus. In his address *To the Reader* that prefaces the first quarto edition of *The Siege of Rhodes*, Davenant studiously avoids the issue of the play's radical status as the first legitimate dramatic production since the 1642 closure and makes no reference to the work as a play at all. Instead, the playwright makes a lengthy apology for its scope, constrained as the producers were by 'the narrowness of the Room', and gives an insight into the logistical difficulties they faced:

> It has been often wisht that our Scenes (we having oblig'd our selves to the variety of Five changes) according to the Ancient Drammatick distinctions made for time) had not been confin'd to eleven foot in height, and about fifteen in depth, including the places of passage reserv'd for the Musick. This is so narrow an allowance for the Fleet of *Solyman* the Magnificent, his Army, the Island of *Rhodes*, and the varieties attending the Siege of the City; that I fear you will think, we invite you to such a contracted Trifle as that of the *caesars* carv'd upon a Nut.[14]

Alongside the familiar apology for the inadequacies of the stage to represent the vastness and variety of a history play is a carefully drawn parallel between Davenant's own 'contracted Trifle' and the legitimising precedent of classical drama. The playwright goes on to justify his use of music, both 'Vocal and Instrumental', and emphasises the innovation of his new style of drama, 'being *Recitative*, and therefore unpractised here; though of great reputation amongst other Nations, the very attempt of it is an obligation to our own' and, similarly defends his 'frequent alterations of measure' on the grounds that a 'variation of Ayres' is more appropriate to the musical accompaniment and better suits the 'heroick Argument'. Thus, Davenant manages to promote the play as being both seductively novel whilst remaining securely and reassuringly rooted in 'Ancient Drammatick' traditions. What is conspicuous by its absence, however, is any acknowledgement of the possible wider significance of the play – for instance, the potential topicality of its subject matter or, indeed, the fact that

[13] Leslie Hotson speculates that, 'it was probably in September, to take advantage of the confluence of gentry to London for the opening of Parliament, and for Michaelmas term at the law courts.' *The Commonwealth and Restoration Stage* (New York: Russell & Russell, 1962), p. 131.

[14] 'To the Reader', A2r–A3v.

the limitations of a confined stage may not have been the only constraints the playwright encountered in his attempt to reconcile public theatre with the ideological exigencies of Protectorate England. Rather, Davenant's preface assiduously stresses the mundane, the politically inert. The deployment of such a strategy is hardly surprising given the politically hostile conditions in which this groundbreaking play operated and in which, in its moment of production, the play text cannot help but intervene. More surprising, however, is the tendency for subsequent commentators to perpetuate the tacit suggestions of Davenant's somewhat disingenuous preface.

That *The Siege of Rhodes* did not operate in a political vacuum was, however, recognised retrospectively by the playwright's younger contemporary, the poet who would ultimately inherit the laureateship from Davenant. In his essay, *Of Heroique Plays*, Dryden describes Davenant's play as 'the first light we had of them on the English theatre' and attributes the nature of this embryonic precursor to the heroic tradition as a direct response to the prohibitive conditions of late Protectorate England:

> It being forbidden in the Rebellious times to act Tragedies and Comedies, because they contained some matter of Scandal to those good people who could more easily dispossess their lawful Sovereign than endure a wanton jest; and he was forc'd to turn his thoughts another way: and to introduce the examples of moral virtue writ in verse, and performed in Recitative Musique.[15]

Dryden's identification of *The Siege of Rhodes* as the origin of an heroic mode of drama destined to flourish on the Restoration stage has, however, tended to detract from the play's problematic engagement with the literary–political conditions of the late 1650s.[16] Davenant's play is clearly more than the straightforward expression of an enforced puritan aesthetic – 'of moral virtue writ in verse'. Moreover, this is not to suggest, as some commentators following Dryden's account have implied, that the play is a deliberate piece of royalist propaganda, ingeniously encoded to evade the attentions of Protectorate censors. Instead, *The Siege of Rhodes* is a particular response both to the exigencies of a reformed stage and the playwright's own expediently transformed identity. The sheer number of innovations that accompanied Davenant's play justifiably distinguish it as a landmark in the evolution of English drama but have tended to obscure the possibility of a more nuanced interpretation of its significance, perhaps the most dismissive example of which

---

15 John Dryden, 'Of Heroique Playes', in *Essays of John Dryden*, ed. W. P. Ker, 2 vols (Oxford: Clarendon Press, 1900), p. 6.

16 Susan Wiseman's account of the play in *Drama and Politics* constitutes a valuable corrective to this tendency. Cognisant of the 'complex significance of the Turk in 1656' (p. 153), Wiseman's reading is an important basis for my own although, as I shall argue, the play's representation of the sultan does not depend upon the diminution of the perceived threat of the Ottoman Empire but a radical reappraisal of its notional relationship with Western Europe and England in particular.

is Chew's verdict that, whilst *The Siege of Rhodes* is 'Of much importance in the history of the theatre, it is of little interest in itself'.[17] As such, the play has commanded critical attention as both the first English opera and, in its first use of moveable scenery, as the antecedent for a more naturalistic mode of drama.[18] *The Siege of Rhodes* also lays claim to being the first to employ a female actress on the public stage – Mrs Coleman, wife to one of the actors, played the part of Ianthe. Consequently, readings have neglected the play as a piece of drama and overlooked both the topical allusiveness of the action as well as the, interrelated, significance of the image of the Turk that lies at its heart. For all its innovative deployment of music and scenery and Davenant's ostensible eschewal of prevailing theatrical norms, however, the play takes many of its cues from the drama's longstanding fascination with the Orient and is particularly sensitive to the problematically fluid, and often contradictory, representations of Islam that come to characterise much of the literature, drama and polemic of the Civil War. In her critical edition of the play, Ann-Mari Hëdbáck discerns the influence of French heroic romance upon Davenant's work, citing *Ibrahim, ou l'Illustre Bassa* (1641) by Mmle de Scudéry as a probable source for the play.[19] Whilst the impact of French and Italian modes of drama upon Davenant's opera is irrefutable (acknowledged in the playwright's reference to 'other Nations' in the play's address *To the Reader*), *The Siege of Rhodes* is also clearly related to a popular strand of English drama. In their portrayal of a specifically feminine Christian virtue, both Bess Bridges of Heywood's *The Fair Maid of the West* (1631) and Despina of Carlell's *Osmond the Great Turk* (1637) suggest themselves as models for Ianthe although, as I shall suggest, Davenant's particular treatment of the binary of Christian maid and Turkish despot represents a distinct development from these prototypes.[20]

By 1656, an increasingly problematised engagement with the East, along

[17] Chew, *The Crescent and the Rose*, p. 496.
[18] Conversely, in her study Laura Brown emphasises the supposed primitiveness of Davenant's production. Arguing that the stylised nature of the action grows out of the physical conditions of its staging, Brown writes that, 'The play's form in itself prescribes that distance, elevation, and stasis. ... The enactment of such a standard is inevitably episodic and static, a series of emblematic scenes that display rather than involve.' Laura Brown, *English Dramatic Form, 1660–1760: An Essay in Generic History* (New Haven and London: Yale University Press, 1981), p. 6.
[19] Ann-Mari Hëdbáck, *The Siege of Rhodes: A Critical Edition.* (Uppsala: Acta Universitatis Upsaliensis, Studia Anglistica Upsaliensia 14, 1973), p. xxxi. The play's French influences are also considered in C. G. Child, 'The Rise of the Heroic Play', *Modern Language Notes* 19 (1904), pp. 166–73. For a recent account of this parallel tradition, see Michèle Longino, *Orientalism in French Classsical Drama* (Cambridge: Cambridge University Press, 2001).
[20] There seems to have been a particular fascination with the dramatic possibilities of the orient concentrated in the latter half of the 1650s. Lodovick Carlell's *Osmond the Great Turk*, first performed in 1637, was printed in 1657, one year after the initial performances of *The Siege of Rhodes* and perhaps in response to the revived interest created by Davenant's play. One year earlier, Robert Baron had published his own treatment of Persian history in the shape of *Mirza*, itself a reworking of an earlier play, John Denham's *The Sophy*. It is interesting to

with the transformative pressures exerted by the Civil War had fragmented the idea of Islam, providing a distinctly double-edged context for Davenant's play. In her study of the period, Susan Wiseman refutes the long-held critical assumption that Davenant subscribed to an unequivocally royalist ideology and characterises his Protectorate operas as plays that mobilise 'old enemies – the Turks, the Spanish – as Islamic or European "others", initially used to define contemporary "Englishness"'.[21] Whilst this is undoubtedly true, I wish to suggest further that *The Siege of Rhodes* exhibits not only contemporary English anxieties but also addresses the crisis of the playwright's own apostasy. Moreover, the figuring of the Turk in Davenant's play is not simply the familiar 'other', a straightforward foil to the English elements of the play, but is at the heart of the play's ideological ambivalence.

Thus far I have confined my comments to the text and circumstances of the play's first appearance in 1656. Any account of *The Siege of Rhodes* is, however, further complicated by the convoluted textual history of the play. In its final form, Davenant's play comprises two parts (and was perhaps in Herbert's mind when he erroneously described *Peru* as containing a 'First and Second parte'). Sometime during the three years following the first performances at Rutland House, Davenant composed the second part, which was itself entered on the Stationer's Register on 30 May 1659. Both parts were reprinted together in 1663 with 'The First Part being lately enlarg'd'. However, whether the complete play, in its final augmented two-part form, was ever performed before the Restoration is not clear. The first extant record of a performance is given by Pepys in his diary entry for 2 July 1661, which confirms that the two parts of *The Siege of Rhodes* constituted a principal element of the inaugural programme for Davenant's new theatre at Lincoln's Inn Fields. It is therefore plausible to imagine that the material had already been tried and tested on audiences at Davenant's embryonic theatre at the Cockpit, during the final years of the Commonwealth. The writings of another diarist, John Evelyn, record that Davenant's theatre was certainly still active at the time of the publication of the second part although, interestingly, not yet immune from imputations of moral laxity, despite the apparent acquiescence of the authorities.

> I went to visite my Bro[ther], & next day to see a new *Opera* after the *Italian* way in *Recitative Music* & *Sceanes*, much inferior to the Italian composure & magnificence: but what was prodigious, that in a time of such a publique Consternation, such a Vanity should be kept up or permitted; I being ingag'd with company, could not decently resist the going to see it, though my heart smote me for it.[22]

---

note that Davenant's 1660 petition for exclusive rights to perform certain plays, specified *The Sophy*, alongside his own and seven of Shakespeare's works.

21 Wiseman, *Drama and Politics*, p. 139.
22 Evelyn, 'Diary entry for May 5, 1659', *Diary*, ed. E. S. de Beer, vol. 3, p. 229.

Evelyn's righteous indignation further illustrates the degree to which the activity of the theatre was inextricably bound up with 'public' life in the period. In its various manifestations, Davenant's play was formulated for both Commonwealth and Restoration audiences, spanning the gap between two epochs of English theatre. The differences between the two versions, as I shall explore later in more detail, throw into relief some critical differences between the dramatic arenas in which the two operate and suggest ways in which Davenant's play was transformed in the short period of transition between a dying republic and a resurrected monarchy. Certainly, the play's treatment of notions of betrayal and apparent reversals of allegiance would have seemed particularly resonant to a playgoer of the early Restoration. As Herbert's attack on Davenant suggests, the question of former loyalties would become a potent preoccupation of the literary thought of the 1660s. Davenant's 1663 edition of *The Siege of Rhodes* is dedicated to the Earl of Clarendon whose own monumental *History of the Rebellion* endeavoured to appropriate the events of the mid-century in the service of a fundamentally royalist ethic. The professed purpose of the narrative is to recognise the few who had 'opposed and resisted that torrent' in the past in order that they might be distinguished from those who had succumbed and implicated themselves in the 'universal apostasy in the whole nation from their religion and allegiance'.[23] Davenant himself was clearly not immune from such an impeachment – as well as the songs to the 'victor' reported as being appended to the performance of his *First Dayes Entertainment*, the poet had also composed an epithamalium to Cromwell's daughter upon the occasion of her marriage to Lord Falconbridge in 1657,[24] although, like the panegyrics of the previous year, no copies have survived. Of course, Davenant was in good company – both Waller and Cowley published poetry in praise of Cromwell, whilst Dryden had himself contributed to a book of verse *Upon the Death of his late Highnesse Oliver Lord Protector of England, Scotland, and Ireland*, only to emerge as staunchly royalist in the very next year.[25] This is not to suggest that Davenant's ability to reconcile his apparently incontrovertible royalist credentials with the expediency of praising the republic in print is evidence of the poet's treachery as Herbert imputed. On the surface, Davenant's decision to cooperate with Cromwell's government simply indicates his overriding determination to reinstate a form of public theatre but, as I shall argue, also betrays a desire to renegotiate the conventional ideological boundaries. This impulse, which finds expression in the extraordinary reversals and subversions of convention that characterise *The Siege of Rhodes*, is an attempt to radically

23 Edward Hyde, Earl of Clarendon, *The History of the Rebellion and Civil Wars in England*, ed. W. D. Macray (Oxford, Clarendon Press, 1958).
24 Davenant's poem, fully entitled, *Epithalamium upon the Marriage of the Lady Mary, Daughter to his Highness, wth the Lord Viscount ffalconbridge to bee sung in Recitative Musick*, was entered in the Stationer's Register for 7 December 1657.
25 Harbage, *Davenant*, p. 141.

reappraise what Clarendon termed the 'universal apostasy in the whole nation', but also responds to the vicissitudes of the dramatist's personal experience.

As a brief account of his eventful biography will testify, Davenant's life appears inextricably bound up with the life of the nation and its theatre.[26] During the 1630s, Davenant became an established playwright for the King's Men and, on 13 December 1638, sixteen months after the death of Ben Jonson, was appointed poet laureate at the particular behest of the queen. In the latter half of the decade, Davenant also achieved distinction as the foremost exponent of a new development in privately staged masques, collaborating with Inigo Jones in the production of splendidly elaborate spectacles for the entertainment of the monarch and his court. As relations between the king and Parliament disintegrated, Davenant's allegiance to the monarch engendered the suspicion of Parliament and, as early as May 1641, he was arrested for his part in the Army Plot. Having been released on bail, Davenant fled the country and joined Queen Henrietta-Maria in her French exile where he acted as emissary to the queen and organised the passage of arms and supplies to the beleaguered king in England. At the outbreak of open hostilities, Davenant seems to have taken up arms for the king and was knighted at the Siege of Gloucester in 1643. Following the execution of the king in 1649, Davenant remained in exile and began composing his epic poem *Gondibert* but, in May 1650, the poet was appointed lieutenant-governor of Maryland by the queen and sent to replace the incumbent governor, a Parliamentary sympathiser. Davenant and his crew never reached Virginia but were captured whilst still in sight of the French coast by a Parliamentary ship. Davenant was imprisoned initially at Cowes Castle and later in the Tower, and was not released until August 1654. The experience of imprisonment seems to have deeply affected Davenant who, judging from his correspondence with Thomas Hobbes and the postscript to his unfinished *Gondibert* (a project 'interrupted by so great an experiment as Dying'), fully expected to be executed as an enemy to the new state. The playwright's rehabilitation, at least in the eyes of the authorities, must have been profound: only two years after his release from the Tower, the quondam gunrunner and confidant of the Catholic queen had secured permission to undertake the revolutionary series of plays and representations at Rutland House. By 1660, however, Davenant had come full circle, joining the host of poets eager to add their voices to the adulating throng, exulting in the vanquishing of the tyrant Protector and rejoicing at the return of the rightful heir:

> When from your Towns all hastened to the shore
> What shame could urge your peoples blushes more,
> Than to behold their Royal Martyr's Son
> Appeas'd, even with the grief for what was done? ...

---

[26] The most recent biographer of the playwright is Mary Edmond, *Rare Sir William Davenant* (Manchester: Manchester University Press, 1987).

No more shall any of the *Noble Blood*
Too faintly *stem* the People's rising *Flood*.
But when the Wind, *Opinion* does grow loud,
Moving like waves, the Many-headed Crowd;
Then those *great Ships* shall fast at *Anchor* ride,
And not be hurri'd backward with the Tyde.

William Davenant, *Poem, Upon his Sacred Majestie's most happy Return to his Dominions*

Notably, Davenant's poem refrains from resorting to the recriminatory rhetoric that characterises many other poetic responses to the king's return.[27] Instead, blame is attributed not directly to the people or the capitulation of the nobility, but to an abstracted wind of '*Opinion*', which whips up the 'Many-headed Crowd', whilst Charles, the 'Royal Martyr's Son', is painted as the embodiment of a Christian ideal of self-sacrifice and forgiveness. Certainly, there is a striking reciprocity between this panegyric and the final two-part version of *The Siege of Rhodes*, which would have been widely circulating by the summer of 1660. As well as the note of reconciliatory understanding that sounds in both the play and the poem, *The Siege of Rhodes* also evokes the same sense of national 'shame' and portrays an analogous conflict between the 'People's rising *Flood*' and the Rhodian ruling class which is central to the play's interrogation of the nature of loyalty and apostasy.

However, the full significance of the play's radical espousal of reconciliation is not fully addressed until the culmination of the second part of *The Siege of Rhodes*. To return to the earliest version of the play, and notwithstanding the equanimity of Davenant's preface, it would seem difficult to underestimate the impact of the play's first performances. The curtain was raised on the first legitimate English stage for fourteen years, since the gathering 'Cloud of Blood' of the Civil War had closed the playhouses[28], and the opening words uttered were a call to arms:

Arm, Arm, the Bassa's Fleet appears;
To Rhodes his Course from Chios steers;
Her shady wings to distant sight,
Spread like the Curtains of the Night.

---

[27] For example, Cowley's poem *Upon his Majesty's Restoration and Return* describes Cromwell as 'that great Serpent' in whose 'posy'nous folds whle Nations Pris'ners made'.

[28] The ordinance which closed the theatres on 2 September 1642 describes the inappropriateness of playacting in graphic language: 'Whereas the distress and Estate of Ireland, steeped in her own Blood, and the distracted Estate of England, threatened with a Cloud of Blood by a Civill War, call for all possible Means to appease and avert the Wrath of God …'. 'Order for Stage-plays to Cease', 3 vols, *Acts and Ordinances of the Interregnum 1642–1660*, ed. C. H. Firth and R. S. Rait (London: Stationery Office, 1911), vol. 1, p. 26.

> Each Squadron thicker and still darker grows;
> The Fleet like many floating Forrests shows.[29] (*1 SOR* I.i. 9–14)

The play narrates the story of the capture of Rhodes by Sultan Suleiman the Magnificent from the Knights of St John in 1522 for which Davenant's main source seems to have been Richard Knolles' influential work, the *Generall Historie of the Turkes* (1603). Nevertheless, contemporary resonances suffuse the play. Since 1645, the Ottomans had been engaged in the epic siege of another strategic Mediterranean outpost, the Venetian territory of Candia and, as discussed above (Chapter 1), English embroilment in the conflict was a diplomatically sensitive issue for Cromwell's regime. In June 1656, and shortly before the first appearance of the play, the Ottomans had suffered an unusual military setback against the Venetian fleet in the Dardanelles, although this does not warrant Wiseman's assertion that 'Davenant was writing of Turkey at a period when it no longer posed such a threat to Europe as it had during the sixteenth and parts of the seventeenth centuries'.[30]

More generally, for the play's first audiences, the image of an island besieged by the apparently inexorable forces of a malevolent and invidious infidel may have seemed uncomfortably reminiscent of the royalist predicament in the 1650s. Certainly, explicit comparisons between the heresy of the Cromwellian regime and the traditional iniquity of the Ottoman Empire might almost be termed a commonplace of the polemical literature of the period and Davenant's dramatic opening makes full use of this familiar and perennially fascinating 'other'. From the outset, the Ottoman fleet is represented as both the military and spiritual diametric of the European forces garrisoning the island, which is itself imagined as a microcosm of Christendom itself:

> Pale shew those Crescents to our bloody Cross?
> Sink not the Western Kingdoms in our loss?
> Will not the Austrian Eagle moult her Wings,
> That long hath hover'd o're the Gallick-Kings?
> Whose Lillies too will wither when we fade;
> And th'English Lyon shrink into a shade. (*1 SOR* I.i.49–54)

Thus, the fate of the entire 'Western Kingdoms' is portrayed as hinging upon

---

[29] This and subsequent quotations are taken from the British Library copy of the two-part edition of the play (1663) unless stated otherwise.

[30] Wiseman, *Drama and Politics*, p. 154. This monolithic and teleological view of the 'decline' of the Ottoman Empire is far from being consistently borne out by contemporary (English) opinion or subsequent events. Although the Venetian victory looks retrospectively symptomatic of a waning of Turkish military superiority, under the reformed viziership of the Köprülüs from the late 1650s on, the empire underwent a resurgence of its expansionist ambitions. By the time the second part of Davenant's play appeared in the summer of 1659, the Dardanelles had long been reopened and Ottoman armies were once more being mobilised against the Hapsburg territories in Transylvania. Candia itself would finally succumb to the Turks in 1669. See Chapter 1, above.

the defence of Rhodes. This monumental clash of competing ideologies is described in terms that evoke the prodigious nature of the Turkish hordes, a familiar characteristic of representations of Islamic imperialism that is emblematically proclaimed by their 'bright Crescents/ ... that encreasing Empire show;/ Which must be still in Nonage and still grow' (*1 SOR* I.i.44–46). By contrast, the powers of Christian Europe are palpably on the wane. In the first entry, Alphonso, the heroic soldier-lover of the play, praises the merits of the various Christian contingents who defend the island – 'the fiery French', 'the grave Italians' and the 'cheerfull English' (*1 SOR* II.i.27–40) – in an evocation of European confederacy that is not borne out by the complacent infighting of the wider Western world. Whilst 'vainly Rhodes for succour waits', the 'triple Diadems, and Scarlet Hats' of Rome are judged guilty of shortsighted parsimony – 'Rome keeps her Gold, cheaply her Warriours pays/ At first with Blessings, and at last with Praise'. Conversely, Catholic Spain is indicted with a profligate imperialism – 'By armies, stow'd in Fleets, exhausted Spain/ Leave half her Land unplough'd, to plough the Main;/ And still would more of the Old World subdue,/ As if unsatisfi'd with all the New'. Even England is deemed culpable of a vague, but perhaps pertinent dereliction of domestic duties: 'the English Lyon ever loves to change/ His Walks, and in remoter Forrests range' and thus, 'All gaining vainly from each others loss;/ Whilst still the Crescent drives away the Cross' (*1 SOR* II.i.13–26). The Ottoman forces, however, appear united in their crusading militarism, their expansionism portrayed as a positively religious tenet. In the third entry, Pirrhus, a 'bassa' (pasha), echoes the conviction, commonly held amongst English writers, that the imperial successes of the Ottomans were directly derived from the teachings of Mohammed:

> 'Tis well our valiant Prophet did
> In us not only loss forbid,
> But has conjoyn'd us still to get.
> Empire must move apace,
> When she begins the Race,
> And apter is for wings than feet. (*1 SOR* III.i.25–30)

The opening exchanges of the play are similarly peppered with allusions to the conventional characteristics of these 'Termagant Turks'. The rapacious nature of the sultan's 'empire'-building is matched by an innate lasciviousness that the Christian forces pledge to defy: 'Our Swords against proud Solyman we draw,/ His cursed Prophet, and his sensual Law' (*1 SOR* I.i.85–6). Solyman's first appearance in the second entry does little to dispel the audience's impression of an archetypal Turk. Infuriated by his army's failure to overrun the valiant Rhodes, Solyman rages at his general Pirrhus, warning that his wrath 'must be quench'd by Rhodian blood or thine' (*1 SOR* II.ii.34). It is, however, the appearance of the captured Ianthe, veiled like 'the Morning pictur'd in a Cloud', that jolts Solyman from his wonted nature.

This is Ianthe, the Sicilian Flower,
Sweeter then Buds unfolded in a shower,
Bride to Alphonso, who in Rhodes so long
The Theam has been of each Heroick Song;
And she for his relief those Gallies fraught;
Both stow'd with what her Dow'r and Jewels bought. (*1 SOR* II.ii. 70–5).

Ianthe's captor, the pasha Mustapha, praises the princess for her martial valour in bringing the jewels of her dowry to redeem her besieged husband, and resisting capture in 'a bloody Fight'. To the play's first audiences, it is plausible that this portrait of the paradigmatic 'Christian wife' may well have called to mind the exploits of Henrietta-Maria and her active participation in the Civil War.[31] For this pivotal moment in the action, Davenant seems to have drawn heavily on Lodovick Carlell's pre-war play, *Osmond the Great Turk*, first performed in 1637. Despite the play's title, Osmond is in fact a Tartar and loyal servant to the Emperor Melcoshus. The play opens *in medias res* with the sacking of an unnamed town – 'The City reekes with the warm blood/ of murder'd Christians whose avarice/ hath made them & their wealth our/ prey' – although the setting may well have been suggested by accounts of the Turkish sacking of Constantinople. Despina, a 'fair Christian Slave', has been captured and two soldiers squabble over the right to violate her honour, whereupon Osmond intervenes, rescuing Despina and, despite his own admiration for her, resolves to present her as tribute to his master. As in Davenant's play, a model of female Christian virtue is brought before an Oriental tyrant and once again she enters veiled. Unlike Solyman, however, Melcoshus unveils his captive and is, of course, immediately spellbound:

… Osmond so well I like, cover her/ face lest I doe surfet with beholding. … Off with/ that vail, the meanest of creatures may behold the Sun:/ and as his beames in showry April breakes through/ the clouds, so does the lightening of her glorious eyes/ breake through their watery circle, and grow more/ powerfull by that opposition; so powerfull, that a conquering/ Prince descends his throne and beggs that hee/ May heare you … (p. 5)

Like Ianthe, Despina's virtuous beauty radiates, sun-like, from beneath her veil. Introduced in Carlell's description, however, is the notion of the powerful and potentially destructive nature of 'this jewell'. Indeed, the rhetoric of Melcoshus' homage to Despina's beauty 'so powerfull, that a conquering/ Prince descends his throne' transpires to be an unconscious prophecy – the king's love for his Christian captive makes him vulnerable to the machinations of the scheming Haly who successfully plots to assassinate Melcoshus.

---

31 Of the queen, Wiseman speculates that 'the female figures in [Davenant's] plays – such as Ianthe – may perhaps bear traces of his admiration of her' (*Drama and Politics*, p. 140), whilst Hedbäck asserts that her 'activities during the first years of the Civil War parallel strikingly those of Davenant's Ianthe' (*The Siege of Rhodes: A Critical Edition*, p. li).

In the meantime, the king has himself murdered Despina in an attempt to assuage public opinion and 'please the ignorant multitude' by making 'a sacrifice of her to them'. Melcoshus is plagued with guilt and vows to commemorate Despina in an act of contrition that perpetuates the strand of light/dark imagery running throughout the play.

> Night, dark thoughts, and justly so, since by/ my cruelties, obscured that light, which was my only/ comfort ... I will erect an Altar in this obscure Walk, and in the dead of night offer thee sacrifice; nay, even at/ noon day would I perform it, and in the sight of all,/ but that I know it must appear too plainly, that I to/ thee performed all rites with greater reverence, than to/ our sacred prophet ...
>
> (p. 53)

These lines capture the play's denunciation of the king's love for Despina, characterised in terms of a pernicious idolatry that ultimately dissolves the bonds of religion upon which the king's power rests. In Davenant's rendering, however, the Christian maiden becomes the means of enlightenment, inspiring Solyman to honour his pasha's pledge (made by the 'Prophets plight') to grant Ianthe unmolested passage to Rhodes. Where the interruption of Carlell's heroine into the Islamic sphere of the play had precipitated a religio-political crisis in Tartar society, the encounter between Solyman and this 'daughter of the Night' exposes a spiritual fragility in the Rhodian camp. This fracturing of the Christian ideal is synecdochally represented in the corruption of the ostensible epitome of conjugal virtue embodied by Alphonso and Ianthe who appear to be, in the sultan's words, 'such a single pair/ As onely equal are/ Unto themselves' (*1 SOR* IV.i.23–5). Instead, Alphonso becomes wracked with a jealousy that threatens to undermine the Rhodian cause. In Act IV, the Admiral relates Alphonso's distraction to Villerius:

> I met him wild as all the winds,
> When in the Ocean they contest:
> And diligent suspision finds
> He is with Jealousie possest (*1 SOR* IV.iii.13–16)

Villerius' disconsolate response – 'Thou sing'st the sad destruction of our Town' – underlines the universal significance of Alphonso's decline, his unwarranted jealousy spilling over into the public sphere of the play. However, the couple's private dialogue in the third act reveals that Alphonso's suspicion is aroused not only by the fact that Ianthe was forced to spend 'two whole nights' as Solyman's prisoner, but has been further aggravated by the uncharacteristic nature of the Turk's behaviour. In an exchange highly suggestive of the play's sophisticated awareness of pre-existing narrative versions of the Turk, Ianthe relates her own surprise to Alphonso that, despite 'All that of Turks and Tyrants' she had heard, the sultan 'seem'd in civil France, and Monarch there' (*1 SOR* III.ii.102). Given the indictment of the failure of the various European powers, including France, to come to the succour of Rhodes, expressed earlier in the play, Ianthe's comparison signals an all-important shift in the imaginative positioning of the Islamic counterpart. Here is a further indication of the play's reluctance, or even inability, to impose a moral definition of Orient and Occident, a disjunction that feeds upon the fluid and conflicted image of Islam in this decade. Instead, Solyman's apparent appropriation of notionally European patterns of morality and 'civil'-ity issues a disorienting challenge to Alphonso, provoking a crisis of identity that the oxymora of his language struggle to contain. Although Ianthe's virtue 'seem'd to civilize a barb'rous Foe', Alphonso remains unconvinced, declaring 'This Christian Turk amazes me' and, in soliloquy, reveals his distrust of such 'wondrous Turkish chastity':

> Oh Solyman, this mistique act of thine,
> Does all my quiet undermine … (*1 SOR* III.ii.141–2)

Meanwhile, Alphonso's jealousy continues to be countered by Solyman's 'stubborn Honour'. On the eve of the Ottoman assault on the island, the pashas Pirrhus and Mustapha counsel their sultan to punish the Christians for their insolent refusal to accept Solyman's offer of amnesty:

> They in to morrows storm will change their mind,
> Then, though too late instructed, they shall find,
> That those who your protection dare reject
> No humane Power dares venture to protect.
> They are not Foes, but Rebels, who withstand
> The pow'r that does their Fate command. (*1 SOR* IV.i.7–12)

Here is the recurring stratagem, prevalent throughout the seventeenth century, of conceptualising the Ottoman Empire as an instrument of 'Fate' and therefore, in eschatological terms, as the providential scourge of Christendom.[32] Latent within this well-rehearsed thesis, however, is a curious distinction between 'Foes' and 'Rebels' that has a particular significance in relation to Davenant's own tentative gestures towards the English political situation in this first version of *The Siege of Rhodes*. In their ultimately futile opposition to the inevitability of fate, a force often evoked in order to account for Cromwell's own prolific success, Ianthe and Alphonso perhaps represent the possibility of virtuous, if misguided rebellion. In the context of 1656, Pirrhus' image appears to mitigate the actions of those who, like the playwright himself, have

---

[32] In this context the Turk was often conflated with the Catholic and the Jew as representatives of the Antichrist on earth who would combine to bring about the apocalypse foretold by St John. Examples of this kind abound in the literature of the period, but one tract, published in 1660, is particularly suggestive of the ways in which these millenarian convictions might feed into political discourse. The exhaustive treatise, fervently and defiantly compiled by Griffith Williams, Bishop of Ossory, is fully entitled, *The Great Antichrist Revealed Before this time, never discovered And proved to be neither Pope, nor Turk, nor any Single Person, nor the Succession of any one Monarch or Tyrant in any Policies BUT a collected pack, or multitude of Hypocritical, Heretical, Blasphemous and most scandalous wicked men* (London, 1660).

been swept along with the political tide and forced to accede to the realities of Protectorate government. In this inversion of the standard narrative, it is those who *fail* to turn Turk who are adjudged rebels, traitors to their fate. Whilst the Turkish generals conform to type, however, Solyman repudiates their blood-lust in an evocation of a, recognisably Christian, conception of ideal government:

> Oh Mustapha, our strength we measure ill,
> We want the half of what we think we have;
> For we enjoy the Beast-like pow'r to kill,
> But not the God-like pow'r to save.
> Who laughs at Death, laughs at our highest Pow'r;
> The valiant man is his own Emperour. (*1 SOR* IV.i.13–18)

Solyman's self-realisation partially derives from contemporary political theory and seems to echo a distinctly Hobbesian analysis of the inherent limitations of a 'Beast-like' human nature. The sultan's final metaphor, however, suggests an evaluation of government based upon a correlation between the individual and society and recapitulates the play's insistent emphasis upon individual responsibility for good self-government. Indeed, if Hotson is correct in his conjecture that the play's first performance took place almost immediately after the play's registration in August 1656, then the sultan's apprehension of government legitimised by military might would have been directly applicable to the shifting power relations outside the world of the playhouse. Since the dissolution of the First Protectorate Parliament in August 1655, the country had been subject to direct military rule with eleven district governors made directly accountable to the Protector; by September 1656, however, Cromwell had called the Second Protectorate Parliament, partly in response to growing civilian pressure to curb the power of the Major Generals.[33] In this context, the play echoes the possibility of concessive reform to a more consultative form of government of the kind that was mooted in the autumn of 1656.

As a man unable to prove 'his own Emperour', therefore, Alphonso conspicuously fails to exercise self-governance; his inability to master his ignoble emotion amounts to a betrayal that is social and political as well as sexual. In the 1656 version, disaster is averted, or at least deferred – Ianthe forgives Alphonso for his 'over-cautious love' and a final chorus of soldiers celebrate the Pyrrhic victory of the Rhodians: 'Whilst we drink good Wine, and you drink but Coffee' (*1 SOR* V.v.32). There remains, however, a tangible sense that the events of the fifth entry have not entirely resolved the unsettling ideological inversions performed in the preceding action. Whilst Solyman vows to starve the 'Audacious Town' into submission, Alphonso remains tormented by his jealousy in a final image of contrition that recalls that of Carlell's fallen

---

33 See Derek Hirst, *Authority and Conflict: England 1603–1658* (London: Edward Arnold, 1986), pp. 339–42.

tyrant cited earlier: 'Draw all the Curtains, and then lead her in;/ Let me in darkness mourn away my sin' (*1 SOR* V.iii.107–8).

'THE PEOPLES VARIOUS MINDS': CONFLICTS OF SOVEREIGNTY IN THE SECOND PART OF *THE SIEGE OF RHODES*

This impression of irresolution is, of course, not least the result of the incontrovertible strictures of historical actuality – as the 1656 audience would have been aware, Rhodes was ultimately destined to fall to the Ottomans. In another sense too, perhaps a sequel was always intended. Davenant's second part builds upon his initial experiment, dispensing with the diversionary choruses between the 'entries', now reestablished as conventional act divisions, and develops many of the ideas that begin to emerge in the first part. This second, and undoubtedly more accomplished piece of drama, however, belongs to an entirely different set of theatrical and political contexts than its pioneering precursor, a transformation that is immediately evident in the contrasting tone of the prefatory material that accompanies the two parts. As opposed to the attenuated apology for the play's 'defects' and the playwright's somewhat tremulous hope to 'advance the Characters of Vertue in the shapes of Valor and conjugal Love' which constitute the prefatory address to the 1656 printing of *The Siege of Rhodes*, the epistle dedicatory to the Earl of Clarendon that introduces the second part of the play is an altogether more strident exposition of the play's meaning and contemporary status.[34]

> Your name is so eminent in the Justice which you convey through all the different Members of this great Empire, that my *Rhodians* seem to enjoy a better Harbour in the Pacifique *Thames*, than they had on the *Mediterranean*; and I have brought *Solyman* to be arraign'd at your Tribunal, where you are the Censor of his civility and magnificence.

Davenant's grateful acknowledgement of the Lord High Chancellor's influential protection draws a parallel between the fictive, and spatially distant, sphere of the play and the real world of the play's production beside 'the Pacifique *Thames*', explicitly suggesting the disconcerting collision between incongruous ideologies and cultures that underpins the rationale behind both parts of *The Siege of Rhodes*. As the epistle goes on to scornfully relate, however, the play is itself besieged by 'vertuous Enemies':

> Dramatick Poetry meets with the same persecution now, from such who esteem themselves the most refin'd and civil, as it ever did from the Barbarous. And yet whilst those vertuous Enemies deny *heroique Plays* to the Gentry, they entertain the People with a Seditious *Farce* of their own counterfeit Gravity. But I hope

---

[34] Hëdbáck states that the dedicatory was first printed in the reissue of Q2 (1663). Hëdbáck, *The Siege of Rhodes*, p. xvi.

you will not be unwilling to receive (in this Poetical dress) neither the Beseig'd nor the Besiegers, since they come without their vices : for as others have purg'd the Stage from corruptions of the Art of the Drama, so I have endeavour'd to cleanse it from the corruption of manners; nor have I wanted care to render the *Ideas* of Greatness and Vertue pleasing and familiar.

Davenant's vigorous defence of his new departure in 'Dramatick Poetry' indicates both the persistence of opposition to the institution of public theatre and as the playwright's new-found readiness to acknowledge, even insist upon, the radical currency of his play. Once more, Davenant's protean sense of self-expediently reflects the status quo, and the playwright is forthright in his denunciation of Puritan hypocrisy and assured of the primacy of his own claim to the moral high ground. Where the first part of the play could only intimate a connection between its own representation of the confrontation of ostensibly inimical ideologies and actual domestic enmities, here Davenant overtly suggests an inverted reciprocity between the Ottoman sultan and factious elements of contemporary London: whilst Solyman manifests a 'civility & magnificence' that refutes his archetypal barbarism, those who malign the theatre in a 'Seditious *Farce* of their own counterfeit Gravity' are charged with affecting a civility that belies their own barbarity. Here too is Davenant's recurring distinction between the 'Gentry' and the 'People' as representatives of potentially conflicting interests – in this case, portrayed as a desire to watch plays and a (misguided) desire to suppress them. As in Davenant's panegyric, *Upon his Sacred Majestie's most happy Return to his Dominions*, the people ('the Many-headed Crowd' of the poem) are imagined as a powerfully volatile and dangerously impressionable component of society that is frequently driven into conflict with the ruling class (the '*great Ships*' of the poem), creating an antagonistic tension that emerges as one of the most prominent themes of the second part of the play.

The scene opens with the Rhodian Council bemoaning the continuing inaction of the Western powers to relieve the island and divided in their proposed course of action. Whilst Alphonso presses for action in a last-ditch attempt to break the Turkish siege, Villerius, the Grand Master of Rhodes, counsels caution, reminding the headstrong knights that a reckless attack will leave the town defenceless, concluding that 'All those attempts of Valour we must shun/ Which may the sultan vex; And, since bereft/ Of food, there is no help but Treaty left' (*2 SOR* I.i.146–8). No sooner is this breach repaired, however, than the counsel and the audience are made aware of a wider division on the island, a split signalled by the stage direction 'A Shout within, and a Noise of forcing of Doors'. Villerius fears that 'Our guards will turn confed'rates with the crowd', in an image of anarchic mob rule dangerously abetted by a militant and intractable army. As Alphonso reports, the experience of war has transformed the people, eroding the deference that sustains the social order:

> These us'd with awe to wait
> Far from your Palace gate;
> But, like lean Birds in Frosts, their hunger now
> Makes them approach us and familiar grow. (*2 SOR* I.i.161–4)

Again, the vicissitudes of public opinion are imagined as a buffeting wind, destabilising the political status quo:

> The Peoples various minds ...
> Were lately as a secret kept
> In many whispers of so soft a breath, ...
> But now, as if they meant to waken Death,
> They rashly rise, and loud in Tumults grow. (*2 SOR* I.i.169–77)

The threat of popular insurrection persuades the Rhodian Council to submit to the people's will and request that Ianthe treat with Solyman on Rhodes' behalf since 'The people find that they have no defence/ But in your Beauty and your Eloquence' (*2 SOR* I.i.227–8), once more hazarding the provocation of Alphonso's pernicious jealousy. Again, the growing desperation of the Rhodian people seems to obliquely refer to the experience of the Civil War. In the second act, the clamour of the 'People within' again penetrates the solemn serenity of the council chamber, creating a sense that the Rhodian rulers are besieged by their subjects as much as by the Turkish hordes, and provoking a debate about the nature of government. Initially, Villerius evokes an image of ideal, perhaps even democratic government, where 'Pow'r is an Arch which ev'ry common hand/ Does help to raise to a magnifique height' (*2 SOR* II.i.11–12). Six lines later, however, the Grand Master is forced to concede the impracticability of effective government without the consent of the people. Despite the ostensible sovereignty of the Rhodian Knights, Villerius recognises the impotence of his authority in the face of popular revolt:

> Ianthe needs must go. Those who withstand
> The Tide of Flood, which is the Peoples will,
> Fall back when they in vain would onward row:
> We strength and way preserve by lying still.
> And sure, since Tides ebb longer than they flow,
> Patience, which waits their Ebbs, regains
> Lost time, and does prevent our pains. (*2 SOR* II.i.18–24)

Here, couched in the same nautical metaphor, is precisely the opposite injunction from that made in Davenant's encomium of 1660, a volte-face that is indicative of the degree to which a transformation in the playwright's own projected identity had been necessitated in the short time between the play's composition and the return of the king. The concessive implications of the play are quickly forgotten in the loyal authoritarianism of the poem to a restored monarch. Like those of '*Noble Blood*', criticised for their negligent quiescence in Davenant's poem, the Grand Master advocates a solicitous passivity in this crucial passage which, in its final couplet, appears to anticipate the changing tide of the Restoration.[35] In the exchange that follows, the Rhodian elite discuss the imperative of appeasing the people in language that suggests a correspondence between theatrical and political arenas – whilst Villerius describes the people's rejoicing as 'applause', the Admiral has the sententious aside, 'Dissembling is an Art above the Crowd', clearly implying that an aptitude for performance constitutes an essential part of the 'Art' of government. In the same way, the terms of Ianthe's valediction emphasise the need for a clear demarcation between private and public shows of emotion. Both Alphonso's 'late ignoble Jealousie' and their trepidatious grief at parting must be concealed from the crowd 'For Rhodes, by seeing us at parting mourn,/ Will look for weeping Clouds at my return'.

In the second half of the act, the scene turns to Solyman's camp and resumes the display of Ottoman unity that has thus far delineated Solyman's forces from the Christian contingents of the play. Pirrhus and Mustapha recite their habitual obsequies to their sultan's 'sway', but in soliloquy Solyman laments the shifting sands upon which his authority is founded:

> Of spacious Empire, what can I enjoy?
> Gaining at last but what I first Destroy.
> Tis fatal (Rhodes) to thee,
> And troublesome to me
> That I was born to govern swarms
> Of Vassals boldly bred to arms:
> For whose accurs'd diversion, I must still
> Provide new Towns to Sack, new Foes to Kill.
> Excuse that Pow'r, which by my Slaves is aw'd:
> For I shall find my peace
> Destroy'd at home, unless
> I seek for them destructive Warr abroad. (*2 SOR* II.ii.53–64)

Evinced here is the same instinctive militarism of Turks 'boldly bred to arms' that informs much of the first part of the play. In this rendering, however, the conventionally ascribed attribute – an innate propensity for war – is stood on its head and posited, not as a measure of the empire's strength, but of its weakness. It is not stretching the terms of the play's ambivalent mediation of contemporary events too far to suggest that Davenant's portrait of an

---

35 If these lines do represent a submerged anticipation of the Restoration, then this would support a case for a later dating of the play's composition, theoretically possible any time from the initial performances of *The Siege of Rhodes* Part One (?September 1656) up until the recording of the second part in the Stationer's Register on 30 May 1659; whilst the Protectorate appeared unassailable in 1656, only two years later following the death of Cromwell and the failure of his successor Richard to consolidate his hold on power, the return of the Stuart heir must have seemed suddenly viable.

isolated and absolute ruler, forced to conduct a policy of restless imperialism, is redolent of Cromwell's foreign policy in the 1650s and, in particular, the so-called 'Western Design' against Spanish-held territories in the Caribbean that foundered in the spring of 1655.[36] Here, more than at any other point in the play, the sultan's vexed authority recalls the predicament of the crypto-monarchical figure of Cromwell who as Lord Protector after 1653, and even more so following the 'Humble Petition and Advice' (1657), began to look increasingly like the absolute ruler he had striven to overthrow.[37] Indeed, such a blurring of political identities is wellsuited to the play's unfolding credo, manifest in its increasing tendency to represent the Turks and the Christians along ever-converging lines. In the second part of the play the distinction between two outwardly inimical systems of government – the absolute rule of the sultan and the collective oligarchy of the Rhodian Council – breaks down and is exposed as an illusion. For all its specious show of unity, Solyman's 'spacious Empire' is, as much as the Rhodian alliance, subject to the tyranny of the people. The shifting signification of the text constantly resists straightforward allegory, and yet within the play's complex parallelism, the play's distinct preoccupation with the ultimately illusive nature of absolute rule must have seemed particularly germane to contemporary play audiences in the political uncertainty of 1659. On 24 May, only six days before the play's registration with the Stationer's Company, Richard Cromwell, the successor Protector ratified by the 'Humble Petition and Advice', had resigned, having been forced to dissolve the Third Protectorate Parliament, under army pressure, and reinstate the 'Rump' Parliament of 1653.

---

[36] Hirst describes Cromwell's venture against the Spanish as 'both economically and politically disastrous', *Authority and Conflict*, p. 330.

[37] Cromwell, of course, famously declined the crown (prompting comparisons with Richard III) and Protectorate government differed from Charles' personal rule in several important ways, not least in how it saw itself. Nevertheless, Cromwell's eventual acceptance of the 'Humble Petition' in its revised form (25 May 1657) did prompt criticism from royalists and republicans alike. In his discussion of the 'drift towards kingship' in the 1650s, Norbrook characterises the ambiguity of Cromwell's position, providing a suggestive context for Davenant's interrogation of legitimate authority: 'In the last period of Cromwell's rule, he seemed in many ways in an unprecedentedly strong position, and opposition was effectively contained. On the other hand, there remained a crisis of legitimacy. If Cromwell became king he would alienate much support and strengthen republican opposition, but as long as he refused the crown his status remained too equivocal to become an effective focus for political loyalty,' *Writing the English Republic*, p. 324.

'A RIDDLE BOTH TO HONOUR AND TO LOVE': REFORMING THE
TURK AND REDEEMING THE APOSTATE IN THE RESTORATION
VERSION OF *THE SIEGE OF RHODES*

The fascination with 'That tide, the Crowd' that permeates this second part virtually qualifies the Hydra-like populous as a distinct protagonist of the play. When the final version of the play was reprinted in 1663, the first part was advertised as 'being lately enlarg'd'. In all, Davenant adds six new speaking parts to his original, for Rustan, Haly, the High Marshal and Roxolana as well as sets of attendants for Ianthe and Roxolana. This was in part, no doubt, simply in anticipation of a more commodious stage than that described in the preface to the 1656 play. Similarly, several of Davenant's later additions and emendations to this first version are partly made to facilitate their introduction to the audience before they are more fully represented in the succeeding part. Of the male additions, the High Marshal seems largely interchangeable with Villerius and takes some of his lines in the first entry. Similarly, Rustan and Haly play little direct part in the action but rather serve as go-betweens for the sultan and his wife. Far more substantive, however, are the additions that concern the two central women of the play. Before the first chorus, Ianthe is introduced, complete with 'Two open Caskets with Jewels' in a new scene that emphasises her selfless valour and introduces the theme of the transformations wrought by love in war:

> Love a Consumption learns from Chymists Art.
> Saphyrs, and harder Di'monds must be sold
> And turn'd to softer and more current Gold.
> With Gold we cursed Powder may prepare
> Which must consume in smoak and thinner Air. (*1 SOR* I.ii.24–8)

The transmutation of Ianthe's jewels into gunpowder underlines that aspect of her story that most closely resembled that of Henrietta-Maria, a comparison Davenant seems more inclined to intimate in his revised version. Ianthe is also given extra lines at the end of the play in the scene of her reconciliation with Alphonso that serve to draw out the agony of his self-recrimination – 'Accursed crime! Oh, let it have no name/ Till I recover Bloud to shew my shame' (*1 SOR* V.iii.99–100). More fundamental, however, is the introduction of an entirely new character, that of Roxolana, wife to the sultan, in three additional scenes before the choruses. At the end of the third entry she arrives from Licia driven, like the people, by a dangerous wind: 'The Tempest' of her jealous passion. Like Alphonso, she is suspicious of Solyman's motives and is correspondingly compelled to resort to metaphors for inversion and paradox in order to explain the strange influence of this Christian princess upon her husband:

> What has your Valour from the Rhodians gain'd?
> Unless Ianthe, as a prize you boast;

120

Who now has got that heart which I have lost.
Brave conquest, where the Takers self is taken! (*1 SOR* III.iii.18–21)

Roxolana's tirade reiterates the familiar parity between amorous and military conquests that surfaces throughout the play, but also suggests the degree to which identity and 'self' are themselves rendered unstable and interchangeable by the crisis of war. With the addition of Roxolana, Davenant expands the theme of the debilitative nature of marital jealousy to symmetrically incorporate the Turkish world of the play. Not only is Solyman compelled to monger war in the name of political expediency, but in a clear reflection of the Rhodian predicament, his foreign policy is hampered by domestic strife, leading the sultan to conclude, 'My war with Rhodes will never have success,/ Till I at home, Roxana, make my peace' (*1 SOR* V.iv.19–20). In its original form, the uneasy resolution to the final entry suggested a precarious truce between Alphonso and Ianthe, disaster being narrowly averted by Christian valour on the battlefield. By the 1663 reprint, however, the failure of Solyman's forces to overpower the island defenders is perceived as being as much the consequence of an internalised wrangling in the Turkish encampment, represented by the archetype of a jealous wife, as in any vindication of Christian merit.

In the second part of *The Siege of Rhodes*, Roxolana develops as the main focus for the play's interrogation of the nature of 'This cursed Jealousie', an endemic apostasy that comes to infect every sphere of the play-action. Sustaining the pattern of even-handed representation instigated by Davenant's revisions to his earlier play, however, Roxolana's suspicion does not supplant that of the Christian protagonists, but positively incites it. At the beginning of Act IV, Alphonso reveals that he has received a letter from the 'Sultana' strongly hinting at an impending assault on Ianthe's virtue and warning of Solyman that 'He to Ianthe lays/ A closer Siege than ere he did to Rhodes' (*2 SOR* IV.ii.31–2). The Rhodian alliance respond with a precipitous decision to abandon policy in favour of military intervention, a privileging of passion over reason and 'Renown' over national responsibility that is clearly signalled by the terms of their rallying cry: 'Then Tell the World that we have joyn'd our Swords;/ But 'tis for griev'd Ianthe, not for Rhodes' (*2 SOR* IV.ii.70–1). Significantly, it is the clandestine jealousy of yet another of the characters that has conspired to undermine the Rhodian cause. In soliloquy, the Admiral confesses his own love for Ianthe and determines to encourage Alphonso's misgivings with 'watchfull fears. ... Till he grow fearfull too'. In a later address, the Admiral imagines himself in the continuum of lovers throughout history.

> Love does Alphonso in a Circle lead;
> And none can trace the wayes which I must tread.
> Lovers, in searching Loves Records, will find
> But very few like me,
> That still would Virtuous be,
> Whilst to anothers Wife I like a Lover woo,

> I use all art
> That from her Husband she may never part,
> And yet even then would make him Jealous too. (*2 SOR* III.ii.114–23)

The Admiral's illicit love is something of a narrative cul-de-sac in the play, apparently forgotten in the mêlée of turns and counter-turns that characterise the final act. Nevertheless, this apostrophe in the action suggests the play's self-reflexive relationship with its own dramatic lineage and evinces Davenant's consciously complex manipulation of pre-existing archetypes, the implication being that straightforward interpretations of such precedential 'Records' have been rendered inadequate and obsolete by the maze-like convolutions of the contemporary political predicament both within and without the fictive sphere of the play. This urgent need for reappraisal underpins the climactic scene of Roxolana's meeting with Ianthe in Act IV, an enactment of the figurative confrontation of honour and jealousy.

Having confided in his lieutenants the marital storm that threatens to undo his reputation, Solyman resolves to send Ianthe to her jealous rival's tent, 'Such a mysterious Present as will prove/ A Riddle both to Honour and to Love' (*2 SOR* III.i.146–7). Oscillating between despair and rage, Roxolana derides Mustapha's invocation of duty as 'officious fear' and ominously enlists the support of her loyal accomplice, the eunuch Haly. When the audience see Roxolana again, she appears in a dramatic tableau of vengeful jealousy, punctiliously described by Davenant's scene direction: 'Being wholly fill'd with Roxolana's Rich Pavilion, Wherein is discern'd at distance, Ianthe sleeping on a Couch … Roxolana having a Turkish Embroidered Handkerchief in her left hand, And a naked Ponyard in her right' (*2 SOR* IV.iii). Deliberately staged, then, this is the sultan's 'Riddle', and interpreting this scene, one of the most visually arresting of the entire action, is at the heart of the ways in which the play dramatically rewrites Oriental conventions and, in so doing, proclaims its own radical meaning. The setting, the eunuch's presence, the sumptousness of the décor, the femininity of the handkerchief and the violence of the naked poniard, in fact every detail of this carefully prescribed tableau is designed to evoke the powerful topos of the seraglio. A source of constant fascination to travellers and dramatists alike, the seraglio functions as the locus for an entire range of preconceived notions about the decadence and deviance of the Turkish court. In his study, *The Sultan's Court: European Fantasies of the East*, Alain Grosrichard highlights the function of the Seraglio as a sexual–political fantasy in terms extremely pertinent to Roxolana's role in the play. Although couched in theoretical and somewhat decontextualised terms, his formulation is a fair summation of the standard narrative that Davenant is actively subverting:

> The seraglio is more then a setting or a scene; it is the supreme tragic site. Shutting out all strangers' eyes by definition, the exclusive realm of a single being, it is the paradise of pleasure only because prohibition surrounds it everywhere. Merely

raising the curtain is already a transgression, therefore, and makes the spectator an accomplice, even before he becomes a witness to the inevitable drama ...[38]

As much a construction of Western imagination as an immediately identifiable, although mysterious, representation of Turkish polity, the Seraglio is also crucially a site of feminised sovereignty. Moreover, it is the natural stage for disaster and, as Roxolana stands poised to plunge her dagger into the sleeping Ianthe, the play teeters dangerously on the edge of tragedy. Moved to compassion, the eunuch Haly persuades Roxolana to postpone her retribution until she has tried her rival's virtue and the waking Ianthe, resolute in her chasteness, wins the sultana's mercy. In her account of the play, Bridget Orr characterises the female opposition of the play as between 'a figure of gentle modesty' and an 'ambitious virago'[39] but Roxolana's failure to conform to her Orientalist stereotype is more evidence of the play's reluctance to enforce conventional binaries such as this. The fact that tragedy is averted and the twin themes of 'honour' and 'love' reaffirmed suggests that generic reform is fundamental to the play's redefinition of a politicised Orient.

When Solyman arrives, Roxolana reproves him for his neglect and, in the ensuing exchange between the sultan and his wife, Davenant consolidates many of the threads of theme and imagery that interlace the play.

> Roxolana: You alter ev'ry year the Worlds known face;
>   Whilst Cities you remove, and Nations chace ...
>   The various mind will wander very farr,
>   Which, more than home, a forein Land preferrs.
>
> Solyman: Strange Coasts are welcome after Storms at Sea ...
>   The wise, for quietness, when civil Warr
>   Does rage at home, turn private Travailers.
>
>   (*2 SOR* IV.iii.215–28)

Here, more than at any other point in the play, Davenant appears to make reference to his own experience of 'civil Warr'. The transformations of identity wrought by foreign war are inscribed even upon the 'face' of the world. Yet more powerful, however, are the effects of domestic conflict, microcosmically represented by the 'Storms' of Roxolana's jealousy, a tempest of such insidious force that the archetype of the invincible Turk becomes transformed into that of the 'private Travailer', a figure of exiled virtue reminiscent of many self-characterisations of royalist luminaries during the 1640s and 1650s, not least those of the Stuart heir and the playwright himself. Roxolana's introduc-

---

[38] Alain Grosrichard, *The Sultan's Court: European Fantasies of the East*, trans. Liz Heron, intro. Mladen Dolar (London: Verso, 1998), p. 124.
[39] Orr, *Empire on the English Stage*, p. 66.

tion into the play is at the heart of this mediation between public and private displays of loyalty.

The final act of the play comprises mainly the decisive battle between the two forces, opening with a sign of the Rhodians' desperate and reckless courage, the scene painted to represent 'a Prospect of Rhodes by night, and the Grand Masters Palace on Fire'. As we might anticipate, the English contingent are here singled out for mention, as elsewhere in the play. For example, the prefatory description of the 'Ornament which encompass'd the Scene' of the play's first performance includes the passing observation that 'The Renown of the English valor, made the Grand Master Villerius, to select their Station to be most frequently commanded by himself'. Similarly, the scene direction appended to the fifth entry of *1 The Siege of Rhodes* calls for a 'Representation of a general Assault', with the 'greatest fury of the Army being discern'd at the English station' whilst, upon learning that Ianthe 'in disguise/ At th'English Bulwark wounded lies', Alphonso consoles himself that 'Ianthe cannot be/ In safer company:/ For what will not the valiant English do/ When beauty is distress'd and Vertue too' (*1 SOR* V.i.105–8). However, these sporadic allusions apart, the battle scene of the first part of the play had been careful to submerge its representation of a specifically English nationhood in the pan-European alliance that comprises the Rhodian Knights. In the corresponding battle of the later play, Davenant seems to be playfully alluding to a more direct and comprehensive resonance between the Rhodian defenders and the English people. Pirrhus announces the English advance to which Solyman defiantly replies,

> Let them proceed!
> Their Cross is bloody, and they come to bleed.
> Set all the Turn-pikes open. Let them in!
> Those Island Gamesters may,
> (Who desperately for honour play)
> Behold fair stakes, and try what they can winn. (*2 SOR* V.i.13–18)

It is not immediately clear as to whom the epithet 'Island Gamesters' applies: the English, or the Rhodians themselves. Certainly, the image of the gambler, compelled by honour to take his chance in battle (against distinctly unfavourable odds) accords strongly with an identifiably cavalier aesthetic of war[40] that the play is far from unequivocally endorsing. Whereas Solyman's submission to the requirements of realpolitick is apparently vindicated by the Turkish victory, the islanders' bravado is portrayed as at best naively idealistic and at worst as the abnegation of national responsibility: Ianthe, and not the Christian citadel,

---

[40] Evident, for example, in John Quarles' *Elegie Upon that Son of Valor Sir Charles Lucas, Who was shot to Death by the Command of the Councel of War, before Colchester* (1648) where the royalist martyr is described as a 'Gamester. … Who lov'd his *King*, and undertook to play/ A noble *Game*, wherein his *honor* lay'.

has become the object of the defenders' misplaced fervour, their battle-cry of 'Ianthe is the Word' once more suggesting an idolatrous elision of religious and erotic zeal.

In Roxolana's pavilion, an analogous interrogation of the nature of national identity and patriotism is taking place. Ianthe has been awoken by the noise of battle and hears conflicting accounts of Alphonso's fate. When the Turkish queen arrives, she at first seems to alleviate Ianthe's fears with news of Alphonso's capture and consignment to her custody before apparently revoking her earlier promise to shelter the Christian princess:

> Soft Fool! Bred up in narrow Western Courts;
> Which are by Subjects storm'd like Paper-Forts ...
> Think'st thou that she, who does wide Empire sway,
> Can breed such storms as Lovers show'rs allay?
> Can half the World be govern'd by a Mind
> That shews Domestick pity, and grows kind? (*2 SOR* V.vi.55–62)

Encapsulated here is a condensed version of the pattern of reversed allegiances and apparent betrayals that suffuse the play. Like the Solyman of Part One of the play, Roxolana performs a *show* of political ruthlessness reminiscent of longstanding representations of harem intrigue and absolves the betrayal of her 'Vows' since their 'Sealing was/ But to a Christian'. Ianthe appeals to a common reverence for 'Religion' but is sharply reproved,

> Religion is but publique fashion here;
> And Justice is but private interest.
> Nature our Sex does to revenge incite;
> And int'rest counsels us to keep our own. (*2 SOR* V.vi.73–6)

As this expression of Roxolana's purported nature indicates, the play is also alert to another archetype, that of the jealous and vengeful woman. In keeping with earlier renditions of Oriental stereotypes, both prove to be illusions, performed by the Sultana in order to test the steadfastness of Ianthe's virtue. Instead, Roxolana is inspired to eschew her baser nature and adds her voice to the play's emergent thesis that 'If mercy were not mingled with their pow'r,/ This wretched world could not subsist an how'r' (*2 SOR*, V.vi. 83–4).

However, whilst Ianthe's influence has allayed the storm of Roxolana's tyranny and successfully induced a show of 'Domestick pity', dissenting voices persist among the Ottoman hierarchy. With the Christian forces defeated, and Alphonso captured, Solyman characteristically decrees that 'Compassion is to vanquisht Valour due'. Pirrhus, however, in keeping with his earlier role as spokesman for an unquenchable militarism, argues for the vigorous suppression of Rhodian resistance:

> Our Sultan does his pow'r from Heav'n derive,
> 'Tis rais'd above the reach of human force:

It could not else with soft compassion thrive:
For few are gain'd or mended by remorse.
The world is wicked grown, and wicked men
(Since jealous still of those whom they have harm'd)
Are but enabled to offend agen
When they are pardon'd and left arm'd. (*2 SOR* V.v.5–12)

Clearly embedded in this conventional expression of Ottoman ruthless-ness, however, are concerns more distinctly contemporary and English than their immediate context might initially suggest. Pirrhus' abhorrence of 'soft compassion' in war combines a rendition of the theory of the divine right to rule with a conviction of the inherently corrupt nature of men in the 'wicked grown' world that held powerful implications for a play audience of late 1659. These, somewhat incongruous, allusions culminate in the double-edged asser-tion that to leave the enemy armed and 'enabled to offend agen' is an example of the worst military folly, an observation that may well have struck a chord with contemporary playgoers as both diagnostic and prescriptive depending on their political sympathies – since Cromwell's death in September 1658, the crumbling Commonwealth had been plagued by the threat of renewed royalist insurrection,[41] whilst likewise, those growing numbers in favour of Charles' return anticipated the need to demilitarise the faltering republic. Whichever the reading, Davenant's by now familiar ambivalence serves to evoke the political dilemmas of contemporary England. The play's resolution, however, repudiates both the dogmatic inviolability of a ruler who 'does his pow'r from Heav'n derive' as well as the cynicism of a conception of a human nature inca-pable of 'remorse'.

By early 1660, of course, the role of the army was emerging as crucial in the delicate power balance between a failing republic and a viably restored monarchy.[42] Dated 23 February 23 1659 in Thomason's copy, the anonymous tract *Learne of a Turk, or Instructions and Advise sent from the Turkish Army at Constantinople, to the English Army at London* makes an ingenious interven-tion into the political discourse of its day and provides a suggestive context for Davenant's own rendition of Ottoman history. Purportedly 'communicated by M. B. one of the Attendants of the *English* agent there', the treatise relates the convoluted history of the bloody power struggle that followed the death of '*Achmat*, eight Emperour of the *Turks*' and draws particular attention to the vulnerability of the Ottoman Empire to its standing army. Osman, rightful heir to the throne, is murdered by the supporters of a rival faction and

41 The playwright was himself implicated in a royalist uprising in August of 1659 and briefly imprisoned for his alleged participation.
42 Davenant appears to have recognised this critical shift relatively early, composing the pane-gyric *To his Excellency the Lord General Monck* in March 1660.

Thus one of the greatest Monarchs in the world was first *affronted* by his mutinied Troops, his own slaves, almost unarm'd, and few in number, no man taking up sword to defend him; and they who first began this madnesse, not meaning to *hurt him,* by the encrease of their own fury, which had no bounds, *deposed him against their own purpose* ; and at *last exposed his life, against their will, to the Counsels of other men, whom they equally hated.*

Thus, Osman's murder begins a cycle of rebellion and retribution that has clear implications for the English situation, a correspondence spelled out in the prefatory address 'To the Reader':

Although thou hast not much skill in *forreign Names,* yet if thou hast any little skill in *Domestick affairs,* thou mayest out of this discourse pick some knowledge of *our Miseries* past : of our *Miseries* present, with the *root* and *spring* of them, and of the most probable *means* of redeeming them for the future. God make our *Grandees* in the Army, *wise by the harmes of others* (they that build much upon the confidence of an Army, build upon a quicksand) And God make them *honest* after the *Example* of others, or else *the men of Niniveh* shall rise up in judgement against this Government, *Matth.* 12.41. And the *Turks Circumcision* shall judge and condemn these mens *Baptisme,* yea, though it be *Anabaptisme.*

Thus, the conventional diametric between Muslim and Christian is employed in the service of an English polemic and thereby reformulated to express the fragmentation of conformity and the breakdown of religious difference, the standard designators '*Circumcision*' and '*Baptisme*' complicated by a third, that of '*Anabaptisme*'. The biblical reference to 'Niniveh', the ancient capital of the Assyrians, again makes the crucial connection between the '*Example*' of the East and the trope of conversion.[43] As such, the treatise participates in an ongoing appropriation of Islamic history and culture, repeatedly invoked in an attempt to comprehend the unprecedented upheaval in '*Domestick affairs*' that, for many writers, threatened to plunge mid-century England into an apocalyptic abyss.[44] By 1659, the Turk is clearly much more than the traditional embodiment of a spiritual and political anathema. As *Learne of a Turk* demonstrates, the old enemy had been accorded a new significance in the decade since the regicide, as the anonymous writer maintains: 'The reading of History having in it no recompense but delight, unless it look forward to use and action,

[43] This New Testament account tells of Christ's reproach to the Scribes and Pharisees, fully: 'The men of Nineveh shall rise in judgment with this generation, and shall condemn it: because they repented at the preaching of Jonas; and, behold, a greater than Jonas is here' (Matthew 12:41). A reluctant prophet, Jonas nevertheless succeeded in converting Nineveh in only three days. Of equal interest to millenarian preachers of the 1650s was that the relapse and divine destruction of the ungodly city was also prophesised (Nahum 1:14); for example, Thomas Reeve, *God's Plea for Niniveh: or London's precedent for mercy, delivered in certain sermons within the City of London* (London: 1657).

[44] On the impact of Osman's overthrow on Ottoman political culture, see Gabriel Piterberg, *An Ottoman Tragedy: History and Historiography at Play* (Berkeley: University of California Press, 2003).

either to correct errors past, or direct wayes for the future.' In his epistle to Clarendon, Davenant clearly imagines the final version of his *Siege of Rhodes* to be similarly didactic, holding a 'Mirrour' up to human nature since,

> ... it proceeds from the same mind not to be pleas'd with Princes on the Stage, and not to affect them in the Throne; for those are ever most inclin'd to break the Mirrour who are unwilling to see the Images of such as have just authority over their guilt.[45]

However, Davenant's account of the play's meaning is characteristically pragmatic, and misleading, in its attempt to suppress the multiple ambiguities of the text in order to suit the predisposition of his official audience, in this case the stern and staunchly royalist figure of the Earl of Clarendon. The achievement of *The Siege of Rhodes* is clearly much more than the straightforward reflection of republican 'guilt' or indeed any consistent system of signification. Rather, Davenant's play takes the topical belief that England might 'Learne of a Turke' a crucial step further, performing an extraordinary refraction of identity upon the already complex and fragmented figure of the Muslim. Solyman, the reformed and transformed 'Turk' at the epicentre of the play's radical vision, represents a groundbreaking inversion of ingrained notions of enmity and apostasy, engendering anxieties that have a clear resonance in the capricious political climate in which *The Siege of Rhodes* operates. In his concluding peroration, the Sultan permits the Rhodians an honourable defeat, granting Ianthe licence to make terms for the town, declaiming 'I am content it should recorded be,/ That, when I vanquisht Rhodes, you Conquer'd me'. In this final confirmation of Solyman's altered identity, a transformation made all the more absolute by his iconic despotism, the Turkish ruler becomes the apogee of a notionally Christian ideal of kingship, the confluence of reason and compassion, honour and love. As the play's reconciliatory finale contends, the answer both to Solyman's own 'Riddle ... to Honour and to Love' and the vexed questions of apostasy and allegiance outside the world of the theatre, lies in a reorientation of longstanding divisions both at home and abroad. Only then, the play suggests, can England avoid that 'fatal desolation'[46] that betrayed her Rhodian counterpart.

---

45 *Epistle*, A3r.
46 From the epistle dedicatory to the 1663 edition of *2 The Siege of Rhodes*. Davenant describes Rhodes as 'the only fortify'd Academy in Christendome where Divinity and Arms were equally profess'd'.

Chapter 5

TOLERATION, TRADE AND ENGLISH MAHOMETANISM IN THE AFTERMATH OF RESTORATION

IN THE LATE 1650s, William Davenant's experimental opera had reintroduced public theatre to Protectorate Britain and, in its revised and augmented form, would inaugurate the strand of heroic drama which, taken up by Dryden and his imitators, dominated the stage for the next twenty years. *The Siege of Rhodes* had portrayed an Ottoman sultan seemingly rehabilitated, reconciled with his Christian enemies in a final display of honourable co-existence. This 'Christian Turk' appeared to embody the spirit of the earliest years of the Restoration, representative of the redemptive possibilities that a return to monarchy seemed to proffer in the early 1660s. At least, this is how the case is generally portrayed in the panegyric literature of the period. Charles' own declaration of intent, issued from Breda in April 1660, was itself painstakingly conciliatory. Not only did the new king promise to pardon retrospectively any 'crime whatsoever committed against us or our royal father' but also seemed to offer a balm to the religious discord that had contributed to the downfall of the previous Stuart government and which had only been exacerbated by the experience of civil war: 'we do declare a liberty to tender consciences, and that no man shall be disquieted or called in question for differences of opinion in matter of religion which do not disturb the peace of the kingdom'.[1] Such salving rhetoric is echoed, not only by Davenant's play, but to varying degrees, by the enthusiastic optimism of those 'royalist' poets who triumphantly serenaded the monarch's return.

'[J]USTICE WEIGHS THE ACTOR, NOT THE ACT': EXPEDIENCY AND EXCULPATION IN BOYLE'S *MUSTAPHA*

Meanwhile, the Turk continued to conquer the restored stage. Two years after the publication of Davenant's complete *Siege of Rhodes*, Roger Boyle's *Mustapha* was brought out at Lincoln's Inn Fields (3 April 1665), to be later

---

[1] 'The Declaration of Breda', in J. P. Kenyon, *The Stuart Constitution 1603–1688: Documents and Commentary* (Cambridge: Cambridge University Press, 1966), pp. 357–8.

performed at the Duke of York's theatre, and is clearly influenced by the earlier play. Like Davenant's opera, *Mustapha* derives its historical setting from the reign of Suleiman the Magnificent, supplanting Rhodes with Budapest as the object of the sultan's seemingly unstoppable westward advance. Also like *The Siege of Rhodes*, Boyle's play opens with a display of Ottoman military might. Having vanquished the Hungarian army and arrived at the gates of 'Buda', Solyman hesitates, considering the conquest of 'a Mourning Queen, and Infant King', too 'low a thing' for his glory. In this qualm of honour, the sultan recalls his counterpart at the end of Davenant's play. However, where Solyman had at first demanded the destruction of Rhodes in the 1656 play, here it is the bashaws who urge their sultan to finish the job. The vizier Rustan gives his monarch a lesson in realpolitik:

> None but the Conquer'd should have sence of shame.
> Shall shows of Vertue darken your bright Fame?
> Success does cover all the crimes of War,
> And Fame and Vertue still consistent are.
> In lazie peace let Christian Monarchs rust,
> Who think no War, but what's defensive just.
> Our Valiant Prophet did by slaughter rise:
> Conquest a part of our Religion is.[2]   (I.19–26)

Where in Davenant's play the vizier Pirrhus had resignedly acknowledged the necessity of war – "Tis well our valiant Prophet did/ In us not only loss forbid,/ But has conjoyn'd us still to get' (*I Siege of Rhodes* III.i.25–7) – here the conviction, conventionally ascribed to the Ottoman Empire, that imperialism was religiously prescribed, is appended to a more thoroughgoing justification for untrammelled expansionism. As the speaker here is acutely aware, 'shows of Vertue' are rendered meaningless by war, when notions of 'Fame' and honour may be designated by the victor at will. Solyman counters this argument by declaring the sheer extent of his imperial ambitions. Buda is not worthy of mercy but indifference: 'To Rome I will my dreadful Ensignes lead,/ … To that great Conquest my designs I bend,/ This Kingdom is my way and not my end.' The bashaws, however, insist upon the imperative of conquest, demanding not only the kingdom but the Hungarian crown in the person of 'the Infant King'. Clearly, the authority of this 'Restoration sultan' rests upon a rather different premise than that of the absolute (and ultimately virtuous) monarch of Davenant's play. Having conceded the strategic importance of the Hungarian city, Solyman crucially devolves responsibility for the fate of the infant heir to the 'Divan', the Ottoman Council of State. Once alone the sultan reflects upon the mechanisms through which his power is divested:

---

[2]   This and subsequent references are to the first London edition of the play (1668).

> Divans like Common-wealths regard not fame,
> Disdaining honour they can feel no shame;
> Each does, for what the publick safety call,
> Venture his Vertue in behalf of all,
> Doing by pow'r what Nature does forbid,
> Each hoping, amongst all, that he is hid,
> Hidden because they on each other wink,
> When they dare act what Monarchs scorne to think. (I.65–72)

Here is the first indication that the play may be concerned not simply with a re-enactment of Ottoman history in the heroic mode introduced by Davenant, but engaged more problematically in an attempt to assimilate the ideological contradictions of England's own recent history. Uppermost in the multi-layered signification of this speech perhaps, the divan is made to suggest the republican parliaments of the Interregnum which, like the larger 'Common-wealth' they represent, are adjudged guilty of subjugating 'Vertue' in the name of 'pow'r'. Moreover, in this image of abdicated and divided responsibility is perhaps a recollection of the regicide, itself frequently portrayed as a crime against 'Nature'. Submerged in this orthodox royalist perspective, however, is a critique of government that may have suggested to Boyle's audience, not only the tyrannical regime supposedly safely eradicated by the Restoration, but, more uncomfortably, the conduct of the restored government itself. Alongside the prevailing censure of evil 'Commonwealths' is a sense of their political effi-cacy, in other words, that 'what Monarchs scorne to think' may also be neces-sary for the maintenance of 'publick safety', a contradiction that resurfaces throughout the play.

The scene that directly follows presents yet another 'parliament', the Hungarian Council in which 'does appear/ Disorder vary'd in all shapes of fear' and who urge their queen to accede to the sultan's demand for tribute and surrender the infant king. Again, their council privileges the common good over an individual act of 'Vertue' (the queen's determination to defy both Solyman and 'Fate'). Significantly, the play makes a cardinal the spokesman for moral pragmatism:

> My way, the worst that can befal our King,
> Is to become his peoples offering;
> Of the two ills, which will the worser be,
> To die for them, or by their Treachery?
> Thus he'l afflict whom he can ne're reclaim,
> For sure the sharpest punishment is shame:
> The worse they are, his fate the better seems,
> When those who him destroy he thus redeems;
> Religion too makes it a greater thing,
> To die a Martyr then to live a King. (I.141–50)

Here is the play's most explicit allusion to regicide and its aftermath. Whereas the old king of Hungary secured honour by dying at the hands of his enemy, his infant heir is bound to 'become his peoples offering' in order to achieve the same apotheosis. Like the martyred Stuart king, posterity will prove him ultimately victorious, consigning his betrayers to the 'sharpest punishment' in the same way that all but the most uncompromisingly anti-monarchical treatments of the regicide, from the *Eikon Basilike* on, had evoked a sense of national 'shame'.

As the cardinal's evaluation suggests, *Mustapha* is overtly preoccupied with the binds of loyalty, both public and private. Although the play's opening scenes establish the familiar predicament of the Hungarian crown – a slaughtered monarch and an heir in exile – the focus of the play soon shifts to the Ottoman camp. In contrast to the imperilled succession of the Christian monarchy, that of the 'Turks' appears secure, safeguarded by not one but two heirs. In their first exchange, Mustapha and Zanger avow their fraternal loyalty:

> Sure, my dear Zanger, those who heretofore,
> The envy'd Crown of this Great Empire wore;
> Nere knew the charms which Friendship do attend,
> Or in a Brother never had such a Friend; (I.193–6)

Intimated here is the conflict between public duty and private conscience that has already arisen in Buda. In this scene, however, the playwright draws upon one of the commonplace features of the Ottoman succession, routinely cited in contemporary treatments of Ottoman history.[3] The younger brother Zanger describes the 'distrust' of the monarch, traditionally eradicating the threat of rival claimants to the throne by a politic fratricide. Mustapha, however, disavows this constitutional precedent and, in so doing, sets in motion the tragic events of the play:

> By our great Prophet solemnly I swear,
> If I the Turkish Crown do ever wear,
> Our bloody custom I will overthrow;
> That debt I both to you and justice owe. (I.117–20)

Whilst Mustapha promises to share the throne if he succeeds, Zanger fatefully seals the bargain by swearing, 'I'le not out-live the day in which you die' (222). This grandiose display of loyalty is, however, also an act of political subversion

---

[3] For example, dynastic murders are frequently recounted in Richard Knolles' *Generall Historie of the Turkes* (1603), which appears to have been the main source for Boyle's depiction of Solyman's dealings with Hungary. It is notable that Boyle departs significantly from Knolles' account, which describes Buda as being taken by stealth and not, as the play would have it, offered to the Turks by the Hungarian queen in a display of honourable self-sacrifice. Of course, this drastically changes the outcome so that, whilst in reality Solyman simply annexed Buda and exiled the queen and her son, in the play-world, the queen's noble fortitude is rewarded with the restoration of her son's throne.

since, as the play goes on to explore, the pursuit of 'justice' may not necessarily be consonant with good and stable government.

In its representation of two brothers, one military, the other amorous,[4] the play may well have prompted its first audiences to contemplate the fragility of their own restored government. Although *Mustapha* resists any consistently maintained parallelism, something of the Stuart brothers is discernible in the figures of Mustapha and Zanger. When the play opened at Lincoln's Inn Fields, Charles II had not yet celebrated the fifth year of his restoration and yet the kingdom had been shaken by continuing religious dissent, constitutional uncertainty and even the threat of renewed rebellion which had dangerously, if briefly, broken out in Yorkshire and Ireland. As for the conduct of the monarch himself, there were already murmurs of disquiet in some quarters concerning the dissolute extravagance of the court which, as in the reign of the elder Charles, were tinged with religious as well as moral disapproval. Not only did the inclusive new government contain several figures whose loyalty to the crown during the Interregnum had been, at best, ambiguous, but there was a growing suspicion in both Parliament and public that Charles' administration was unduly tolerant of Roman Catholicism, indeed that popish interests had infiltrated government to the highest level.[5] Although James did not officially convert to Catholicism until the 1670s, the dubious sympathies of Charles' younger brother constantly threatened to undermine the king's religious and thereby his political authority. If James was associated with a less than strict observance of Anglicanism in government, then he also came to represent the militarism of the new regime. Having served with the French and Spanish armies whilst in exile, James had established a formidable reputation as a military leader and, with control of the armed forces placed firmly in government hands by the Militia Act of 1661, he played a prominent part in conducting England's foreign policy abroad, leading a naval force to an early victory against their old trading rivals, the Dutch, after a declaration of war in February 1665. Many in England, however, mindful of the role the army had played in deciding the country's destiny, were anxiously aware of the continuing potential it held as an instrument for imposing political will at home as well as abroad, an anxiety sharpened by the perceived influence of a Catholic faction.[6]

Again, Boyle's play can be read as a critique of such contemporary polit-

---

4   Although both brothers are 'conquer'd' by their love for the Hungarian queen, it is Zanger who first succumbs to her beauty and claims precedence for his suit: 'You are the Heir to Empire, I to Love;/ You as the Eldest may the Scepter bear,/ You first the world did see, I first saw her' (III. 112–14).

5   See John Miller, *Popery and Politics in England, 1660–1688* (Cambridge: Cambridge University Press, 1973).

6   See Ronald Hutton, *The Restoration: A Political and Religious History of England and Wales, 1658–1667* (Oxford: Clarendon Press, 1985); J. R. Jones, *Britain and the World 1649–1815* (Brighton: Harvester Press, 1980).

ical concerns. In the second act, Rustan, the scheming counsellor of the play, inflames Solyman's jealousy of his son in order to provoke a crisis in the succession. As he reports to his cohort Pyrrhus, 'Last night some words I artfully did say,/ From Fame, not from my self, of Mustapaha,/ Which might the Sultan's jealous anger raise,/ Not words of accusation, but of praise' (II.121–4). Later, we learn that Rustan has singled out Mustapha's popularity with the army in order to exploit Solyman's fear of disloyalty. When, through Rustan's machinations, Solyman decrees first the exile and then the execution of his son, his fears are ironically realised and the army rises in mutiny. If the audience have been in any doubt as to the wider repercussions of Solyman's political mismanagement, the playwright overtly signals the didacticism of his story in Act IV. Having been humiliatingly forced to negotiate with his rebel forces, the sultan soliloquises on his altered fortune:

> My race of Glory did proceed too fast.
> My Armies now grow weary of my haste.
> And yet, though tir'd, they shout and gladly run
> To see me over-taken by my Son ...
> Though Mustapha by Heavens decree was sent
> To warn great Monarchs by my punishment
> Yet he does Heav'n offend, offending me.
> What means our Prophet by this mistery? (IV.368–81)

For all the play's insistent allusiveness, however, his question remains largely unanswered, and an audience might well have been as puzzled as Solyman as to the true meaning of this 'mistery'. The sultan invokes his derived divinity as proof of Mustapha's offence, but whether the play ultimately endorses this view of the inviolable authority of the monarch is not immediately apparent. Whilst Solyman is clearly guilty of needlessly endangering the succession – Mustapha is innocent and has remained loyal to the sultanate – the real source of conflict is not the sultan's claim to absolute power but the manipulation and subversion of that power by unscrupulous counsellors. Although Solyman believes himself to be an example to 'warn great Monarchs', *Mustapha* is clearly not simply a straightforward allegorisation of the contemporary political scene. Nevertheless, in its suggestive critiques of sovereignty, the play does address, albeit ambivalently, the domestic anxieties that attended the early years of the Restoration.

As in the case of *The Siege of Rhodes*, *Mustapha*'s preoccupation with conflicts of loyalty and expediency may be usefully illuminated by considering the ebb and flow of the playwright's own allegiances in the treacherous political waters of 1642 onwards.[7] When the political tide returned the monarchy

---

7 'Many of the dramatic conventions used in the heroic subgenre, undoubtedly rooted in earlier drama and in history, also come from Orrery's life.' Maguire, *Regicide and Restoration*, p. 251, n. 2.

to government in 1660, Boyle, formerly Lord Broghill, was soon created Earl of Orrery and, later that year, appointed as one of the lord justices of Ireland, being responsible for devising the act of settlement there. When his *Mustapha* opened in 1665, Boyle was a prominent member of the political elite, his celebrity perhaps partially responsible for the interest generated by the play's inaugural run and the enduring popularity of the piece. Up until his death from gout in October 1679, Boyle maintained a reputation for dedicated and able statesmanship, so much so that he was offered the post of Lord High Chancellor upon Clarendon's resignation, an honour he declined on the grounds of ill health. What was extraordinary about the now earl's apparently unimpeachable loyalist credentials post Restoration, however, was the degree to which Boyle, in his previous manifestation as Lord Broghill, had been implicated in the public life of the Protectorate regime.[8] Like Davenant, Boyle was a royalist who had apparently abandoned resistance when the cause seemed hopeless and not only reconciled himself to the new order, but positively courted it. Where the future poet laureate's tergiversation had been painfully accepted only after long periods of exile and imprisonment, however, Boyle's 'conversion' was as swift as it was expedient. Having served the king's cause in Ireland, fighting in the battles of Lismore and Liscarrol, Boyle was eventually forced to capitulate to the parliamentary forces and, upon the execution of the king, began a period of retreat from public life. However, Boyle's ambition made this neutrality short-lived. As posterity remembers it, on the pretence of visiting a German spa he conspired to arrange a meeting with the exiled Charles II, but whilst awaiting permission to travel he received word from Cromwell of an unexpected visit. Cromwell warned him that his design was known and that only his own intervention had prevented his arrest. According to the version of the story that emerged after the Restoration, it was at this moment that Boyle found it expedient to throw his lot in with Cromwell.[9] If such an account of Boyle's defection may be believed, it is testament not only to the effectiveness of Cromwell's intelligence network, but to the pragmatism that characterised Boyle's political dealings throughout his career. Even if, as the report suggests, the would-be agitator had little choice in accepting Cromwell's commission, Boyle's subsequent success in subduing the Irish and participation in the parliaments of the mid-1650s demonstrates his genuine commitment to the regime.

As noted earlier, such pragmatism finds expression in the play as the sententious exhortations of the worldly cardinal. When, in Act III, the queen declares

---

8   Harbage distinguishes Boyle's service under Cromwell as 'one of the most freakish political alignments of the epoch'. Alfred Harbage, *Cavalier Drama: An Historical and Critical Supplement to the Study of the Elizabethan and Restoration Stage* (New York: Russell & Russell, 1964), p. 251.

9   According to Boyle's entry in *The Dictionary of National Biography* 'Broghill thanked Cromwell warmly for his kindness, and asked his advice as to what he should do whereupon Cromwell offered him a general's command in the war against the Irish.' *DNB*, p. 124.

herself 'in a lab'rynth left' by the rival suits of the two Ottoman princes, the cardinal urges her to favour Mustapha, who 'must by succession reign' and thus redeem the Hungarian crown. In her central speech at the end of the third act, the queen describes her political and spiritual paralysis in terms that both encapsulate the paradox of honour ('Vertue') at the heart of the play and strongly suggest the religious dislocations that had increasingly dogged the nation throughout the period. Speaking of the 'Turks', she says,

> Them for their false Religion I eschew
> Though I have found their Vertue ever true.
> And when Religion sends my thoughts above,
> This Card'nal calls them down and talks of Love ...
> He would, bold with Ambition lead through all
> The dark and crooked walks where Serpents crawl.
> His Priests to what he counsels gravely bow;
> Whilst other Priests condemn what those allow:
> Those would by Pious craft restore our loss;
> These scorn the Crescent should redeem the Cross.
> Zeal against Policy maintains debate;
> Heav'n gets the better now, and now the State.
> The Learned do by turns the Learn'd confute,
> Yet all depart unalter'd by dispute. (III.555–70)

Whilst the Christian party are riven by the competing claims of 'Heav'n' and 'State', the 'Turks' initially exhibit a unity in religion which, although deemed 'false', is undoubtedly an effective political weapon. In their first confrontation, Roxolana, the sultan's wife, taxes Rustan with the conventional amorality of the stock Machiavellian politician:

> Religion now does many faces bear,
> And all resemble those, who Copy her;
> You States-men in your own resemblance draw
> Her shape, by which you keep the world in awe   (I.306–9)

Significantly, Rustan does not refute the charge, but rather implies that the function of religion is to vindicate rather then dictate policy:

> Fair Empress, when Religion does oppose
> What custom plants, or in our nature grows;
> We are incens'd, and yet we then forbear
> T'accuse the Law, but tax th'Interpreter; (I.310–14)

Although this scheming courtier is representative of a pernicious influence within the Turkish court, the play as a whole does have some sympathy for such a view. Like the cardinal, his mirror image in the Christian camp, Rustan astutely recognises the interdependence of religion and statecraft whilst the unequivocally 'vertuous' characters of the play – Mustapha, Zanger, the widowed queen – are hampered by a moral absolutism that equates with political naïveté and precipitates the tragic annihilation of the succession. The brothers' noble pact of friendship and the queen's pious reluctance to regain the crown by marriage to 'an Infidel' are portrayed both as individually right-eous but collectively dangerous.

Interestingly again, particular details of the playwright's biography lend a peculiar resonance to the duality of *Mustapha*'s representations. By the late 1650s, Cromwell's confidence in his Irish general was such that he was appointed to a special council that convened to advise the Protector upon important affairs of state. Amongst the more radical of the committee's recommendations was the proposal of a marriage between Cromwell's daughter Frances and Charles II – the moral equivalent of marrying off one's daughter to a Muslim. Rather like the queen of Boyle's play, the Protector must have considered such an unholy alliance beyond the pale although Boyle's prominence in advocating the reconciliation indicates his instinct for political compromise. More realistic, perhaps, was the committee's recommendation that Cromwell take the title of king. The proceedings of the meeting are recorded in a document entitled *Monarchy asserted to be the best, most ancient, and legall form of government, in a conference held at Whitehall with Oliver Lord Cromwell and a Committee of Parliament*, published in 1660. Again, Boyle's contribution provides a particularly suggestive context for his later play.

> Your Highness the last time this Committee had the honour to wait on you, seemed to be of opinion, that it was not necessary that you should assume the Title of *King* to exercise legally the office and duty of supreme Magistracy of these three Nations; because that the Title of *Protector* is by the authority of Parliament made the title of the chief Magistrate, would do as well and answer all ends of Government as fully, as that which now the Parliament does desire and advice your Highness to take upon you: but to effect this, either all the powers and limitations of a *Protector* must be more particularly enumerated, or he must under the name have all the authorities with a *King*, as a *King* has by the Law. (pp. 67–8)

Evinced here is an awareness of the significance of names and titles in defining and, ostensibly limiting, political authority. In fact, as the terms of Boyle's supplication imply, such signifiers are 'legally' expedient but cannot in themselves confine or control the exercise of power – after all, Cromwell (his 'Highness') is already in possession of the prerogative, if not the precise title of kingship. Moreover, the title '*Protector*' remains linguistically un-appropriated, a fluid designation the true function of which is to legitimise, and not regulate, the existing power system. In the event, Cromwell did not feel obliged to acquiesce with his council, declining the title of king, whilst assuming one of the definitive trappings of hereditary monarchy: the right to choose his own successor. When composing his *Mustapha*, Boyle seems to have been still preoccupied with distinguishing between rival definitions of authority. As Derek Hughes observes in his survey of the period, *English Drama 1660–1700*, 'To subvert the sign … is here the work of anarchic villains, such as the Vizier Rustan in *Mustapha*, whose success in persuading Solyman to execute his virtuous son is persistently associated with corruption of signs and the bonds which they record.'[10] Thus, as Hughes notes, the bond of friendship is, for Mustapha, 'a stronger tye than that of blood' (I.227) but for Rustan exists as 'a meer name 'twixt those who covet power' (II.116).

Whilst these contrasting appraisals are undoubtedly central to the play's interrogation of genuine versus constructed codes of moral conduct, it seems a simplification of the play to conclude, as Hughes does, that 'Language in Orrery is a stable bond between individual and community, and a mirror of the moral order that sustains society.'[11] Rather, I would argue, *Mustapha* is embroiled in a far more sophisticated representation of this relationship and is consequently a more problematic treatment of contemporary dilemmas than has been generally acknowledged. Far from offering an unequivocal vision of linguistic stability, the play constantly suggests the arbitrary nature of language as a system of names and 'titles':

> How can that wisdom in our Sultans be,
> Which of it self is fear and cruelty?
> If titles change th'intention of the Fact,
> Then justice weighs the Actor, not the Act; (I.209–12)

What Mustapha inadvertently acknowledges in this idealistic repudiation of the customary fratricide is that titles *do* 'change th'intention of the Fact' in the Ottoman court; in other words, that the instability of language renders the identification of any kind of objective notion of 'justice' an impossibility. Villains like the Vizier Rustan do not themselves 'subvert the sign[s]' of loyalty but are simply more cognisant of the subversive potentiality inherent in language. As Roxolana, a character torn between the virtuous and villainous factions of the play, becomes increasingly implicated in Rustan's conspiracy, she too recognises the slipperiness of signification:

> Friendship, to Love and Pow'r, seems but a name.
> Though Mustapha has Virtue and Renown …
> Yet when he shall th' Imperial Scepter bear
> He must become my Zanger's Murderer.
> For that is made a righteous Law by time,
> Which Law at first did judge the highest Crime. (IV.114–22)

In the event, Roxolana's misgivings are unwarranted and Zanger dies by his own hand, the tragic fulfilment of his oath not to outlive his elder brother. Nevertheless, the play suggests, it is the very fact that Mustapha refuses to place

---

10 Derek Hughes, *English Drama 1660–1700* (Oxford: Clarendon Press, 1996), p. 33.
11 Hughes, *English Drama*, p. 48.

the interests of 'Love and Pow'r' above those of fraternal loyalty that enables Rustan to frustrate the legitimate succession. By the fifth act, the prince's 'Virtue and Renown' have been completely subsumed by this corruption of titles, to the extent that the sultan warns his wife that the very 'name of Mustapha infects your breath' (V.9).

When Mustapha's innocence and Roxolana's guilt are finally exposed, *Mustapha* culminates in a puzzling final scene, which shifts the focus from the slaughtered succession to the sultana's arraignment, presenting a pattern of imperial justice that conspicuously fails to allay the troubling questions of authority and succession raised earlier in the play. Studiously ignoring the part his own jealous rivalry has played in 'this bloody day', Solyman portrays himself finally, not as the victim of unscrupulous counsellors, but of love, since 'Beauties fair hand has many a mighty name/ Too foully blotted in the Book of Fame' (V.575–6). In an extraordinary display of self-justification, Solyman attempts to appropriate the judgement of imagined posterity by forcing his wife to write a confession before his sentence of death is carried out. Roxolana humbly submits, offering to die in order that the 'People, Armies, and the State' may admire the sultan's justice. Solyman rather deflates this declaration of heroic self-sacrifice for the public weal by declaring his concern only to be that women consider him just:

> But, that your Sex may ever think me so,
> You must a form of process undergo
> Which strict necessity does make me use.
> You must, under your hand, your self accuse.
> Which, as a true Record, may rescue me
> From false opinions of my crueltie. (V.63–7)

The portrait of a ruler enervated by a predilection for the female sex may well have reminded audiences of their own, infamously amorous monarch. Alongside this intimation of mild censure for the king's lifestyle, however, is a rather more unsettling image of royal justice. His marriage to Roxolana, it transpires, is itself illegal:

> Though the strict Laws of Ottoman's high Race
> Did not allow our Sultans e're should grace
> The Mothers of their Sons with privilege
> Of Marriage, yet your Sex I did oblige,
> And lifted you above the scorns of life,
> When I, by sacred forms, made you my Wife. (V.632–7)

Thus we discover retrospectively that it was the sultan's marriage that exemplified the play's very first subordination of public to private interests. Like his two sons, Solyman has subverted a traditional principle of the imagined constitution, creating a conflict of interests that undermines the stability of the realm and initiates the tragedy. The analogy is obscure – representative of the breakdown of monarchical authority in the 1640s but also offering a salutary warning to the restored government of Charles II, a sophisticated backward- *and* forward-looking gesture that is characteristic of early Restoration drama.

More evident is the play's self-conscious problematising of the standard narrative of restoration. Whilst, at the opening of the play, it is the predicament of the Hungarian crown that appears to represent the subjugation of legitimate monarchy, it soon becomes clear that not only do the ostensibly inimical 'Turks' manifest the characteristic attributes of Christian 'vertue' but that the Ottoman succession may also represent the redemptive possibilities of a restored morality, perhaps even in the form of a Muslim–Christian marriage alliance. As the Ottoman hierarchy threatens to collapse under the weight of treachery and rebellion, the plight of the Hungarian infant king is largely forgotten until, towards the play's dénouement, his throne is suddenly restored at the behest of the dying Zanger. In further corroboration of the play's complex mirroring, however, the cardinal reports that, whilst the queen has been negotiating with the Ottomans, a crisis is brewing at home:

> You, with the Infant, should to Buda haste;
> Which, now disloyal grown, will scarce with stand
> The worst of all your Foes, King Ferdinand.
> For whilst the Turk invades us from the East,
> Th'un-christian King assaults us in the West.
> With craft and wealth he has advanc'd his pow'r. (V.140–5)

What may have been anticipated as the glorious resurrection of the rightful dynasty is rather more problematically delivered by the play. Beleaguered on two fronts and threatening rebellion, Buda is critically unable to distinguish between its enemies within and without, the inversions of the cardinal's rhetoric suggesting the breakdown of the putative distinctions between Christian ally and Islamic foe. If the Hungarian succession appears dangerously uncertain by this point, then that of the Turkish empire seems utterly devastated. Having commuted Roxolana's death sentence to exile, the play ends with an image of the isolated sultan bewailing his diminished majesty: 'But Oh, how little I esteem a Throne/ When Love, the Ornament of Pow'r is gone!' (V.94–5). Like Davenant's play, therefore, *Mustapha* employs a strategy of disorientating representations, including several characters whose paradigmatic 'vertue' within the heroic mode of the play seems to belie their designation as infidels, a contradiction that reflects the playwright's own experience of civil war. Crucially in Boyle, however, theirs is a 'fatal vertue' (V.471). Where *The Siege of Rhodes* had been enthused by the possibility of co-existence in its radical vision of spiritual and political rapprochement, in *Mustapha* the promise of restored virtue remains unfulfilled, murdered by the sultan's inability to control the various factions who seek to influence the succession. As early as 1665, the play suggests, even royalists such as Boyle were beginning to perceive cracks in the image of idealised monarchy. As in Davenant's play, however, the distinction between infidel and true believer is deliberately obfuscated in recognition of the conflicted allegiances of public life; at this point in the first decade of Restoration, it was increasingly unclear as to who had re-turned 'Turk' and who had turned again.

THE BUSINESS OF EMPIRE: PAUL RYCAUT'S DIPLOMATIC WRITINGS

Instrumental both to the prosperity and reputation of the Levant Company in the period was Paul Rycaut, initially secretary to the ambassador at Istanbul (or Constantinople as the English still termed it) and later consul to the English factory at Smyrna. Shortly after the Restoration, Rycaut was appointed private secretary to Sir Heneage Finch and, when his employer was awarded the embassy at Constantinople, found himself bound for Anatolia as part of the earl's entourage. Rycaut soon established himself as an able administrator, adept at juggling the interests of the company with those of the crown, but what is most extraordinary, insofar as posterity is concerned at any rate, is the assiduity with which he resolved to document his experiences. In the prefatory address to his *History of the Turkish Empire* (1679), Rycaut describes how 'from [his] first entrance into those Countries', he determined 'to note down in a blank Book what occurred in that Empire, either as to civil or military affairs; with what Casualties and Changes befel our Trade, that so both one and the other might serve for Examples and Precedents to future Ages'. This method-ology, to mine Ottoman society for universally applicable precepts, beneficial for 'future Ages', underpins much of Rycaut's writing. His first publication may have been the anonymous pamphlet, *A Narrative of the Success of the Voyage of the Right Honourable Heneage Finch*, published in 1661, which dealt with the journey to Constantinople and the reception of the Englishmen by the sultan there.[12] The secretary's first acknowledged work, however, was *The Capitula-tions and Articles of Peace betweene the Majestie of the King of England, Scotland, France and Ireland &c. And the Sultan of the Ottoman Empire*, published in 1663. This document listed the concessions negotiated by the English embassy in relation to trade in the region, consolidating and augmenting the existing charter between the two nations. The updated version, the first English work to be printed in the Ottoman territories[13], was clearly much in demand among the merchantmen of Aleppo, Smyrna and Constantinople, but it seems prob-able that *The Capitulations* were also circulating back in England. The epistle address is dedicated to Sir Andrew Riccard, governor of the Levant Company,

---

[12] 'Rycaut's authorship of the original narrative has never been remarked on, but there is over-whelming internal evidence for it, particularly in the description of Winchelsea's reception at court.' Sonia P. Anderson, *An English Consul in Turkey: Paul Rycaut at Smyrna, 1667–1678* (Oxford: Clarendon Press, 1989), p. 29.

[13] Anderson, *An English Consul*, p. 30.

and provides a telling insight into English perceptions of the Turk and his trading empire.

> The Capitulations the Grand Sig. Gives to us, & other Christians that traffick With him, are (in my opinion) of an other nature & forme, then articles of peace are usuall to bee betweene two nations; for hee requires no counterpart from his Majestie, Whereby to oblige him to performe the same conditions with himself; but as if hee needed, & expected nothing from the English conferres on them severall Imperiall imunities, & priviledges, as his Charter, & Acts of grace, Without demand of any returnes Which hee accounts as a dimunition to his all containing Majesty to bee needfull, or Wanting of. And this pride, is so naturall to the Turkes, & so necessary to bee flattered by those, Who Would maintaine the intercourse of peace, & trafficke with them, that it is no mean Art to know well, how to nourish, & dally with their barbarous humour … it is for my Lord, to bee Master, & profoundly versed in them; who knows the times, both to threaten, & to flatter, & when with resolute words, or soft speeches to dispearse, & calme those stormes, which wee who live, under the arbitrary will of Tyrants, doe often foresee, & yet dissolve, before the fury reach, & arrive you. This is the care, & study of his Excellencie, who hath many times occasion to bee more tender of your safetie, then his owne, & to interpose himself, & his, betweene you, & the barbarous rage.[14]

Here is oft-rehearsed figure of the Oriental tyrant: proud, temperamental and given to fits of 'barbarous rage'. Alongside this conventional caricature, however, is a tacit acknowledgement of the incontestable supremacy of the Ottoman sultan by whose sufferance the whole enterprise of English 'trafficke' may be conducted. Moreover, Rycaut implies, the combined eminence of the Company, enjoying the full sanction of the English king and his representatives, does not guarantee the sultan's cooperation; *this* sovereign's will may only be coaxed, not coerced. The fact that these 'articles of peace' are unilateral only serves to emphasise the self-confident pre-eminence of the Grand Signor. In the early years of his secretaryship, Rycaut had occasion to note the importance of Turkish countenance in the affairs of Levantine trade. When Algiers refused to guarantee the right of British merchant ships to ply the Mediterranean unmolested, precipitating war between the two, it was thanks to Finch's adept diplomacy that the sultan's support was enlisted, and the Algerines forced to comply.

More ambitious than Rycaut's work to date was *The Present State of the Ottoman Empire*, which contained the secretary's first-hand observations upon Turkish government, religion and the composition of the military. This time the dedication was to Lord Arlington, the Secretary of State and, in keeping with his earlier design, the professed purpose of the study was instructive:

---

14 Rycaut, *The Capitulations*, pp. 6–7.

but perhaps without disparagement to your Lordships profound Wisdom ...
I may confidently draw a rude Scheme before your Lordship of the Turkish
Government, Policies, and Customs; a Subject which Travellers have rather
represented to their Countrymen, to supply them with discourse and admiration,
than as a matter worthy the consideration, or concernment of our Kings or our
Governors.[15]

Unlike previous accounts, Rycaut's volume properly belongs in the statesman's
study, its analysis of the Ottoman administration germane to the conduct of
English government. The first edition of *The Present State* was published in
London in August 1666, but one month later, the stock was decimated in the
Great Fire, so that demand for Rycaut's work far outstripped supply.[16] A second
edition appeared in 1668 and was followed by two more in 1670 and 1675, as
well as numerous translations in French, Italian, German, Dutch and Polish.[17]

Rycaut's work caters to the same contemporary fascination with the Ottoman
East that drew audiences to Boyle's play and successive others. Although the
immediate source for their narratives was almost invariably Richard Knolles'
Generall Historie of the Turkes[18], something of the drama's ambivalent representation of the Turk is also intimated in the tone of Rycaut's preface. In the
four years that had lapsed between his epistle dedicatory to Riccard and this to
Arlington, experience seems to have modified Rycaut's opinion of his 'barbarous' hosts:

The speculation of what is contained in this following Discourse may seem
unworthy of your lordships precious hours, in regard of that notion of Barbarity
with which this Empire is stiled. ... This Present, which I thus humbly consecrate
to your Lordship, may be termed barbarous, as all things are, which are
differenced from us by diversity of Manners and Custom, and are not dressed in
the mode and fashion of our times and Countries; for we contract prejudice from
ignorance and want of familiarity. But your Lordship, who exactly ponderates
the weight of humane Actions, acknowledges reason in all its habits, and draws
not the measures of Economy or Policy from external appearances or effects,
but from the fundamental and original Constitutions; so that your Lordship will

---

[15] Rycaut, *Present State*, A2r.
[16] The fire seems to have ensured that at first the book was almost exclusively the preserve
of statesmen. In his diary entry for March 1667, Pepys proudly records his purchase of a
coloured copy of Rycaut's book, 'of which there was but six books done so, whereof the King
and Duke of York and Duke of Monmouth and Lord Arlington, had four ...'.
[17] See Anderson, *An English Consul*, p. 44; Appendix 1.
[18] In 1679, Rycaut became the latest author to 'continue' Knolles' history. Originally conceived
as an autonomous work, his narrative was extended backwards to 1623, where the previous
continuation of Knolles had left off, and given the title *The History of the Turkish Empire from
the Year 1623 to the Year 1677*. That the author was not entirely comfortable with this association is suggested by his response to the inevitable decision to publish both authors in a single
reprint: 'I cannot but with some regrett thinke it a great disparagement to that Worke to see
it Crouded into 50 sheetes, and to become an appendix to an old Obsolete author.' Anderson,
An English Consul, p. 231.

conclude, that a People, as the Turks are, men of the same composition with us, cannot be so savage and rude as they are generally described; for ignorance and grossness is the effect of Poverty, not incident to happy men, whose spirits are elevated with Spoils and Trophies of so many Nations...[19]

Rycaut's personal 'familiarity' with the 'Manners and Custom' of the Ottomans may have engendered his belief that supposed barbarity is merely a measure of cultural difference, but the relativism expressed here is also both contributory to and a reflection of an ongoing process; throughout the century, and given further impetus by the ideological dislocation of a civil war, English writers were engaged in a sustained re-evaluation of the Ottoman Empire, its peoples and religion. For men like Rycaut the pressing business of trade simply made that process all the more urgent. This economic expedient is, however, substantiated by the more current conviction that a nation may be measured by its military might; thus the very existence of an Ottoman *empire*, vaunted in the 'Spoils and Trophies of so many Nations', belies any imputation of savagery. According to the diplomat, Christian complacency continues to aid the expansion of this rival empire:

It hath been the happy fortune of the Turk to be accounted barbarous and ignorant; for upon this perswasion Christian Princes have laid themselves open and unguarded to their greatest danger; contending together for one palm of land, whilst this most puissant Enemy hath made himself master of whole Provinces, and largely shared in the rich and pleasant possessions of *Europe* ...[20]

For readers and audiences alike, it must have seemed that very little had changed since the loss of Constantinople more than two hundred years earlier. Not only had the Austrians failed to capitalise on early military successes against the Turks, losing their influence in Transylvania following the Treaty of Vasvar (1664), but in 1669, the Venetian garrison at Candia had finally been overrun after a siege lasting more than twenty years. Everywhere, it seemed, the forces of the crescent were in the ascendancy. Rycaut, however, is careful to distinguish between the prevailing misrepresentation of the Ottomans in Europe and English attitudes towards her powerful trading partner.

We cannot now but pity those poor Borderers in *Hungary, Syria, Croatia*, and other parts subject to the Incursions of this cruel enemy. ... This consideration ought to move us, who are barracado'd and fortified by the Seas from the violence of our Enemies, to bless God we are born on so happy and so secure a Country, subject to no dangers but from our selves, nor other miseries but what arise from our own freedom and two much felicity; we ought to consider it as a

<hr>

19 *The Present State of the Ottoman Empire*, 'To the Right Honourable Henry Lord Arlington', A3r–A4v.
20 *The Present State of the Ottoman Empire*, 'To the Right Honourable Henry Lord Arlington', A3v.

Blessing, that we have never felt any smart of the Rod of this great Oppressor of Christianity, and yet have tasted of the good and benefit which hath proceeded from a free and open Trade, and an amicable Correspondence and Friendship with this People; which having been maintained for the space of above eighty years, begun in the reign of Queen *Elizabeth* of blessed Memory, preserved by the Prudence and admirable Discretion of a series of worthy Embassadors, and daily improved both in Business and Reputation by the excellent Conduct and Direction of that Right Worshipful Company of the *Levant* Merchants, hath brought a most considerable benefit to this Kingdom, and gives employment and livelihood to many thousands of people in *England*; by which also His Majesty without any expence, gains a very considerable increase of His Customs.[21]

At the heart of this special relationship is profit. Notwithstanding the iniquity of 'this Great Oppressor of Christianity', it is clearly not in the interests of the Company or the Crown to malign the source of so lucrative a 'livelihood'. Ironically, Rycaut's sedulous pragmatism entails a radically new representation of the Ottoman nation based not on religious enmity but commercial interest:

And as some study several ways, and prescribe Rules by which a War may be most advantagiously managed against the Turk; I, on the contrary, am more inclinable to give my judgement in what manner our Peace and Trade may best be secured and maintained.

Of course, for all this *laissez-faire* liberalism, Rycaut remains the staunch Anglican, loyal to the king and his church. Having emphasised the relevance of his survey to 'Kings' and 'Governors', in 'The Epistle to the Reader', Rycaut is anxious to circumscribe the inferences of his wider readership:

If (Reader) the superstition, vanity, and ill foundation of the Mahometan Religion seem fabulous, as a Dream, or the fancies of a distracted and wild Brain, thank God that thou wert born a Christian, and within the Pale of an Holy and an Orthodox Church. If the Tyranny, Oppression, and Cruelty of that State, wherein Reason stands in no competition with the pride and lust of an unreasonable Minister, seems strange to thy Liberty and Happiness, thank God that thou art born in a Country the most free and just in all the World; and a Subject to the most indulgent, the most gracious of all the Princes of the Universe; That thy Wife, thy Children, and the fruits of thy labour can be called thy own, and protected by the valiant Arm of thy fortunate King: And thus learn to know and prize thy own Freedom, by comparison with Foreign Servitude, that thou mayst ever bless God and thy King, and make thy Happiness breed thy Content, without degenerating into wantonness, or desire of revolution.[22]

In this disclaimer, Rycaut simultaneously acknowledges the radical potential of his material whilst attempting to defuse the implications of the kind of

---

21 *The Present State of the Ottoman Empire*, 'The Conclusion', p. 217.
22 *The Present State of the Ottoman Empire*, 'Epistle to the Reader', A5r.

parallelism endemic in *The Present State*. The explosiveness of the comparison was clearly recognised by playwrights of the late 1660s on, for whom Rycaut's portrait of a state run by a proud and 'unreasonable Minister' must have seemed a suggestive model for a dramatic treatment of 1660s and 1670s England. Nevertheless, the treatise is essentially conservative in design (if not implication), its comparative strategies advocating reform and not 'desire of revolution'. Rycaut's balancing act in the Levant, like the fluid allegiances of Boyle's play, themselves contribute to the increasingly contradictory idea of Islam; the Turk remained both infidel and business partner, tyrant and emperor, enemy of Christianity but also scourge of Catholic Europe. The perceived bivalency of Islam, however, was still available for writers of diametric political and religious positions.

For a new generation of playwrights, Islam continued to exert a fascination, seemingly in proportion to the disjunctured state of the English political scene. First performed at the Lincoln's Inn Fields theatre in 1667, Elkanah Settle's tragedy *Cambyses King of Persia* returned to familiar territory in its own rendering of the perennial problems of loyalty and legitimacy. Set in the period of Persia's ancient history most consonant with dynamic empire building, Settle's treatment of a specifically pre-Islamic history allows a shift of emphasis from the Prophet to a more broadly pagan conception of religion. Nevertheless, Settle's prologue ignores the immediate setting of the play and anachronistically invokes the fratricide for which the Ottoman and Persian empires were notorious, initially suggesting that a generally similar system of eastern tropes and images might underpin the drama, as those that had informed Boyle's earlier 'Turkish' play. Adapting the conventional appeal for an audience's indulgence, Settle alludes to the narrative crux of the earlier play:

> You no more Mercy to Young Writers show,
> You damn and blast 'em e're they've time to grow.
> Thus you have learnt the Turkish Cruelty,
> When Elder Brothers Reign, the Younger dye.
> But as those Turks, when they're for Death design'd,
> This favour from their Cruel Brothers find,
> Strangled by Mutes, who fitted for the Fact,
> Want Tongues to speak the Cruelty they Act.
> Knowing the dangers of a publick shame,
> Our Rhimer hopes his Fate may be the same:
> He humbly begs, if you must cruel be,
> You'd make no noise when you his doom decree,
> But if you damn him, damn him silently.[23]

---

23 Elkanah Settle, *Cambyses King of Persia* (London, 1671), B1v. This and subsequent quotations are taken from the first London edition of the play (1671).

Settle's play was a great success, enjoying full houses for its opening run and attracting the patronage of such influential figures as the Earls of Rochester and Mulgrave for Settle's subsequent theatrical ventures. Indeed, *Cambyses* initiated a whole series of dramas taking the Orient as their setting, manifesting a sustained fascination with Islam within the work of a single playwright of the period. For all its flippant ingenuity, the prologue reveals Settle's preoccupation with the ethics of succession. In the opening exchange between Cambyses and the Princess Mandana, Settle recapitulates the familiar figures of conquering tyrant and disinherited feminine virtue and, fairly typically, the amorous victor finds his advances checked by a bastion of chaste loyalty: 'Whence is your Title, that this pow'r you have/ Thus to degrade a Monarch to a Slave?' (I.i.59–60). However, the play complicates this formula with the addition of a rival king, Smerdis, younger brother to Cambyses. In its portrayal of antagonistic brothers, the plot seems initially to be the inverted image of *Mustapha*, an initial indication of the reverse political corollary of Settle's chosen narrative. In accordance with the archetypal ruthlessness of the Islamic despot, Cambyses has ordered his servant Prexaspes, the stock false favourite of the piece, to murder the rival heir. When news of a popular rebellion raised in Smerdis' name reaches the king, he fatally alienates his appointed murderer, accusing him of treacherous neglect. The actual turn of events has rather more intriguing implications for the play's interrogation of legitimate authority. Smerdis, we learn in the third scene, is an impostor, treacherously advanced by Patasithes, the Persian regent during the king's conquest of Egypt:

> 'Twas by Heaven's pleasure, and our wills decreed,
> To place the Crown of Persia on your head.
> Let dull successive Monarchs idly wait
> To be enthron'd by the slow hand of Fate...
> You by a Nobler force have Empire gain'd,
> Wresting the Scepter from Cambyses hand. (I.iii.1–8)

Thus Smerdis embodies the figure of the usurper in what would appear to be a fairly straightforward re-enactment of illegitimate ambition in the Cromwellian mode. Like Cromwell, Smerdis derives his position from a de facto authority – 'Thus Kings and Beauty in this Title share,/ 'Tis the adorers eye makes Beauty fair./ The Persians thus by their Allegiance show,/ You're the true Prince, if they but think you so' (I.iii.55–8). Such a philosophy has clear repercussions for the subjectivity of morality in the play which, like *Mustapha*, seems to articulate a growing suspicion that 'Kings make Justice, and not Justice Kings' (i.iv.106). As such, notions of loyalty are rendered not only problematic but absurd by the counterfeit authority of the false king. Where bonds of love and friendship were noble, if fatal manifestations of loyalty in Boyle's play, in *Cambyses* they are often made to seem parodic. At the beginning of the second act, Theramnes, the play's principal exponent of unswerving allegiance, finds himself in a double-bind of loyalty versus honour. Having gallantly undertaken to take revenge for an affront to Phedima, a Persian lady, Theramnes supplicates King Smerdis for help in unmasking the perpetrator, only to find that king and 'Offender' are one and the same. In a parody of regicide, Smerdis directs Theramnes' sword to his breast and urges him to fulfil his pledge. In this rendition, however, the loyal subject is paralysed by reverence – 'Though Vows are sacred, so are Monarchs too' (II.i.46) – and instead of performing the 'Champions part', agrees to contrive a meeting between the impostor king and the object of his lustful advances. When Phedima is brought before Smerdis, the purported embodiment of justice in her cause, she pertinently assures Theramnes, 'you mistake the Throne, or I the Prince' (II.ii.3). Having thus made a mockery of the notion of the sanctity of monarchy, the play represents a parody of regal justice in which judge becomes advocate and accuser becomes judge. As if to underline the degeneracy of justice these contortions of role-play signify, Phedima steps into the throne, creating an image of sacrilegious sovereignty: 'what strange Interlude must here be shown?/ A woman seated on the Persian Throne!' (II.ii.36–7), the irony of course being that Smerdis has no more right to the throne than this 'woman'. If any further proof of the illusory nature, not only of the inviolable authority of the monarch, but of the unquestioning obedience of his subjects were needed, it comes with the revelation that Theramnes is himself an impostor, a disinherited Syrian prince who 'came to Persia in a borrow'd Name' to exact revenge upon Cambyses.

As such convoluted refractions of identity suggest, *Cambyses* betrays deep misgivings concerning the legitimacy of succession. Amidst these anarchic plot reversals both true and usurping king are killed, Cambyses by his scheming parasite, and Smerdis by a company of Persian noblemen who after several false starts finally discover his imposture. The Persian crown then falls to Otanes as the legitimate heir to Cambyses' throne who, in a moment of supreme bathos, immediately passes it to the noble Darius. Thus, just as the forces of legitimate sovereignty appear to have reasserted themselves, the succession is perverted by an act of arbitrary will. In keeping with the chaotic applications of justice elsewhere in the play, the new king, having been invested by an act of dubious legality, feels obliged to observe the rule of law. His first duty is to decree death for the captive princess who has been wrongly indicted for Cambyses' murder.

> But e're we Crown you King, 'tis just you knew
> Our Laws are sacred next our gods, and you;
> Laws, which by Monarchs too must be obey'd,
> And in their right I now am bound to plead.
> 'Tis written, Sir, in Persia's strict Decrees,
> If any Persian King by Treason dyes,
> That day his Heir does his high seat supply,
> His Predecessors Murderer must dye. (V.iii.163–70)

The play's resolution, then, only serves to compound the vexed question of legitimate authority, looking askance at the procedures and institutions of 'sacred' government. Significantly, Mandana's wrongful execution is averted not by the rigorous application of judicial procedure or the clemency of a virtuous king, but by the intervention of the villainous Prexaspes, who confesses, vaingloriously revelling in the magnitude of his crimes. Though paradigmatic of eastern empire building, the great Persian state is shown to be nonetheless vulnerable to the moral failings of its ruling elite.

DEFENDING THE STATE AND VINDICATING THE PROPHET: STUBBE'S BIOGRAPHY OF MOHAMMED

Perhaps the most radical exponent of this movement towards relativism in the period is Henry Stubbe. If the writings of Boyle and Rycaut, to distinct ends, manifest the need to depict Islam and Christianity along ever-converging lines, those of Stubbe take the impulse a crucial step further, proposing an historical account of the two religions that reveals a common heritage. Where Rycaut's *Present State* had simply outlined the 'material points of the Mahometan Religion', the title of Stubbe's study of Islam proclaims its deliberately unorthodox polemic: *An Account of the Rise and Progress of Mahometanism with the life of Mahomet And a Vindication of him and his Religion from the Calumnies of the Christians*. Of course, Stubbe's *Account* is as much concerned with the 'Calumnies' of the established Christian church against the author's own heterodox beliefs as with mounting a rational account of Islam. Nevertheless, with Stubbe's proselytising *Christian* agenda came a genuine desire to dispel the old myths ascribed to 'Mahometanism', and the most sympathetic account of Islam and its founder yet written in English.

Not published until 1911, *An Account* was circulated in manuscript form, and was written sometime between 1671 and the author's death in July 1676.[24] Best known for his attacks on the Royal Society, Stubbe was a prolific polemicist and, in common with many of the English writers drawn to Islam in this period, his life and work is characterised by apparent reversals of allegiance and ideology. In 1641, Stubbe entered Westminster School where the headmaster, Richard Busby, added the study of Arabic to the curriculum alongside the conventional Greek, Latin and Hebrew. Busby also introduced the young Stubbe to a former pupil, Sir Henry Vane, who would become his patron and mentor. Having graduated from Christ Church, Oxford, in 1653, Stubbe fought for the Parliamentary cause for two years before returning to the college to further his studies. As the Commonwealth began to look vulnerable

---

[24] In his *An Epistolary Discourse Concerning Phlebotomy*, published in 1671, Stubbe digresses upon his intention to make some 'political reflexions upon the rise of Mahomet'. For an analysis of the dating and attribution of the treatise, see James R. Jacob, *Henry Stubbe, Radical Protestantism and the Early Enlightenment* (Cambridge: Cambridge University Press, 1983), pp. 64–5.

and Vane himself came under increasing attack from both resuscitated royalists and orthodox Presbyterians, Stubbe continued to defend his radical and
Independent principles in print, justifying his patron in *A Vindication of that
Prudent and Honourable Knight, Sir Henry Vane* in 1659. At the Restoration,
Vane, although not a regicide, was excluded from the Act of Indemnity and
finally executed on Tower Hill in June 1662. Stubbe, meanwhile, had successfully managed to shake off the associations of former acquaintances, taking the
oath of allegiance and conforming to the Church of England. In the early years
of the Restoration, Stubbe apparently transformed himself into the champion
of monarchy and established church. In 1672, he even wrote *A Justification of
the Present War against the United Netherlands* on behalf of the government.
The degree to which domestic opposition to the war was predicated upon a
perceived religious, and thereby political affinity with the Dutch Republic,
is suggested by the rhetorical strategy of Stubbe's follow up piece, *A Further
Justification of the Present War against the United Netherlands*, published early
in the next year. In order to shift the terms of the debate from co-religion to
antagonistic national interest, Stubbe points out the need to oppose the Dutch
in their rivalrous trading ambitions. In these terms, Charles' proposed policy
of Indulgence is cast a financial as much as a religious policy, since economic
survival is seen to be dependent upon the unity of the nation, bound together
by a mutually beneficial subordination to monarchical authority.[25] This appeal
to the self-interest of England's merchant class leads to a particularly suggestive renegotiation of the theoretical justification for England's apparent alliance with Catholic absolutism to the detriment of European Protestantism:

> If we consult the law of nature, the respect we owe to our lives, liberties and
> estates requires … that we preserve ourselves, and if we cannot effect thus much
> by our domestic forces, we must recur to foreign assistance: the law of grace doth
> not destroy that of nature; hence it is that the obligation doth still remain, and
> that those alliances made by kings with infidels and heretics, when profitable or
> necessary, may not justly be blamed.[26]

In the immediate context of the argument, the resort to 'foreign assistance'
necessitated by protection of the national interest alludes to the French alliance but, in the light of the emphasis upon trade in the preceding account,
surely the empires of Islam are purposely invoked here too among the 'infidels and heretics'. In an essay that sets out to explicate the sudden shift in

---

25 'Indulgence, he claimed, would increase trade and hence national wealth because it would
keep English Dissenters from emigrating for reasons of conscience and equally because it
would persuade Dissenters elsewhere to resettle in England in order to escape persecution.'
Jacob, *Henry Stubbe*, p. 114. The same justification appeared in the terms of the Declaration
itself: 'for inviting strangers in this conjuncture to come and live under us, and for the better
encouragement of all to a cheerful following of their trade and callings'. Kenyon, *The Stuart
Constitution 1603–1688*, p. 407.
26 Henry Stubbe, *A Further Justificiation*, p. 22.

public opinion against the conduct of the third Dutch war mid-way through its progress, Steven Pincus challenges what he sees as the prevailing assumption amongst historians that European affairs impinged little on the popular imagination, arguing that to the contrary that,

> ... there was a native and lively popular discussion about European affairs in England throughout the later seventeenth century, and ... this discussion had always connected domestic and foreign concerns. In England, as in the rest of Europe, this debate turned on the proper identification of the universal monarch. The third Anglo-Dutch war proved to be a time in which two rival interpretations – the one claiming that the republican Dutch, the other that the absolutist French, were seeking universal monarchy – could be tested.[27]

This is a useful formulation of the ways in which the English political crisis of the 1670s was intricately bound up, not only with the suspected popery of the presumptive heir, but with the choice between two monolithic ideologies of *Western* Europe embodied in their national representatives. This, however, is clearly only part of the story. For centuries there had been another power bloc with imputed ambitions towards a 'universal monarchy': the Ottoman Empire. *This* 'rival interpretation' of empire was long established and, in pursuit of its territorial ambitions from the 1660s onwards, was a very real consideration for those attempting to read the delicate balance of power in Europe. Moreover, by the 1670s as a paradigm of statehood, the Ottoman Empire was more conceptually ambivalent than ever; whilst its perceived subjection to the sultan's personal rule meant that it was frequently aligned with French absolutism, its military campaign against the Hapsburgs appeared to designate it a friend of Protestant Europe.

Having posited the necessity of heterodox alliances, it is significant that Stubbe's *Further Justification* turns to the early history of the Christian church in order to legitimise the Act of Indulgence. By drawing explicit comparisons between the king and the Emperor Constantine, the parallel manages to emphasise the purity of the national churches they represent, as well as the political and economic efficacy of a policy of religious inclusiveness. On the face of it, the comparison is unproblematic, flattering Charles II by association with a prototype of Christian kingship. In the light of Stubbe's subsequent exegesis of comparative religious histories, however, the precedent of Constantine may be seen as sharply double-edged. In his more private writings, Stubbe appeared in no doubt as to where the true inheritors of Constantine polity might be found: in Constantinople.

Only one year after his proselytising efforts on behalf of the crown, Stubbe had become disillusioned with events at court and, in the *Paris Gazette*

27 Steven C. A. Pincus, 'Republicanism, Absolutism, and Universal Monarchy: English Popular Sentiment during the Third Dutch War', in Gerald MacLean, ed., *Culture and Society in the Stuart Restoration* (Cambridge: Cambridge University Press, 1995), pp. 241–66.

(October 1673), anonymously attacked the marriage of the Duke of York and Mary of Modena. The author was quickly traced, arrested and 'was hurried in the dark from one prison to another, threatened with hanging, and was put to a great deal of charge'.[28] The twentieth-century editor of Stubbe's manuscript considers it 'probable that he wrote his *Rise and Progress of Mahometanism* some where about this period, but the reason for its non-publication remains a mystery'.[29] What the non-publication of the account surely demonstrates is the author's awareness of its political sensitivity. If, as seems likely, *An Account* was conceived around the time of Stubbe's defection from government propagandist to spokesman for a proto-opposition,[30] then its heterodox treatment of 'Mahometanism' may be explained in terms of a timely critique of Christianity, as much as an overdue vindication of Islam itself. Moreover, the consistency of the historiography propounded here and in the *Further Justification* suggests that Stubbe's abrupt change of allegiance in these years signified more the apostasy of the Stuart–Anglican regime in his eyes than any fundamental recantation on the author's part.

As has been noted in regard to the Ottoman possession of Constantinople, Islam had long been associated with religious tolerance. Since the Restoration, Charles' policy had vacillated between the desire to heal the religious divisions that had wracked the nation for much of the century, and the need to enforce Anglican conformity, not only to combat the explosion of sectarianism that had fragmented the church, but to dispel rumours of an encroaching popery in public life. In the heated controversy generated by the king's various legislative interventions in matters of conscience, the 'Turkish' example was frequently cited. For example, writing to the king in 1670 in relation to a proposed Conventicle Act, John Lerie urges,

> Pray consider what a strange rigour it is to force and violate men's consciences … I hope your Majesty will not forget your former declarations that you were against persecution for conscience's sake … I think that those persons who make such noise in forming these coercive laws are those that have the least sense of religious duties, and are of debauched practices. Will the wealth and honour of the nation, the rents of land, or the customs duties, be increased thereby, or sobriety, piety, and the peace of the people, be established? The Turks have a more tender sense and respect for those Christians who live among them, and

---

28 Anthony Wood, *Athenae Oxonienses* (London, 1817), iii, p. 1082. Quoted in Jacob, *Henry Stubbe*, p. 133.

29 Henry Stubbe, *An Account of the Rise and Progress of Mahometanism with the life of Mahomet And a Vindication of him and his Religion from the Calumnies of the Christians*, ed. Hafiz Mahmud Khan Shairani (London: Luzac & Co., 1911), p. xx.

30 According to Jacob, at this early stage, Stubbe was already in contact with the Earl of Shaftesbury, around whom an opposition to the succession of the Duke of York would congregate. Stubbe's account of Islam was propagated in letters written by Charles Blount, another prominent member of the Green Ribbon club. See P. M. Holt, *A Seventeenth-Century Defender of Islam: Henry Stubbe (1632–76) and his Book* (London: Dr Williams's Trust, 1972).

suffer no one to interrupt or infringe on their liberty in worship; I trust that we shall not be less compassionate, or more unreasonable, than those deluded Mahometans, and that we shall not resort to the old paganish and anti-Christian mode of forcing men to religious ways of worship, as men drive sheep into Smithfield, or destroying them because they will not be so driven.[31]

Here is the standard rendition of the Ottoman policy of 'liberty of worship' as seen through seventeenth-century English eyes. According to this, presumably non-conformist or Catholic writer, religious coercion will not enhance the financial or social stability of the nation, two of the benefits of toleration conventionally ascribed to the Ottoman Empire. Also characteristic, however, is the unquestioning assumption that the Muslims follow a false prophet; thus, the 'Turkish' regard for tender consciences does not lend credence to the Islamic faith, but rather shames those Christians who resort to such 'old paganish' practices as even the 'deluded Mahometans' have eschewed. Stubbe's *An Account* draws upon a similar tradition of Turkish toleration whilst turning the conventional opprobrium of 'Mahometanism' on its head.

From the outset, the author proposes an account of religious history that will necessitate a revision of historiography itself. Rejecting the providential schema of orthodox religious histories replete with their 'miraculous accidents, unimaginable effusions of the Holy Ghost, and such like, which no reason can comprehend nor example parallel',[32] Stubbe insists upon the place of human agency in the formulation of religious belief.[33] *An Account* then proceeds to relate the origins of the early Christian church and its inheritance of a strict monotheism from the Judaic tradition. The author goes on to document what he sees as the corruption of this pure state of Christianity by such pagan dogmas as the sanctification of temples, the intercession of a priesthood between individual consciences and God and, most heinous to Stubbe, the cult of the Trinity. By contrast,

> Their Articles of Faith are few and plain, whereby they are preserved from Schisms and Heresies, for altho' they have great diversity of opinions in the explication of their Law, yet, agreeing in the fundamentals, their differences in opinion do not reach to that breach of Charity so common among the Christians, who thereby become a scandal to all other Religions in the world. Their notions of God are great and noble, their opinions of the Future State are consonant to those of the Jews and Christians.[34]

Earlier in the century, writers like William Bedwell and Edward Pococke had begun to explore the common theological precepts of the three mono-

---

[31] *C.S.P.*, 1670, p. 124.
[32] Stubbe, *An Account*, p. 39.
[33] Jacob accordingly categorises Stubbe as a 'Hobbesian secular historicist'. For a detailed analysis of the parallels between Stubbe's account of Islam and the description of natural religion contained in Hobbes' *Leviathan*, see Jacob, *Henry Stubbe*, pp. 70–3.
[34] Stubbe, *An Account*, p. 168.

theisms whilst never allowing their mask of orthodoxy to slip. Stubbe, on the other hand, draws upon the same exegetical tradition whilst abandoning the impulse towards confutation that features in every other account of Islam in the century. He then turns to the foundation of Islam itself; enter Mohammed, the opportunistic beneficiary of Christianity's degradation. The Prophet, according to Stubbe's detailed account, exploited the corruption of Arian Christianity in order to establish his new religion, which is presented as the true heir of the early Christian church. This radical contention lies at the heart of Stubbe's work and pervades his characterisation of Islam throughout.

> It were an endless Task to descant upon the particular Motives upon which depends the Excellency of his Laws. What a discourse might be made upon his uniting the Civil and Ecclesiastical Powers in one Sovereign! Upon his rejecting all the Christian Scripture rather then decide amidst so great Uncertainty of Books, and so difficult Rules to Judge of the Right, and to reconcile the different Sects & opinions, was it not prudently foreseen that it would be more easy to introduce a new Religion then to Reform such a one? and well conjectured that all interested parties would more willingly submit to a novel Doctrine then yield themselves to have been all in an error except one party.[35]

In tone and argument, this passage is typical of *An Account*. Stubbe offers a portrait of Mohammed as a shrewd politician without the customary accompanying condemnation. Instead, the 'Excellency of his Laws' derives directly from their pragmatism and his ability to harness the natural religious inclination of humanity in the furtherance of empire is deemed positively praiseworthy. In this respect, Stubbe's explicit acclamation of the political and religious unity of the Islamic state – the union of 'the Civil and Ecclesiastical Powers in one Sovereign' – is reminiscent of the same, albeit more tentatively expressed sentiment, identifiable in both Boyle and Rycaut. Elsewhere in *An Account*, Stubbe similarly enumerates the historical contingencies for every aspect of Islamic belief and doctrine, as formulated by the Prophet. So, the famed polygamy of the Islamic nations is attributed to the need to propagate and sustain an empire[36] whilst the hardship and austerity of prescribed pilgrimage and fasting would have the added benefit of generating a populace of pliant subjects and disciplined soldiers.[37] Stubbe does not refute the standard depiction of an empire driven by the sword but makes a crucial distinction between religion and nation that signals an entirely new conception of Islam: 'It is manifest that the Mahometans did propagate their Empire, but not their Religion, by force of arms.' By pointed contrast, Christian princes seem bent upon the persecution of their own people in the name of religion. Rather, a degree of religious

35 Stubbe, *An Account*, p. 178.
36 Stubbe, *An Account*, p. 173.
37 Stubbe, *An Account*, p. 169.

toleration is conducive to good empire-building as Stubbe maintains in an uncharacteristically direct allusion to present-day Islam:

> ... the vulgar Greeks live in a better Condition under the Turk at present than they did under their own Emperours, when there were perpetual murders practised on their Princes, and tyranny over the People; but they are now secure from injury if they pay their taxes. And it is indeed more from the Interest of the Princes & Nobles, than of the People, which at present keeps all Europe from submitting to the Turks. (p. 183)

This assessment of the Ottoman hegemony clearly has revolutionary implications. The conventional depiction of a providentially divided Europe, contested by the forces of virtuous Christianity versus iniquitous 'Mahometanism', is utterly confuted. In its place is the unprecedented notion that the real conflict of interest lies, not in religion, but in rank; the scourge of Europe is not Islam, but the tyranny of Christian princes. Just as Mohammed chose to institute a new faith rather than attempt to 'reconcile the different Sects & opinions' of the old, so England requires an entirely new religion based upon the interest of the people and not 'the Princes'. What this, and the entire thrust of *An Account* amounts to, then, is not simply a case for toleration, but a manifesto for fundamental religious and political reform for which Islam provides the precedent.

Stubbe's English 'Mahometanism' is the apogee of sympathetic treatments of Islam in the century. Other writers would recruit the 'Turk' in the service of often conflicting political and religious causes, but none would engage with the history and religion with such a free-thinking liberality. Of course, even Stubbe's account does not simply constitute the historical observations of a disinterested commentator but is, like just about every mention of Islam in the decade, directly and vitally linked to the crises of constitution and state religion that looked set to permanently hamstring the authority of the monarchy, if not bring it crashing down altogether. Nevertheless it, like *Mustapha* and Rycaut's meticulous account, is representative of a new and more probing interrogation of Islam. Energised by religious controversy at home, and problematised by a burgeoning trade abroad, the longstanding English fascination with the many faces of Islam took a different turn in the 1670s. No longer straightforwardly representative of an external despotism, for some, the absolutism of the sultanate was looking more like an admirable, even desirable alternative to the chronic inefficacy of an emasculated monarchy. By 1678, Charles had switched allegiances once more, preparing for war against the French. True to form, the 'Turk' was swiftly implicated, at least in the imaginations of some fanciful onlookers convinced by the rumour of a 'match betwixt the Turk's daughter and the Dauphin'.[38]

---

[38] *C.S.P. Domestic*, Car. II. 398, no. 186.

Chapter 6

PLOTTING THE SUCCESSION: EXCLUSION, OATES AND THE NEWS FROM VIENNA

FOR THE YEAR 1670, the *Calendar of State Papers* reports the circulation of a pamphlet, instigating,

> 'all gentlemen, apprentices, and journeymen inhabitants of London and the suburbs, acquainting them that we are impoverished by foreign nations, especially by the French trading with England, and that we are also in fear of our lives', and calling upon them to procure arms, and meet in Moorfields between 8 and 9 p.m. of May-day, it being resolved to suffer it no longer; ending, 'So God save the King and all the royal family. Procure what arms you can, for we are resolved to do it'.[1]

This May Day protest was apparently frustrated and the would-be rioters were brought before the Lord Mayor, Sir Samuel Starling. The ringleader, it transpired, was one Robert Plowman, a tailor who had been a soldier 'in Col. Read's regiment under Lord Monk, when he came out of Scotland'. Upon examination, he explained that,

> The contemplated rising arose from the number of French in London, and the talk about the joining together of the French and Turks, and their intention of coming to make war with England, which he related to his fellow workmen, who becoming excited, agreed to issue an address, which he wrote, to their fellow apprentices, to meet together, and to set up a copy of it at Whitehall.

Another examinant testified that Plowman had become incensed 'on being informed of the news that the French and Turks had taken English ships'. Rather than signifying any real threat of invasion, however, the imagined alliance of these two perennial bogeymen suggests the political insecurity that was creeping into the public life of the nation; the vague, but tangible sense that the professed values of the restored and reformed kingdom were stealthily under threat. As the, rather muddled manifesto of Plowman and his fellow tavern-goers indicates, the mounting resentments of the early Restora-

---

[1] *C.S.P.*, 1670, p. 204.

tion had not, by 1670, coalesced into any meaningful opposition to Charles himself – these disaffected Londoners are still careful to declare themselves for 'the King and all the royal family'. Nevertheless, the xenophobic, small-scale rabble-rousing of a handful of apprentices would prefigure the savage hysteria of the Popish Plot only eight years later. Throughout the decade, the conviction that the nation was beset by a shadowy enemy within gained increasing momentum; the evidence seemed to point not only to foreign insurgents but to the monarchy itself.[2]

When the king's brother and heir presumptive refused to take Anglican Communion on Easter Sunday 1673, serious credence was lent to the imputations of popery and attendant arbitrary government that would dog the Stuart dynasty for the remainder of its incumbency. Precipitated by the Duke of York's subsequent resignation from the Admiralty and marriage to the Catholic Mary of Modena, the Exclusion Crisis rekindled the controversies of religion and monarchical authority that had plunged the nation into civil war thirty years earlier. Once again, the 'Turk' was a prominent, if contradictory, figure in the war of words that followed.

Settle's next play was *The Empress of Morocco*, performed in the summer of 1673, and topically placed to respond to English relations with the North African state in its dealings over Tangier. Complete with what the title page describes as 'Sculptures', the detailed stage directions also stipulate spectacular scenic innovations including a 'glorious Fleet of Ships', 'a Prospect of a Clouded Sky' complete with a shower of hail and, in what must have been the visual centrepiece of the play, 'a Hell, in which Pluto, Proserpine, and other Women-Spirits appeared seated attended by Furies'. Such marvels would, however, have to compete with the dramatic pyrotechnics on offer. As in Settle's earlier play, *The Empress of Morocco* abounds in scenes of mistaken identity, perverted justice and elaborate intrigue. Again, the play explores the problem of distinguishing between legitimate and illegitimate rulers – in place of *Cambyses*' rival kings are the virtuous Muly Labas, vicariously murdered and usurped by the evil Crimalhaz. There is, however, an intriguing addition, which seems to offer a direct commentary upon the conditions in which the play was first performed. Crimalhaz's treasonous co-conspirator is the exuberantly malevolent figure of the queen mother (Laula), a feminisation of the earlier role of Prexaspes and equally determined to undermine the legitimate succession by foul means: 'A States-mans Breast should scorn to feel remorse;/ Murder and Treason are but things of course' (I.i.195–6). Having already poisoned her husband the old king, Laula plots to engender a division between her son and the army. Once effected, the queen mother and her nefarious lover will seize power and execute the rightful king:

---

2   For a recent overview of the period, see John Spurr, *England in the 1670s: 'This Masquerading Age'* (Malden, MA and Oxford: Blackwell, 2001) and in relation to 'Mutinous Assemblies' in the latter part of the decade, especially ch. 9.

His Pow'r once gone, we'l act his Death in state,
And dash his Blood against his Palace Gate.
Great Deeds should in the open day be don,
As Sacrifices offer'd to the Sun. (I.i.225–8)[3]

No doubt Laula's bombastic rhetoric is meant to recall the execution of Charles I, the royal 'Sun' martyred before his own palace of Whitehall. In the event, however, Muly Labas is murdered in an elaborate spectacle, which undermines the straightforward allegorisation of his overthrow, shifting the signification from remembrance of Charles I to remonstrance of Charles II. In the fourth act, the queen mother persuades the young queen to 'lay by Majesty for Masquerade' (IV.iii.14) and take the part of Eurydice in a courtly revel which, in the height of its extravagance, will demonstrate the loyalty of Crimalhaz.[4] Having similarly convinced her son that he must disguise himself as Orpheus in the forthcoming masque in order to thwart Crimalhaz's murderous plot, she tells the young queen that Crimalhaz himself intends to take the part of Orpheus and will murder the king and force her to 'his foul Embrace' (IV.iii.111) under cover of 'the noyse of Drums, and Trumpets' (114). Thus, when the masque calls for Orpheus to rescue his lover from the underworld, the young queen draws a concealed dagger and kills her husband, believing him to be the evil Crimalhaz. This confusion of identities – a rightful king mistaken for his usurper – is further complicated by the dramatic action of the masque itself. As Orpheus, Muly Labas challenges divine authority and accuses the king of the underworld of an illegal tyranny. Pluto's reply articulates a version of monarchical absolutism that haunts this, and much of Settle's drama:

Dares a weak Animal of Mortal Race,
Affront a God t'his Face;
And of a Crime Impeach a Deity?
Thy Breath has Damn'd Thee, thou shalt Die. (IV.iii.166–9)

At Proserpine's entreaty Pluto's sentence is revoked, only for Orpheus/Muly Labas to die at the hands of his own 'fair Treasure' (201). Where, in the earlier *Cambyses*, the body politic was poisoned by the actions of an evil counsellor, in *The Empress of Morocco*, the canker has spread to the family state. When the loyal general Muly Hamet is falsely accused of her rape, the queen mother convinces the king of his guilt by virtue of the familial bond – 'And since her Blood does run within my Veins,/ By instinct I know she all that's base disdains' (III.i.268–9). The success of her masqued conspiracy demonstrates not only the

---

3 This and subsequent quotations refer to the edition of the play held in the British Library (1673).

4 Of Settle's spectacular set-piece, Gilman adjudges that, '*Orpheus and Euridice* provides the finest example of an integrated masque in a Restoration tragedy.' Todd S. Gilman, 'London Theatre Music, 1660–1719', in Susan Owen, ed., *A Companion to Restoration Drama* (Oxford and Malden, MA: Blackwell, 2001), p. 254.

dangerously illusive potential of these 'shows of Loyalty and Friendship' (IV. iii.30) but the utter degeneration of such 'instinct[ive]' bonds of allegiance.

Certainly, the months leading up to the first performance of Settle's most successful play were fraught with increasing public and parliamentary disquiet concerning the tendencies of the government and the true complexion of its most likely heir. Charles appeared to be making overtures to Louis XIV, the most powerful Catholic monarch in Europe. The religious convictions of his brother were also put beyond doubt by events of 1673. When, in March of the previous year, the king had issued his Declaration of Indulgence, suspending 'penal laws in matters ecclesiastical, against whatsoever sort of nonconformists or recusants', many perceived Charles' regard for 'tender consciences' as a smokescreen for a stealthy introduction of Catholic toleration. In response, Parliament demanded a Test Act, obliging all public office-holders to forswear the principle of transubstantiation and to publicly take the oath of allegiance and supremacy.[5] On Easter Sunday, James refused Anglican communion and, unable to comply with the new act, resigned his position as Lord High Admiral soon afterwards. Meanwhile, Charles had declared war on the Protestant Dutch in an ill-advised attempt to curb the influence of this trading rival that only seemed to confirm the influence of French and Popish interests over the king's foreign policy. The returning navy of Muly Hamet, represented at the beginning of the second act of *The Empress of Morocco*, recalled the Dutch war, suggestively alluding to an ambiguous enemy which, by the end of the play, is itself pitted against the invidious factions of the Moroccan court. Moreover, it is perhaps significant that Settle chooses to have the Moroccan succession subverted by a specifically female agency, not only that of his mother, but of his wife. James' first wife had died in 1671 and, by the likely date of the play's composition, the Queen's continuing inability to produce a Protestant heir combined with the revelation of the Duke's recusancy had heightened anxieties concerning the object of his next marriage alliance and the possibility not merely of a Catholic monarch, but a Popish dynasty. In its portrayal of perfidious femininity, Settle's play seems particularly attuned to the vulnerability of the succession to what the queen mother herself describes as 'A Masculine heart linkt with a Female Hand.' (V.i.135); uncannily concurrent with the play's opening run, such fears were substantiated with the announcement of James' marriage to the Catholic princess Mary of Modena. As a spectacular and hugely successful portrayal of intrigue, treason and illegitimate kingship, *The Empress of Morocco* is an early response to the Exclusion Crisis that would gather increasing momentum during the remaining years of the decade.

Similarly responsive to James' perceived apostasy and also turning eastward in the following year, was Henry Neville Payne's *The Siege of Constantinople*, a play with a comparable taste for the gruesomely spectacular. More so even than Settle's suggestive representations of court machinations in an Oriental

---

5   See John Kenyon, *The Popish Plot* (London: Heinemann, 1972); Miller, *Popery and Politics*.

setting, Payne's play is unflinchingly topical, evincing an allusiveness that was not lost on his contemporaries. Writing in 1680, an anonymous pamphleteer describes the playwright thus: 'Then he composes a Tragedy of a certain Emperor of Constantinople, whom he never knew; but in whose person he vilifies a certain Prince, whom he very well knows.'[6] In fact, this is a fairly comprehensive misreading of the play. Unlike the corrupt courtiers of Settle's identifiably Whiggish critique of monarchy, Payne's hero, whilst undoubtedly redolent of the Duke of York, is vindicated and not vilified by the action.[7]

The scene opens with the Byzantine emperor and his brother 'Thomazo' discussing the plight of the city. In a familiar rendition of a factious Christian counsel,[8] Thomazo maintains the folly of majority rule:

> It is by strength of Argument & Reason;
> Since they've the major part: yet I'll confess
> I'm unconverted still. This Rule of most
> Appears to me stark madness; (I.2–5)[9]

In this clear indictment of parliamentary government, Thomazo takes a staunchly absolutist standpoint against the emperor's observance of the rule of law, introducing a fundamental opposition that propels the entire action. Constantine cannot believe the counsel to be anything but 'honest' since the entire fate of the West depends on their decision:

> The grand concern this Councel has debated
> Affects no less than all the Christian world:
> It is indeed, chuse Christ or Mahomet,
> Whose Law shall have the universal sway,
> And can a Christian think that Christians would
> Give selfish Councels in their Saviour's cause? (I.36–41)

In accordance with just about every contemporary account of the siege, the conflict is portrayed as the monumental clash of two competing ideologies, the stark choice to be made between 'Christ or Mahomet'. More particular to

6   Quoted in Willard Thorp, *Henry Nevil Payne, Dramatist and Jacobite Conspirator* (Princeton: Princeton University Press, 1935), p. 9.
7   Payne's Jacobite convictions become increasingly apparent in the following decades. As the Popish Plot was gathering momentum in 1678, he was seized for composing a seditious elegy to Coleman. Secretary to the Duke of York, Coleman had been executed following accusations of treasonous communication with the French made by Oates. In 1690 the playwright was arrested for his part in the Montgomery Plot, the first Jacobite conspiracy, and became the last man to be judicially tortured in Scotland.
8   Significantly, an equivalent debate features in Davenant's archetypal heroic play *The Siege of Rhodes* (1663). Where Davenant's play had suggested the potential fragility of coalition rule, by 1674 *The Siege of Constantinople* depicts the corruption of government by consultation: 'For such aren't Counsellors but Advocates,/ And plead the cause of their own Interest' (I.9–10).
9   This and subsequent references are to the first London edition of the play (1675).

Payne's rendition is the emperor's fatal inability to distinguish between personal political and universal religious motives, an oblique but unequivocal allusion to the king's wrangling with Parliament over the Declaration of Indulgence (1672) and a recurring theme of the play. When, in the following year, Charles was forced to withdraw his declaration and impose the Test Act to exclude Catholics from public office, the precariousness of the political consensus was manifestly exposed. Unlike Davenant's play of the previous decade, the opening speeches of *The Siege of Constantinople* propound the perils and not the virtues of consensual politics. In his emphatic response to the emperor's ingenuous idealism, Thomazo appears to speak with the full force of the play-wright's own conviction:

> Christian! Ay that's the word; but Interest
> Is the thing. That Damn'd Chancellor,
> *Romes* Pentionary lately, now the *Turks* – (I.46–8)

Much of the ensuing play action is concerned with the scheming attempts of this 'false *Chancellor* with all his tricks ... of cokesing parties' (I.414–15) to undermine the position of the valorous Thomazo in a fairly unalloyed evoca-tion of the Earl of Shaftesbury's manoeuvrings to discredit the Duke of York. The influence of Charles' chancellor, a former Cromwellian and Presbyterian, was resented by the more Anglican royalist elements of the government and he was widely perceived as a malignant voice in the king's ear.[10] These lines contain the play's first mention of a compact between the chancellor and the infidel 'Turks', a correspondence that has clear implications for the political signification of the action. Moreover, the chancellor is representative of a dangerously capricious allegiance that is expressed in terms of a commonplace analogy between Romish and Turkish influences. The standard denigration of these two lieutenants of Antichrist is, however, somewhat complicated by the historical contingencies of the play, reflecting the ambivalence of the play's religious positioning. Although ostensible allies of the Greek government at Constantinople, the forces of Rome are, as the chancellor is shrewdly aware, motivated by self-interest:

> I know their minds –
> The Turk must take this Town, and then the Pope
> Will have no Rival Bishop in the World.
> Let them have their design, so I can be
> Grand Vizier to this growing Monarchy. (I.253–7)

This is one of several references to the 'long continu'd Schisme' (I.176) within Christendom that prevents the galvanisation of an effective opposition to

---

10 See J. R. Jones, *The First Whigs: The Politics of the Exclusion Crisis 1678–1683* (London: Oxford University Press, 1961); K. H. D. Haley, *The First Earl of Shaftesbury* (Oxford: Clarendon Press, 1968).

the Ottoman menace. Illustrative of two rival systems of government, the Ottoman may boast a 'growing monarchy', whilst the republican government at Constantinople is riven with conflicts of interest which reflect the inter-necine strife of the wider western world:

> I wish your Eminence, would press them hard
> For speedy succors, and that his Holiness
> Would interpose his sacred admonitions
> To reconcile the Kings of *France* and *England*,
> That private discords, lay'd by them aside,
> They might assist the general Christian Cause: (I.182–7)

Treasonously collaborating with the Ottomans, the chancellor is able to advo-cate a Christian alliance, secure in the knowledge that the English and French will not make peace in time to relieve Constantinople. Again, this allusion to longstanding Anglo-French enmities would have sounded with a particular resonance in the playhouse of 1674. In the early years of the decade, Charles had cultivated increasingly close relations with Louis XIV and, in 1672, had jointly declared war on the Dutch, disquieting those who construed a reli-gious dimension to the king's foreign policy; not only was Charles supporting an absolutist Catholic monarch against the Protestant Dutch but the troops mustered for the war remained garrisoned at home, inciting wild rumours that the army was poised, not to fight the Dutch, but to join with the French in facilitating the forced introduction of popery into England.[11] In its remem-brance of the ruinous effects of the Hundred Years' War (the 'private discords' above), the play implicitly endorses royal policy, suggesting that opposition to Charles, like that of the Emperor, is based upon petty religious differences. Later in the play, the parallel is further emphasised in relation to the senate's reluctance to finance the war effort, 'And mony 'tis, if any thing can save it,/ All Councels that retard that, scarce are honest' (III.329–30). Whilst the Turkish forces surround the city and the prospect of foreign intervention is thwarted, the chancellor schemes to drive a wedge between the emperor and his legis-lature: 'for the Senate,/ I'le still possess with jealousies and fears/ Of Laws subverting, and religious change,/ That they no aid shall to the Emperor give' (I.227–9). In the months leading up to the play's first performance (November 1674), Parliament had similarly refused to authorise further money to finance the war, and the king was forced to make peace with the Dutch. Within the

---

[11] Suspicions of this kind seem to have been only partially misplaced; in 1670 Charles had signed the secret Treaty of Dover in which he agreed to publicly declare his Catholicism in return for financial assistance from Louis. For an account of the war in relation to Charles' toleration policy, see J. R. Jones, *Charles II: Royal Politician* (London: Allen & Unwin, 1987). Also John Miller, *Charles II* (London: Weidenfeld & Nicolson, 1991). A more specialised account of the war itself is in C. R. Boxer, 'Some Second Thoughts on the Third Anglo-Dutch War', *Transactions of the Royal Historical Society* 19 (1969), pp. 67–94.

loyalist framework of the play, Payne is anxious to emphasise the dire consequences of vitiating the monarch's authority.

In common with many of the playwrights treating episodes of Turkish history in the period, for the outline of his narrative, Payne seems to have relied upon Richard Knolles' *Generall Historie of the Turkes*, first published in 1603 but reprinted and augmented throughout the century. In his account of the siege, for example, Knolles relates how the Christian citizens of Constantinople famously demurred from contributing to the defence of their city. Payne was also clearly inspired by the historian's description of the 'Emperor of Constantinople, a Prince of a mild and soft spirit, fitter for the Church than for the field'[12] and a 'great Chancellor of Constantinople, a man of greatest account next unto the Emperour himselfe'[13] who is finally executed by the victorious sultan. Knolles, however, makes no mention of the chancellor's collaboration with the 'Turks' and, beyond a handful of incidental details, Payne has freely adapted his source material to suit the remit of a pointed critique of the contemporary political scene. Indeed, the playwright omits some of the most inherently dramatic aspects of the famous story of the siege, namely, the deployment of a gigantic brass cannon against the city defences and the extraordinary feat of military ingenuity by which Mehmed II gained entry to the seaward side of the city, dragging his navy out of the water and over dry land to the bay beyond.

In Knolles, Payne also found his heroine, Irene, the fair Greek maiden whose beauty enthrals the Ottoman sultan. In the *Generall Historie*, as well as in several contemporary treatments of her famous story, Irene is sacrificed to appease the will of the people who suspect their sultan of neglecting his public duty for his private infatuation with the Christian captive.[14] Performed by the sultan himself, her summary execution is elsewhere representative of the subjugation of the monarch's desire to the common weal. The Irene of Payne's play, however, is rather more than the straightforward embodiment of Christian virtue martyred by 'Turkish' tyranny. Not only does Irene evade the sultan's ardent attentions, being mistaken with and substituted by the chancellor's daughter Calista, but she remains exasperatingly reluctant to own her love for Thomazo and graciously admit his suit. Instead, in her recourse to disguise and dissimulation, albeit in the name of modesty rather than machiavellianism, this Christian princess appears to have more in common with the scheming chancellor than the 'honest' Thomazo. In this sense, Irene is subsumed in the nightmarish vortex of confused allegiance and identity that constantly threatens to tear the Christian play-world apart. The play's dark and

---

[12] Knolles, *Generall Historie*, p. 340.
[13] Knolles, *Generall Historie*, p. 347.
[14] Gilbert Swinhoe's *The Unhappy Fair Irene* (1658) and the anonymous *Irena* (1664) provide direct analogues for the character. More generally, the trope of the captive Christian princess permeates the Oriental drama, as epitomised by William Davenant's *The Siege of Rhodes* (1663).

disorienting representations have been identified by Parker with an ongoing dramatic tradition:

> Beginning with the grotesque masque in Act 1 and continuing throughout the play, Payne utilises to the full the range of techniques bequeathed to him by the Jacobean playwrights. These techniques render the sense of reality problematical: disguises, multiple deceptions, rapid shifting of dramatic tone, exaggerated disjunction between word and deed, and between the verbal and the scenic …[15]

Whilst there are clear precedents for the macabre spectacle of the play, Payne's troubled portrayal of court life and government is also the unmistakable correlative of the political uncertainty of the early 1670s. The 'grotesque masque' of Parker's description consists of

> a Dance led by Ambition, Represented by a Monster with many Bodies, and but one Head, with a Crown upon it, follow'd by War, Famine, Murder, and Death: The Dance brought up by Fame, represented by one Body, and several Heads and Hands, each having a Trumpet in it.

Usurping the masque and subverting the symbolic bringing of harmony to chaos in the person of the monarch, the twin figures of Ambition and Fame cipher a, literally monstrous, body politic. In the context of the play's earlier treatment of absolute versus collective means of government, the image signals yet another uneasy rendition of a parliamentary monarchy, that unwieldy deformity comprising 'one Body, and several Heads and Hands'. In the scene directly following, Thomazo mistakenly woos the chancellor's daughter, 'supposing her to be Irene by her Habit', a confusion of identities that signifies a deeper crisis of government. As Derek Hughes argues, the play's puzzling representation of Irene is related to Payne's reluctance to acknowledge any kind of moral absolute: her 'reticence leads to a particularly striking failure of woman to control the posthumous narrative of her life … Irene cannot fix her own story.'[16] More than this, however, Irene's voiceless impotence is rendered in pointedly political terms. Thomazo entreats Irene, 'I desire you would not mix/ Affairs of State with my free Love', but what the ensuing action goes on to demonstrate is precisely the impossibility of separating the amorous from the political, the private, from the public spheres. Whilst the turbulent courtship of this royal couple is reminiscent of the Duke of York's ill-favoured match with the Catholic Mary of Modena, Irene's particular dilemma reflects that of the loyal subject, and by implication, that of the playwright himself. Having rebuffed Thomazo's suit, Irene describes herself as,

15 Gerald D. Parker, 'History as Nightmare in Nevil Payne's *The Siege of Constantinople* and Nathaniel Lee's *Lucius Junius Brutus*', *Papers on Language and Literature* no. 21 (1985), p. 11.
16 Hughes, *English Drama 1660–1700*, p. 96.

> Like a just Favourite, who from his Prince
> Refuses to accept some mighty Grace,
> 'Cause it may bring his Masters prudence into question;
> I, through your proffer'd friendship, Sir, can well
> Discern the Crime of state I should commit
> Both 'gainst your Person and this Empire too,
> If I should suffer you to make me yours. (I.274–80)

Irene's moral paralysis, then, suggests the problematic nature of loyalty in a world where unquestioning obedience may also be construed as treason, a 'Crime of state'. She must remain, like Thomazo's actual 'Favourite', mute:

> My Love, like *Mutantrope*, your Highness Boy,
> Does now and then make signs, but cannot speak;
> This difference only is, my Love can hear,
> Though dumb, like him it must for ever be. (I.319–22)

In common with several of the play's subordinates, however, and as his name emphatically denotes, Mutantrope is not all he seems but a spy instigated by the chancellor to observe Thomazo. It is only when the sultan proposes to make him his eunuch, since 'a Natural Mute' is 'properer for Secrets', that Mutantrope cries out, betraying himself and losing his tongue as punishment for his deception. Such swift transformations of allegiance, feigned and genuine, punctuate the action of the play. By the fourth act, the chancellor has succeeded in discrediting Thomazo who, once again is condemned by his own misplaced silence: 'Then silent Sir as Death, I'l hear my honour/ Be blasted by his Breath' (IV.381–2). With his brother accused of conspiring with the Turks, the emperor is plunged into confusion, his lament amounting to a state-of-the-nation address for the 1670s:

> What a sad Fate have Princes that are born
> To bare the Fate of sinking Monarchy;
> Those actions which we judge will prop it most,
> Produce its speedier Ruin: Faction grows
> And spreads itself through Councel, Court, and Nation,
> And nothing can be heard but accusations … (IV.409–14)

Drowned out by the babble of 'accusations', Thomazo's voice is reduced to that of the madman. In a crucial passage, the distracted prince enters 'Solus with a Book in his hand' (IV.547). Hamlet-like, he rails at the inadequacy of language and reason to signify 'Truth', the book offering only an illusion of order in the midst of chaos: "Tis meerly words: They'r Sinowy Sillogismes/ By which they puzle both themselves and us,/ Are perfect Ropes of Sand' (IV.550–2). The book contains, perhaps, the kind of political theory that was being deployed in the contemporary battle being waged in print to either legitimise or attack the Stuart regime in the early 1670s, although, given the censure of 'State Pamplets

... and Ballets' (IV. 603) that follows hard on this passage, may simply signify the degeneration of all printed language. Most notorious of all was still *Leviathan* (1651) with its justification of the ecclesiastical and civil authority of an absolute sovereign and, paradoxically enough, Hobbes himself formulates a comparable analysis of language in Chapter 4, identifying four 'abuses' of signification since words may be used 'in other sense than that they are ordained for, and thereby deceive others'. For Thomazo, however, the failure of language equates with the destruction of any kind of moral certainty:

> Avant substantial thick *Ægyptian* darkness,
> [*Throws away the Book.*]
> Rank mist of words be gone; there's nothing true,
> No nothing: Good and Ill are only Names
> Stampt by our Interests; farewell all Books,
> I'le Study nothing but my Misery, (IV.565–9)

With its biblical connotations, the story of the Israelites' deliverance from the '*Ægyptian* darkness' was frequently invoked in connection with the peoples of the world who had failed to accept the full truth of Christian revelation.[17] With the forces of Islam closing in, Thomazo's symbolic divestment of the book may also gesture towards the commonplace contention that Ottoman law forbade printing, particularly of religious material. For example, in *Areopagitica*, Milton argues that licensing of books is aimed at obscuring religious truth, 'little differing from that policy wherewith the Turk upholds his *Alcoran*, by the prohibition of printing'. The Ottoman ban on printing was well known and apparently enforced against visitors to the Porte. In 1626, a printing press had been seized by the Turkish authorities, having been imported into Constantinople from London for the distribution of Christian works for the Greek Orthodox population.[18] Unlike Milton, however, the playwright suggests the strict prohibition of printed 'State Pamplets ... and Ballets' (IV. 603) to be positively utopian.

Betrayed by the chancellor, the town falls to the Ottoman forces whilst the turncoat faction look on, symbolically accoutred 'like Turks' in anticipation

---

17 In his essay *A Needful Caveat* in defence of the translation of the Qur'an (1649), Alexander Ross cites as his ninth point the fact that knowledge of the 'Alcoran' might allow Christians to better appreciate their not being oppressed by a 'more then palpable Egyptian darkness'. In his essay on the 'Reasonableness of Christianity' (1695), Locke makes precisely the same distinction as Thomazo between rationalised argument and faith in strikingly similar terms: 'The belief and worship of one God, was the national religion of the Israelites alone; and ... it was introduced and supported amongst that people by revelation. They were in Goshen, and had light, whilst the rest of the world were in almost Egyptian darkness, without God in the world.'
18 The printer took refuge in the house of the English ambassador Sir Thomas Roe and, when the Jesuits attempted to pursue the matter, Roe's influence led to the expulsion of the Jesuit order from the city. M. A. Cook, ed., *A History of the Ottoman Empire to 1730* (Cambridge: Cambridge University Press, 1976), p. 151.

of their reward. It is at this point in the narrative that Payne diverges most significantly from Knolles' account. The *Generall Historie* describes in some detail how the emperor is ignobly crushed in the general retreat and 'miserably ended his daies, together with the Greek empire'; the play, however, has him die heroically in a final, hopeless battle against the Turkish hordes. According to Knolles, the emperor 'whose head being cut off, was ... thrust upon the point of a lance, and in great derision carried about as a trophy of his victory'. Perhaps Knolles' account was too uncanny in this respect, his representation of the emperor's death, a curious anticipation of the beheading of the Stuart martyr, combined with the ritualistic mutilation of his successor's corpse – soon after the Restoration, the Protector's body had been exhumed and 'executed' at Tyburn. The real object of Payne's attention is not Charles, or Cromwell, but the crisis provoked by their legacy, the unresolved conflict between what the play calls 'the Liberty o'th' Subject' and the 'Natural Law of Pow'r' (IV.651, 658). In Payne's rendition, the retribution of a judicial execution is reserved, not for the sovereign, but for his pernicious counsellors so that the final stage direction calls for '*a great Number of Dead and Dying men in several manner of Death's. The Chancellor, Lorenzo, and Michael Empal'd*' (V.583). However, not only does Payne spare his Christian king the ignominy of a brutal death, but the sultan is also made magnanimous in victory, at least towards the nobler of his Christian foes. Where his source maintains the famed ruthlessness of the sultan, permitting his soldiers three days to despoil the city and its inhabitants, the finale to *The Siege of Constantinople* is altogether more reluctant to propagate the standard narrative. Crucially, it is the Ottoman sultan who brings justice to Constantinople whose 'riches ... are found prodigious;/ Though basely they deny'd their Prince assistance' (V.555–6). Again, the play returns obsessively to the business of finance and seems to endorse the Pasha Synan's view that captivity is a 'just reward' for their treacherous parsimony. The surviving Christians mouth a conventional lament for the 'sad sight' of their impaled countrymen, but the play's resolving conviction is left to Synan, simply: 'This is the way to govern: Severity, not Mercy, strengthens power' (V.589–90). In this context, Thomazo's observation that, 'This *Turkish* way of rule threatens the world,/ As if their Crescent would at last be full,/ And rule it all.' (V.586–8) appears only as a statement of political reality. Once the demands of honour have been served, Thomazo, it seems, can happily join the 'Turks' as the vassal-king of the Ottoman province of Morea. What this ending craves is the exercise of untrammelled monarchic authority in the face of factious sectarianism; in terms of the political conditions in which the play was first performed, it asserts the ultimate transcendence of loyalty over ideology. Like Davenant's own siege-play of the early 1660s, *The Siege of Constantinople* represents a kind of reconciliation between age-old enemies. Profoundly unlike the earlier play, however, *The Siege of Constantinople* represents an Islamic sovereign every bit as autocratic as his fearsome reputation. Where Davenant's 'Christian Turk' had come to manifest a degree of uncharacteristic virtue, Payne instead makes a virtue of one of the most characteristic aspects of 'Turkishness' ascribed by English writers: despotism.

To some extent, this fundamental shift of emphasis arises from Payne's subject matter – the fall of Constantinople in 1453 could not be seen as anything but an abject defeat for the Christian powers of Europe, bringing the infidel to the very doorstep of Christendom. Indeed, the symbolic significance of Constantinople's cataclysmic loss is central to the play's rationale, the ascendancy of the forces of Islam made directly analogous to the politico-religious crisis facing Britain. Above all, though, Constantinople represents the disastrous consequences of internal dissension. For Payne's purposes, not only did the story of Constantinople serve as a timely reminder of the folly of a self-serving, and ultimately self-defeating fiscal policy, but the fall of the city had long been associated with the betrayal of Christians by fellow Christians. As the play and its chancellor are acutely aware, however, history is a matter of interpretation. Speaking to the cardinal, Rome and the Western Church's representative, the chancellor impugns Thomazo for harbouring an age-old grudge.

> There's rooted in his soul the Antient hate
> This Empire shew'd in the first holy War,
> When they betray'd those pious, valiant Knights,
> *Godfrey* of *Bulloign*, *Robert* of *Normandy*,
> And all the holy Cruciado'd Pilgrims ... (I.107–11)

The historical rift between the two branches of Christianity is evoked in terms familiar to the English playgoers of 1673, prompted to reflect on the double-edged nature of betrayal and the ongoing remembrance of 'Antient hate' in their own recent history. Like England, Constantinople is vulnerable precisely because of its compunction to rehearse deeply 'rooted' grievances, undermining itself from within. For Payne, Constantinople is more than an admonitory example of bad tactical planning; it is the site of an ancient and ongoing contention between East and West both within and across religious divisions.

Throughout the period under consideration, however, Constantinople held more than an historic significance for English writers and commentators. Following his conquest Mehmed II ('the Conqueror') had largely rebuilt the city, neglected by the declining Byzantine Empire, and repopulated it with peoples from throughout his territories and of several religious denominations. By the time of Mehmed IV's ascension to the throne in 1648, Constantinople (now Istanbul) was a thriving metropolis, the hub of a vast empire that stretched almost as far as Vienna in the west and to the shores of the Caspian Sea and Persian Gulf in the east. Visitors to the city described its sumptuous mosques and the splendid palace or Seraglio, which, following its institution by Mehmed II, had become the official residence of the sultan. Above all, however, European commentators were struck by the multiculturalism of this bustling entrepôt, accommodating communities of Muslims, Christians and

Jews permitted to practise religion without state interference. Of the many English travel accounts published in the seventeenth century, that of William Biddulph is typical in this respect. Having described the 'savage cruelty' of the Turkish invasion, the English preacher goes on to recount the 'history' of Constantinople as he understands it:

> This lamentable loss of Constantinople, being chief of the Oriental Empire, and likewise of the city of Perah ... was in the year of Our Saviour 1453 ... after it had remained under the dominion of the Christians [for] 1198 years ... Muhammed, after he had thus taken the city, resolving to keep there the seat of his Empire, caused (with diligence) the walls to be new made, and certain other ruined places to be repaired. And instead of the great number of people that were there slain and carried away as prisoners he caused to be brought thither, out of all the provinces and cities by him conquered, a certain number of men, women and children, with their faculties and riches, whom he permitted there to live according to the institutions and precepts of such religion as it pleased them to observe; and to exercise with all safety their handicrafts and merchandises; which ministered an occasion unto an infinite number of Jews and Maranes, driven out of Spain, to come and dwell there; by means whereof, in very short time the city began to increase in traffic, riches, and abundance of people.[19]

Viewed through Western eyes, this city of contradictions encapsulated the enigma of the Turkish Empire. For writers like Biddulph, Constantinople was synonymous with both barbarism and liberality, a constant reminder of the threat posed by the infidel war machine, and yet living proof of the economic and cultural benefits of religious tolerance. Religious refugees were not the only beneficiaries of the city's enlightened attitude towards foreign nationals, however. Constantinople was also one of the main conduits for commerce between the Mediterranean and the East, and merchants from virtually every European power plied their trade at the port. As described in Chapter 1, since 1581, the Levant Company had held a monopoly for English trade east of the Mediterranean; the business of profit-making had survived the upheaval of civil strife at home and ongoing war in Europe so that by the mid-seventeenth-century, the Levant Company was the premier trading company resident at Constantinople.

Like Rycaut's earlier representation of the Islamic superpower, *The Siege of Constantinople* is an endorsement of military might, and of the desirability of empire. Both play and treatise participate in the same discourse of absolutism in which imperial supremacy is adjudged to be an *a priori* justification for strong leadership, regardless of issues of religion or morality. In the opening exchange of the play, Thomazo contemptuously dismisses the prospect of a treaty with the sultan: 'as if a *Turk*/ Regarded any Title but Possession' (I.54–5).

---

[19] William Biddulph, *The travels of certaine Englishmen* ... (1609). On Biddulph, see also Gerald MacLean, *The Rise of Oriental Travel: English Visitors to the Ottoman Empire, 1580–1720* (New York and Basingstoke: Palgrave Macmillan, 2004).

By the end, Thomazo is reconciled to the destruction of the Byzantine Empire, but his evaluation of its Ottoman usurper remains the same: 'This *Turkish* way of rule threatens the world,/ As if their Crescent would at last be full,/ And rule it all' (V.586–8). With the 'Turkish' sway comes order and an end to the vexed ambiguities of allegiance that have riven the Christian court, confusing the 'best and truest Friends, for Enemies' (III.62–3). Significantly, it is not Muslim, but Christian soldiers who wreak havoc in the name of the Turk. Symbolically disrupting the decorum of the masque, two Genoese mercenaries mock the officious attempts of the lord chamberlain to restrain them:

> How the old Creature raves: Prithee Good man,
> Consider *Turks* are coming. *Turks* d'you hear! –
> What place will then be Sacred, if we don't
> By our undaunted Courage keep them so! (I.484–7)

Here is the play's recurring contention that the real threat to the civilised state is posed, not by the advancing Ottoman Turks, but by seditious elements already operative within the city walls. The scene re-enacts the widespread fear of the early years of the decade, that the king might deploy foreign troops to enforce his domestic policy whilst simultaneously problematising the whole question of knowing the enemy. In Payne's rendition, the spectre of alien forces infiltrating the body politic has already materialised. Disingenuously exploiting public hysteria at the approaching menace, in order to disguise their own insubordination, the soldiers' stratagem recalls that of Shaftesbury and his faction, and condemns what the playwright sees as the profane attempts of an enemy within to undermine the monarch's authority, whilst masquerading as the loyal guardians of the 'Sacred' tenets of Christian civilisation.

Payne's ending, then, is both warning and wish-fulfilment, poised between the salutary memory of the triumph of religious heterodoxy and admiration for the staunch absolutism of the Ottoman regime. Performed against the backdrop of renewed hostilities between Hapsburg and Ottoman power blocs in Europe, the play's dualism reflects a contemporary English attitude towards the 'Turk' that is similarly evinced in Rycaut's *Present State*.

In March 1676, Settle returned to the ever-popular subject of the reign of Suleiman the Magnificent, producing his *Ibrahim the Illustrious Bassa* for the Duke's Company. The extent of Settle's obsession with Oriental themes and settings is exceptional in the drama but the particular fascination of this radical playwright-cum-controversialist is indicative of the innate political explosiveness of his subject material. Departing from the convoluted plot and multiple identities of his earlier spectaculars, Settle focuses upon the conflicts of love and honour created by a Muslim monarch's illicit desire for a Christian captive. Initially, the sultan appears the model of conquering virtue, making the captured Persian prince his honoured guest and rewarding the victorious bashaw Ibrahim with his daughter's hand in marriage. Even when Ibrahim refuses this honour, bound in love to the Christian princess Isabella, the enraged sultan honours his vow to preserve the life of his valiant general: 'I swear by Alla ... Whilst Solyman Lives, his Ibrahim shall not dye/ By any violent death' (I.221–4).[20] In the second act, Isabella miraculously finds herself kidnapped and delivered to the Ottoman court where she is amazed to find 'such vertue out of Christendom' (II.212). In an apparent reincarnation of Davenant's earlier sultan, Solyman blesses the couple in a show of royal munificence, gently chiding the stupefied Ibrahim, 'is Justice in a King/ So strange, and so astonishing a thing?' (II.207–8). Of course, in the context of Settle's representations of kingship elsewhere, the scene certainly is 'strange'. Isabella praises the sultan for his self-conquest, believing that 'Solyman does Solyman subdue' (II.251); his asides, however, reveal the true extent of his inner turmoil: 'From Ibrahim's Friend, I am his Rival grown' (II.10). From this point on the sultan degenerates into the familiar figure of the criminal tyrant who seeks to subordinate monarchical obligations to an arbitrary will. Significantly, in *Ibrahim* the anxiety over the succession has been supplanted by a preoccupation with infidelity expressed time and again in terms of a religious apostasy. In loving Isabella, Solyman has forsaken Roxolana:

> Her right I, irreligious I, have stole;
> She, who so long has singly sway's my soul;
> To whom I've sworn that Faith should ne're remove,
> And dedicated an immortal Love;
> A Love so sacred, as should neither have
> An end of this side, nor beyond the Grave:
> Down go her Altars, and her pow'r decays;
> To a new Saint I a new Temple raise. (II.376–83)

Twice referred as an 'Apostate Lord' (512) elsewhere in the act, Solyman is accused by Roxolana herself of lapsing into 'Idolatory' (480), a charge that seems particularly pointed in the context of the religio-political crisis of the 1670s. Significantly, such an inconstancy in love and an associated heresy in religion are not confined solely to the absolute monarch but permeate the Ottoman court. The illegitimacy of Solyman's desire is replicated in a series of parallel acts of unrequited love that intersperse the play. Thus Ulama, the Persian prince, describes his love for Roxolana as equally idolatrous, finally confessing himself a 'Convert' and her 'a Saint above'. Similarly, Ibrahim is himself given to religious rhetoric that burns with more than a whiff of popery. Although he is the object and not the advocate of her infatuation, Ibrahim declares that when Asteria dies he will venerate her as a relic, 'with as true/ A Zeal, as the fam'd Vestals ever knew:/ With Piety more constant and entire/ Your ashes I'le adore, than they their fire' (III.313–16). Crucially,

---

[20] This and subsequent quotations are taken from the first London edition of the play (1676) held in the British Library.

the audience learn in the first scene of the play that the empire's champion is, by birth, a Christian. In the second act, Ibrahim narrates his history, further suggesting a dualism in allegiance that may not be entirely compatible with his role as defender of the Islamic polity:

> By the ill chance of War, 'twas our hard doom,
> In three set Battails, to be overcome:
> My Family destroy'd, my hopes undone …
> I strait took Ship, and for new aids did flye
> To our Allies, the States of Sicily.
> And taken Prisoner by the Algereens,
> I to that Voyage owed my Turkish chains. (II.30–6)

As a Christian in the military service of Islam, Ibrahim is both hero and apostate; in his own words, a 'Criminal … below the state of Infidels' (I.281). Conjoined by their rivalry for Isabella, both Ibrahim and the sultan are prone to 'Irreligious thoughts' (IV.133); problematising the play's conventional depiction of Christian fortitude versus 'Turkish' despotism is the figure of Isabella, described upon her arrival as possessing a 'mistaken Innocence' (II.97). As the ambivalence of the epithet suggests, the Christian princess becomes associated with a destabilising religious fervour. Conversely, it is the Ottoman queen who increasingly embodies religious orthodoxy. Roxolana describes the vacillations of Solyman's devotion in terms that suggest a larger ideological dimension:

> Yes Sir; you rais'd me to a Crown, forsook
> The rude delights your wilde Fore-fathers took.
> When from the feeble Charms of multitude,
> And change, your heart with one pure flame endu'd
> Was all entire to Roxolana giv'n:
> As Converts quit Idolatry for Heav'n. (III.475–80)

However, it is in the conflict between public and private shows of religion that the play seems to most directly critique Charles' administration. Having determined that his rival must be eradicated, Solyman's only qualm is his public oath to preserve Ibrahim's from a violent death: 'I must be Perjur'd when I take his Life' (IV.195). As in Settle's earlier plays, it is an ambitious counsellor who proposes a characteristically expedient solution: 'Send for the Mufti, Sir, consult with him:/ He may repeal that Vow your rashness past;/ And find your promise does not bind so fast' (IV. 207–9). With a deft bit of sophistry, the priest finds that, since Solyman only swore to uphold Ibrahim whilst he lived, the execution may properly take place when the sultan is asleep, since 'whilst you sleep you are not living' (IV.368). Evinced alongside the generalised anti-clerical satire of this episode is a more sustained suspicion of the role of the church in justifying the actions of an arbitrary government and perhaps a direct representation of the Earl of Danby, a figure who attracted growing resentment as the agent of repressive Anglicanism throughout the latter part of the decade.[21]

The play's resolution, perhaps the bleakest of those addressed thus far, signals the desolation of the Ottoman court. Awaking from his sacrilegious idolatry, the sultan declares that his 'long benighted Soul is with new light array'd' (V.522), but not before the climactic deaths of his wife, daughter and the Persian prince whilst Ibrahim and Isabella ('that Inchantress and her Favourite' (549)) are condemned to mourn their losses in exile. In *Ibrahim*, the tragedy is not that the succession has been perverted, but that the sultan's tyranny has gone unchecked and his kingdom wasted. Settle's emphatic denunciation of subverted orthodoxy here is a fair reflection of popular disillusionment with the king's ability, or even the desire, to prevent England's surrender to the absolutism of France or the heresies of Rome. In the same year as the publication of *Ibrahim*, Andrew Marvell produced his influential pamphlet, *An Account of the Growth of Popery and Arbitrary Government in England* (1677), which expresses a comparable apprehension of malign influences in the kingdom. As in the play, such insidious forces are made all the more pernicious by their subterfuge.

And as we are thus happy in the Constitution of our state, so are we yet more blessed in that of our church; being free from that Romish Yoak, which so great a part of Christendome do yet draw and labour under, that Popery is such a thing as cannot, but for want of a word to express it, be called a Religion. ... Were it ther open Judaism, or plain Turkery, or honest Paganism, there is yet a certain Bona fides in the most extravagant Belief, and the sincerity of an erroneous Profession may render it more pardonable: but this is a compound of all three ...[22]

Such was the strength of resentment that pope-burning ceremonies had become a regular feature of popular political expression in the 1670s. By the end of the decade, the anti-monarchical tendencies exhibited in the drama were coalescing into a coherent opposition to the Stuart regime and, in 1680, Settle was himself chosen to organise the pope-burning procession to take place in commemoration of Queen Elizabeth's birthday (17 November), in recognition of his staunchly Whiggish credentials. By 1681, the notorious Popish Plot was already on the wane, but the fears of invasion and insurrection that had fuelled Oates' remarkable hoax persisted.[23] In that year, at the height

---

[21] See Mark Goldie, 'Danby, the Bishops and the Whigs', in *The Politics of Religion in Restoration England*, eds. Tim Harris, Paul Seward and Mark Goldie (Oxford: Basil Blackwell, 1990), pp. 175–05.

[22] Andrew Marvell, *An Account of the Growth of Popery and Arbitrary Government in England ...* (London, 1677), p. 5.

[23] Unsurprisingly, the plot and its subsequent exposure provided rich material for several dramatists of the period. Perhaps most notorious is Crowne's *City Politiques* (1683), which

of the Exclusion Crisis, the playwright published his own polemic in the form of *The Character of a Popish Successor*, which evoked a storm of remonstrance: his 'personal attacks upon the Duke of York are said to have involved him in a dual with Thomas Otway'.[24] More remarkable, however, is the complete *volte-face* performed by Settle only two years later, taking the occasion of the plot's decline humbly to recant his former opposition and 'first libel' (presumably his *Character of a Popish Successor*), and firmly to align himself with the king's party. More revealing than the rambling *Narrative* itself, however, is Settle's *Epistle Dedicatory* in which the playwright confesses that he took the opportunity of the plot to wreak his 'own private Spight and Revenge … under the umbrage of a popular Champion'. Considering the European implications of the plot, Settle writes,

> 'Tis but insinuating into the Brainless heads of the People that the King himself (as I told you) is leaguing with *France* to bring in the Pope : and though the *French* King has his Sword in the very Bowels of *Flanders*, against the Faithfullest Son of *Rome* the King of *Spain*; though he can scarce keep his profane hands even from *Italy*, the seat of the Roman God himself; though he has pyrated the very best flower in the Popes Garden the Regalias of his Empire, and shaken the very Papal Supremacy, even to the pulling down of that dreadful Curse of Excommunication, had the Pope but courage to pronounce it; nay though he has promoted the Protestant Rebellion in *Hungary*, and brought the very Turk into Christendom, possibly not many years journey from the very gates of *Rome*; yet all this while this very King of *France* shall be the Popes right Hand, his Spear, his Shield, his every thing, and is setting up the Romish Interest with all the Industry and Vigour in the World : And to compleat this Mountainous Monster of a Conspiracy, the King and Court of England (for Plots and Popery make all things go down) shall be as deep in it as He.[25]

Perhaps tellingly, the proselyte author does not deny the influence of Louis XIV in English affairs so much as dispute his confederacy with Rome. Moreover, in recounting the many military triumphs of the French king, Settle, perhaps somewhat pointedly, revives the longstanding belief that Islam would eventually prove the scourge of Christendom as the Turkish Empire advanced inexorably westwards, now 'not many years journey from the very gates of *Rome*'. That Protestant Europe and, in particular, the Protestants of an embattled Britain, might find ideological points of contact with the religion of Orient

directly satirised Oates in the guise of a slanderous 'Doctor'. Situated at the opposite end of the political spectrum is the anti-Catholic invective of Shadwell's *The Lancashire Witches* (1681). Having been indoctrinated by an Irish Catholic priest, the maverick of the play is asked whether he believes in 'the plot' to which he suggestively replies, 'No, But the damn'd Presbyterian Plot I do: I would be a Turk before I would be a/ Presbyterian, Rogues, Villains', p. 36.

24 See Settle's entry in the *DNB*, p. 297.
25 Elkanah Settle, *A Narrative of the Popish Plot* (1683), p. 8.

was nothing new. Often, as in the 1648 tract *Liberty of Conscience*,[26] the Islamic paradigm was cited in order to condemn a malignant non-conformity in the English church. A religious and geographical survey of 1683, however, adds anti-Catholic sentiment to the mix and produces a rather different assessment of Turkish tolerance:

> Hence I have heard many say, that it is better for a man that would injoy liberty of Conscience, to live in the Countreys professing Mahometanism than Papistry: for in the one he shall never be free from the Bloody Inquisition; in the other he is never molested …[27]

Whilst the Restoration settlement had averted the immediate crisis of 1660 – the imminent collapse of the republican regime – the compromise of Parliament and monarch had done little to heal the fundamental divisions of the country. Over twenty years later, however, little appeared to have been resolved. Written in 1683, the pseudonymously authored *News from Vienna* satirises the continuing fragmentation of religious opinion in strikingly familiar terms:

> Great and Thorow Reformations, such as is intended by the Turk and You, is never brought to pass without Blood, Treason and Massacre, wherein the True Protestants (to give them their due) have quite out-stript the worst of Turks, [Witness that never to be parallell'd Reformation begun in 1641. O that memorable Act committed before White-hall in cold blood, by form of justice, by True Protestants, for Protestantism, in the face of the Sun!] What Turk or Pagan after this will stand in competition with you![28]

The appeal to Protestantism of the notion that 'Mahometanism' might provide a foil to Catholic hegemony in Europe sheds some light on the matrix of images that make up the ingeniously coded *News from Vienna*. The writer's assertion that the Turks intend a covenant with 'True' English Protestants to be enshrined in 'one Volume Dr Oates' Narrative and the Alcoran, with Liberty of Conscience for everyone' exemplifies a strain of anti-Whig propaganda that seems particularly virulent in 1683 and derives much of its force from the commonplace representations of Islam made by English Protestants (presumably like 'R. D' above) throughout the period.

The direct prompt for the pamphlet is the besieging of Vienna by the Turks in 1683. Their subsequent defeat marked the high tide of Ottoman expansion in Europe and, following the treaty of Carlovitz (1699), set in motion the decline of an empire which, since its capture of Constantinople two hundred and thirty years earlier, had established itself at the very borders

---

[26] *Liberty of Conscience Confuted by Reasons of Argument and Policie* (1648).
[27] R. D., *The Strange and Prodigious Religions, Customs, and Manners, of Sundry Nations* (1683), p. 54.
[28] 'Calvin Bassa', *News from Vienna, Contained in a Letter from a True-Protestant-Turk* (1683), p. 1.

of Christendom, a rival civilisation both spiritually inimical and militarily formidable. The contradictory response this complicated cultural interaction often provoked, veering from fear to admiration to vituperative condemnation, feeds into the ambivalence of the figure of the Turk and goes some way towards explaining the extraordinary political and religious resonance of the Orient by the second half of the century. As here, Islam is held up as a mirror to Christendom. In its juxtaposition of political events at home and abroad, this fascinating 'letter' subscribes to a recurrent polemical strategy of the period, damning the opposing faction by association with the infidel Turk. Thus 'Calvin Bassa' rehearses one of the conventional characteristics of many Islamic representations; the Turk is cruel and treacherous, his political culture steeped in 'Blood, Treason and Massacre'. More particular to the political climate of 1683, however, is the Ottoman disposition for imperialism, exhibited here in a tendency to bring about 'Great and Thorow Reformations' in otherwise legitimate nation states. England is imagined, like Vienna, besieged by an enemy intent on imposing its own invidious ideology. Purportedly reporting an alliance between the 'Turks' and English Prebyterians, the self-styled 'True Protestants' of the satire, the wonderfully hybridised 'Calvin Bassa' goes on to enumerate the tenets of the 'True-Protestant-Turk':

> … for we are contriving a solemn League and Covenant between the Mahumetans and Presbyterians, and there is just now a Bill of Comprehension drawing up for uniting the two churches. The preliminary points are already adjusted, which are these, viz.
>
> 1. That the Old and New Testament, because they were received as Gods Word from the testimony of the Church of Rome, shall be cast aside as Popish Reliques: and instead thereof, shall be bound in one Volume Dr Oates' Narrative and the Alcoran, with Liberty of Conscience for everyone, (provided he remain a true slave to the Grand Seignior) … (p. 1)

As the author's earlier references to 'that never to be parallell'd Reformation begun in 1641' and 'that memorable Act committed before White-hall' demonstrate, the experience of rebellion and regicide continued to cast a deep shadow over political events long after the restoration of Stuart government. Despite the scrupulously worded sanction of Charles' 'manifesto', quoted above, 'Liberty of Conscience' continued to be one of the most divisive issues of the day. In 1678, religious antagonism and political anxiety surrounding the succession had culminated in the extraordinary sequence of events initiated by Titus Oates and his denunciation of a Popish Plot to assassinate the king and establish Catholic rule. By the time *News from Vienna* had been written, 'Dr Oates' Narrative' had been discredited, its contents now fit to be categorised with those of the 'Alcoran' as the apostatical utterances of a false prophet. Nevertheless, the widespread hysteria with which Oates' inflammatory allegations were initially received testifies to the fragility of the religious settlement in the period.[29] Between 1678 and 1683, Oates' testimony resulted in the judicial murders of some 35 men, and his transformation from loyal Englishman to perjured rabble-rouser is frequently and intriguingly bound up with the ubiquitous figure of the Turk.

The immediate prompt for the amalgam of Turk and Oates may well have been suggested by a story of the notorious 'Salamanca Doctor' that was circulating in the same year. The *Calendar of State Papers* reports that

> There was a dispute at the Amsterdam Coffee-house, last Thursday, in effect whether the Turks or Christians were the honester men. A gentleman siding with the Christians and being a little too familiar with the Salamanca Doctor, Oates told him he was a rascal and struck him two or three blows over the head with his cane. The gentleman was wedged in on the wrong side of the table and could not make a return, but only with a dish of warm coffee in the eyes of him.[30]

An account of the same episode contained in the newsbook the *Observator*, quoted in Lane's biography of Titus Oates, gives a more colourful, and a more suggestively satirical version of the doctor's dubious allegiances:

> There's a Report about the Town as if Dr Oates had taken up Arms for the Turk and Advanc'd his Pastoral Staff at the Coffee-house, in the honour of Mahomet. ... Why I'le tell ye what he said then, upon Saturday last was Sennight, at the same Place. 'We are waiting here' (says Titus) 'to hear the Good News that the Turk has taken Vienna. I hope they get the Town, and subdue the Army.' 'What?' (sayd a Gentleman) 'Turks against Christians?' (Dr) 'Christians! Ay, the Turks are as good Christians as they. I don't there's any Papist in the World a Christian.' (Gent.) 'Say ye so, Doctor? That's very Hard. I believe you are turn'd Turk.' (Dr) 'Well Well! 'Tis my Opinion. You don't know 'em so well as I do. I don't question but there's a great many Honest Men of my Opinion.'[31]

In terms of the mythology that had grown up around Oates, the strict veracity of this story (the two accounts disagree as to the precise day of Titus' altercation) is unimportant. What the range of representations of Oates, clustered around 1683 demonstrate, is the persistent ambivalence and irresistible potency of the Islamic idea; for those opposed to the Stuart succession, the comparison merely highlighted a more heinous apostasy within the establishment, whilst for those anxious to preserve the political status quo, the Turk could be made to represent the extremity of those factions seeking to subvert the crown and drag the country into a second civil war. Moreover, the inherently double-faced nature of religious representations of Islam seemed to correspond directly with the constantly shifting terms of the English religious

---

[29] Jonathan Scott, 'England's Troubles: Exhuming the Popish Plot', in *The Politics of Religion*, eds. Harris, Seward and Goldie, pp. 107–32.

[30] *C.S.P.*, 1683, pp. 351–2. Of course, with its Turkish and subversive associations, a coffee house was a fitting place for Oates' imagined declaration for the Ottomans.

[31] Jane Lane, *Titus Oates* (London: Andrew Dakers, 1949), p. 297.

debate. Liberty of conscience, for example, a doctrine known to be practised in Islamic countries, was associated both with nefarious attempts to introduce popery into England, but also with the increasingly vociferous dissenters of which Oates and his confederates were an example.

Ironically, one of Oates' many allegations had itself included an imputation of 'Mahumetanism'. In one of his more extended flights of fancy, Oates had impugned the Reverend Adam Elliot, an acquaintance of his university days, with being not only a popish priest, but circumcised, a charge afforded a thin veneer of credibility by his experience of capture by Turkish pirates whilst returning from a trip to the eastern Mediterranean when a young man. The first part of his *Modest Vindication of Titus Oates the Salamanca-Doctor from Perjury* (1682) relates his enslavement and dramatic escape from captivity (ostensibly in order to refute Oates' slander, although the inclusion of such sensationalist material seems likely to have been a selling point in is own right), before turning to a rather more prosaic vindication of Elliot's innocence. In his introduction, the indignant reverend makes an indicative distinction between the two charges:

> ... he asserted, that I was a Mahumetan, and had been thereupon Circumcised; and that also I was a Popish Priest, having received orders from the see of Rome: by the former charge making we unworthy of credit or reputation, uncapable of the advantages of converse amongst Christians; and by the later, the milder indeed of the two, aiming only at my life, which as being a Popish Priest, is forfeited to the Law.[32]

Here too, the explicit comparison of these two heterodoxies, one considered 'milder' by the Anglican author, indicates the significant, if contradictory role Islam played in the imaginative positioning of competing ideologies by the 1680s. Published in 1682, the *Modest Vindication* may itself have contributed to the spate of satires and treatises that identified Titus and the Turk in the following year. Again dated 1683, an anonymous squib comically imagines Oates' exile, entitled *Dr Oats' last Legacys and his Farewel Sermon. He being sent for to be high Priest to the Grand Turk*. Having bequeathed his library of heretical texts (including his own '*Narrative*' and the '*Alcoran*'), Oates addresses an imaginary congregation:

> My Friends, *I* imagine you expect a Lecture or a short Exhortation at parting & as *I* am not over stockt with Rethorick, unless my infallible Tallent for swearing, I'll be short with you: for my Text, *I* will not look for it, for *I* am almost as great a stranger to the *Alcoran*, as yet, as to the Bible, *I* preach all by Inspiration. Oh! Popery, Popery's coming in upon you, have a care *I* say, of *Anti-Christ*, and Popery ... (p. 2)

---

[32] Adam Elliot, *A Modest Vindication of Titus Oates the Salamanca-Doctor from Perjury* (London, 1682), A2r.

178

BOB. FERGUSON *or the* Raree-Shew *of* Mamamouchee Musty

Titus, Teck Titus, *view this* Figure *well*, | Here Cloak, *there* Coate *his equall Deference*
True Lines of an INCARNATE Imp *of* Hell : | *To* CALVIN IACK, *and* IACK *of* LEYDEN *too* .
No Doctor, *nor No* Saviour *of a* Nation ; | *Whilst one hand holds a* FLAYL, *the t'other* Swo
But skill'd in Turkish *and* Italic Fashion . | *It Paints a Modern* HOLDER-FORTH *oth'* Wor.
In whom the ELDER's MAYD *and* GREEN *Combine*; | BUTTON'D SCHISMATIC CASSOCK, GIRDED *not*
Both Fleshly *given, and yet Both* Divine . | *An* Odd Amphibious Animal *like* O——
Hence Cap *and* Turbant *both his* Noddle *grace*; | *Who for a* Doctorship *nere paid* Ten Groat
his Mouth's *the* Center *of* Protesting *face* . | *But* Length *of* Chin *bewrays his* Want *of* Sens
Cravatt his Neck *doth yet unstretch'd, Environ*, | *Which makes him* APE *an* IRISH EVIDENC.
his RASCALL SIDE *is guarded with cold Iron* . | *View him* All *ore, he's* QUAKER, PRESBYT
| MUSULMAN IESUITE *and for* HIM, *not* HE

Figure 4. 'The Raree-Shew of Mamamouchee Musty' (1685). Satirical print of Titus Oates reproduced in Jane Lane, *Titus Oates* (London: Andrew Dakers, 1949).

Underpinning this relatively unsophisticated lampoon, however, is the same rhetorical strategy manifest in *News from Vienna*. By 1683, Oates was a figure of ridicule, apparently easy prey for the satirists. However, what emerges as a virtual commonplace of the literature – an identification of Oates with Islam – functions in a decidedly double-edged manner. On one hand, such responses are representative of a strategy of containment: Oates and his heretical prophecies are fit only for the 'Alcoran'. In the context of the Ottoman advance on Vienna, however, the analogy is, characteristically, explosive. Lurking within the conventional condemnation of the religious and political treachery of the Titus/Turk figure is an acknowledgement of the potentially irresistible forces that he represents. Although the plot itself had been safely discredited, the deep anxieties that had set it in motion were still keenly felt. Similarly, although the majority English writers had long sought to reassure themselves of the innate superiority of the West, and in particular, of their own brand of Christianity, that sense of superiority must have seemed particularly fragile in the opening months of 1683.

The dualism this conflicting representation engendered is perhaps most clearly evident in one of the many prints of Oates that were circulating by the mid-decade. Depicting a figure half Jesuit, half Turk, the *Bob Ferguson or the Raree-Shew of Mamamouchee Musty* (1685) (see Fig. 4) suggests not the impotence, but the persisting menace of Oates' legacy. The text appended below the print denounces his contemptible hybridity. Thus Oates is 'No Doctor, nor no Saviour of a Nation;/ But skill'd in Turkish and Italic Fashion.'; he is 'An Odd Amphibious Animal ... Quaker, Presbyter, Musulman, Jesuite and for Him not Her'. The description of an unnaturally indistinct creature (even down to an imputed homosexuality)[33] is, however, somewhat belied by the imposing figure above. Redolent of a dangerous doubleness, the figure holds a flail in one hand, whilst the other rests on that symbol of Ottoman power, the sword. The final defeat of the forces of Islam at the gates of Vienna signalled the beginning of the end of this extraordinary empire, but the representations of Islam forged in the experiences of Civil War, Republic and precarious Restoration would persist well into the next century. With the heirless Charles dangerously ill, and the long-dreaded Catholic autocrat poised to take the throne, the English Turk must have seemed in more vigorous health than ever. The political and religious crises of the 1670s appeared to revisit those of the Civil War and its aftermath but there would be no equivalent revival in the intellectual engagement with the cultural legacy of Islam that had flourished in the earlier part of the century. Between this high point of English Arabism and the advent of Empire and Orientalism in the succeeding century, for all its potent signifi-

---

[33] For an analysis of homosexual representations of Oates, see Paul Hammond, 'Titus Oates and Sodomy' in *Culture, Politics and Society in Britain, 1660–1800*, eds. Jeremy Black and Jeremy Gregory (Manchester, Manchester University Press, 1991).

cance, an objective understanding of Islam's own rapidly changing empire took second place to the primary consideration of the polemics: to finally win the battle of ideas that had provoked Civil War and had only been deferred and not resolved by Restoration.

CONCLUSION: 'IF WE OUR SELVES, WOULD FROM OUR SELVES EXAM'NE US'

Worlds of examples, I could here denote
As well in ancient dayes, as moderne times:
What were these Pagans past? what were they not?
What are our present judgements? for like crymes?
May not their Alcoran, serve to condemn us?
If we our selves, would from our selves exam'ne us.
William Lithgow, *The Gushing Tears of Godly Sorrow*, 1640

Appearing in 1640 and riven with unanswered questions, Lithgow's poem expressed the endemic spiritual and moral uncertainty that troubled many private consciences in that decade and would dramatically shape public life for the remainder of the century. In the same year as the poem, Charles' abortive attempts to impose a religious settlement on the Scottish Church through military force had fatally exposed the breach between the English king and his Parliament, stretching bonds of loyalty and tradition beyond breaking point. The war and revolution that followed irrevocably altered the face of the nation, transforming not only its social, political and religious institutions but perhaps most fundamentally shifting the very terms by which the nation imagined itself. What we now think of as the 'literary' expression of the period – particularly drama for the purposes of this study– was inevitably caught up in this process, along with the outpourings of treatises, newsbooks and printed polemic most commonly thought of as 'political'. As this book has sought to demonstrate and as Lithgow's poem synecdochally epitomises, Islam was an ever-present touchstone for a whole range of writers struggling to find meaning in the chaos, or determined to impose a meaning of their own.

If Islam was available as a means of reorientation of one kind or another, however, it was far from being a fixed or stable point of reference. As a rival religion, attractive though it was, it continued to be strenuously refuted, and negative comparisons between the myriad divisions of Christian opinion engendered by revolution and the heretical imposture of 'Mahometanism' abound throughout the period. And yet, there was acknowledgement of the power and relevance of this great monotheism, even in the zealousness of that refutation. Lithgow's poem is an early and radical example of a comparison that does not simply damn the present degeneracy of the Christian faith but articulates the possibility of an entirely new perspective that is itself made possible by the pervading sense of spiritual dislocation. Of course, as in the case of all representations, the precise relationship between the original and its refracted, sometimes grossly distorted projection is difficult to trace and highly individual. In one sense, Lithgow's specific allusion – to the '*Alcoran*' – need not in itself be predicated upon any first-hand knowledge of the Islamic holy text. Rather, it stands for a whole range of alternate religious possibilities that turn orthodox theological principles on their head. In a new world devoid of absolutes, Scriptural interpretation is itself called into doubt: if 'Worlds of examples' may be used to vindicate Christian (in this case Protestant) belief, may not the same examples be used to condemn it when viewed from the opposing position? In fact, the Scots writer had more experience of that position than most, having travelled extensively throughout Europe and the Middle East, staying with the English ambassador at Constantinople en route.[1] Nevertheless, his poem does not depend upon empirical experience of life inside Islam in any clearly definable way, but rather upon the revolutionary idea that a traditionally anathematised religion might hold answers to some of the most vexed questions of the day. Although the full implications of Lithgow's extraordinary relativism were not to be taken up until Stubbe's *An Account of the Rise of Mahometanism* (c.1673), in modified forms the same impulse to reassess the present through the eyes of another culture and religion – 'If we our selves, would from our selves exam'ne us' – is fundamental to all the English treatments of Islam addressed in the preceding chapters.

And yet, as we have seen, understanding of Islam was far from being purely theoretical. The Islamic empire most frequently, but by no means exclusively, evoked was that of the Ottomans. Gleaned from widely available travel accounts such as Lithgow's *Totall Discourse* as well as diplomatic and frequent news reports from Constantinople, information about the Ottoman Empire was common currency in seventeenth-century London as never before. In the ale houses and coffee shops of the capital, as reports of Titus Oates' altercation of 1683 suggest, news of the Turks' military campaigns was discussed in the same breath as domestic affairs. Throughout the period under consideration, English politicians trod a delicate path between expressing qualified solidarity with fellow Christians under threat from the Ottoman war machine whilst maintaining cordial relations with the Porte at all costs. Cromwell seems to have been particularly adept in this regard, receiving deputations from the Venetians whilst refusing to be drawn into their long-running conflict with the Ottomans over the disputed island of Crete. At the heart of it all was the lucrative Levant trade. In Aleppo and Izmir as well as at Istanbul, English merchants competed with their French and Dutch counterparts in a situation in which they, and not their powerful Ottoman hosts, were the cultural and religious

---

[1] Lithgow's account of his travels, including the episode of his torture at the hands of the Spanish Inquisition, made for popular reading and was reprinted throughout the century. William Lithgow, *The totall discourse, of the rare adventures, and painefull peregrinations of long nineteene yeares travayles, from Scotland, to the most famous kingdomes in Europe, Asia, and Affrica* (London, 1632).

outsiders. The passage of trade placed English ships within range of the Barbary corsairs and continued the possibility of renegade Englishmen who had converted upon capture or simply chosen to defect for profit and expediency. The constant traffic of the Levant trade even provided the principal means for the procurement and dissemination of Arabic manuscripts to meet the demand of the flourishing industry of scholarship that grew up around the two Arabic chairs at Oxford and Cambridge. Revolutionary England proved the ideal breeding ground for Arabic study.

Herein lies the contradiction. By mid-century, the idea of Islam was a volatile mixture of longstanding anxieties centred upon the Ottoman Empire as a spiritual and military threat, combined with esteem for its cultural and imperial achievements. As much of the source material for the drama suggests, the figure of the Turk was Janus-faced to an extraordinary degree, being infidel and trading partner, benighted barbarian and custodian of classical wisdom, enemy of Christianity and yet scourge of Catholic Europe. In matters of religion he could be cast as both cosmopolite respecter of tender consciences and unyielding doctrinaire. In matters of state he was both petty tyrant and glorious emperor. As addressed above in relation to specific plays, this exhilarating valency goes a long way towards explaining the particular appeal of Islam to writers of every political allegiance. The drama in particular was drawn to Islamic subjects and settings partly because of this innate plasticity of meaning, but as my readings of several of the plays also suggests, this could be a double-edged sword. Writing specifically in relation to plays of the Exclusion Crisis, Susan Owen offers a useful formulation for a 'drama of contradiction' that holds true for many of the plays I have examined:

> These texts were closely and ferociously engaged with their times. Of course they are written within the dominant discourse of their times, which they in turn employ and embody, but the playwrights also, successfully or unsuccessfully, wrench these discourses to their purpose. … Unexpected and undesired results may arise as internal contradictions within the text … or it may occur in a conflict between the author's aims and the play's reception.[2]

The gap between authorial intention and subsequent interpretation is notoriously treacherous, but particularly so when it comes to dealing with such a slippery set of contradictions as those congregated around seventeenth-century notions of Islam. As a political and religious paradigm, Islam was uniquely available for skilful manipulation, but as a dramatic idea it was also prone to those '[u]nexpected and undesired results' that seem to go hand in hand with ideologically driven theatre. In the case of *The Famous Tragedie*, the subject continually threatens to spill over its ideological parameters as Cromwell's imagined scene with the 'English Alchoran' unexpectedly legitimises him to an extent surely unintended by the royalist author. In other cases, this tension is

---

2 Susan J. Owen, *Restoration Theatre and Crisis* (Oxford: Clarendon Press, 1996), pp. 21–2.

evident in the gap between the dramatic action itself and the framing textual material with which the author attempts to contain or direct interpretation, a tendency particularly evident in Baron's *Mirza* which, despite its copious annotations, singularly fails to contain the radical ambivalence of its critique of English/Persian tyranny.

Despite such indeterminacy, however, broad patterns are discernible in the dramatic responses identified here. An early emphasis upon the religious implications of Islam in the wake of the collapse of the English church and the first appearance of a translation of the Qur'an gives way to a more sustained engagement with the East as a site of imperial ambition and paradigmatic statehood. Similarly, recurring tropes of plays treating Islam – tyranny, toleration and primogeniture – may be tracked in relation to their shifting meanings through Revolution and Restoration. The charges of tyranny that frequently attended Charles' personal rule were clearly transformed and transferred by the experience of regicide and yet again by Cromwell's autocratic rule in the 1650s, only to re-emerge in a new guise as fear of 'arbitrary government' in the 1670s; as specific plays demonstrate, concepts of 'Turkish tyranny' were equally transformed in the process. 'Liberty of conscience' too, a characteristic commonly ascribed to the Ottoman state by virtue of its diverse religious population, carries seditious connotations throughout the period although for very different reasons. In Baron's play of 1655, for example, toleration is depicted as a dangerous incitement to popular insurrection. By 1670, however, a regard for 'tender consciences' is regarded as a mask for popish and arbitrary rule and the means by which government might be nefariously sustained, not overthrown, a sense reflected in Settle's Whiggish drama of that decade. Similarly, the perennial English fascination with the bloody history of Ottoman and Persian succession and legitimacy by 'force of arms' finds very different expression in the immediate aftermath of the king's execution compared to the drama of the Exclusion Crisis, where the usurper was no longer a demonised Cromwell but the king's own brother, and fears attending military mobilisation were transferred from a puritan New Model Army to the spectre of a Catholic French invasion.

As these complex and shifting correlations suggest and as the diversity of representations described in the preceding chapters surely demonstrates, the current postcolonial view of England's relationship with the East is no longer adequate. In the course of her discussion of English incursions into the New World, Ania Loomba breaks off to describe how

> Medieval notions of wealth, despotism and power attaching to the East (and especially to the Islamic East) were thus reworked to create an alternative vision of savagery understood not as a lack of civilisation but as an excess of it, as decadence rather than primitivism.[3]

---

3   Ania Loomba, *Colonialsim/Postcolonialism* (London: Routledge, 1998), p. 109.

By jumping from the 'Medieval' to an identifiably Saidian and eighteenth-century conception of Eastern 'decadence', such a reading glosses over and distorts the intensity of English identification with Islam in the seventeenth century, and a sense of reciprocity that rendered any straightforward categorisation of the East an impossibility. By rereading the drama in the context of mostly unexplored archive material, I hope to have made a case for a re-evaluation both of the importance of Islam to the literary and political expression of the later seventeenth-century but also of a still unfamiliar and little recognised period in Anglo-Islamic relations. There are, however, inevitable omissions and whilst there remains a great deal more archival evidence still to be adduced from the wealth of documents bequeathed to us from that period, there is further scope for the work of other dramatists of the period – perhaps most obviously the now canonical authors Behn and Dryden – to be relocated in the light of the dramatic tradition I have delineated.

By tracing the intensely pervasive and politicised place of Islam in the drama of the second half of the century, this book has attempted to explain how a set of pre-existing ideas loosely associated with the East became newly invigorated and urgently available to English writers during the course of the English Civil War. Not only did this set of ideas provide an ideological context and apparatus for writers to address the crises of national identity experienced in these revolutionary decades but, by the same token, those ideas were themselves transformed in the process of assimilation. Although it has been one of my aims to transgress conventionally held boundaries of historiography, the sequence of events beginning in 1688 known as the 'Glorious Revolution' represents a genuine turning point in the story of England's vigorously creative engagement with the culture of Islam. As the chronic political and religious uncertainties so characteristic of the seventeenth century were overwritten by a confident narrative of a parliamentary monarchy seemingly vindicated by the prosperity of its maritime empire, so the role of Islam in the formulation of that history has been erased. Resituating Islam in the cultural and political context of England's most turbulent century will do much to discredit the worldview of those seeking to portray East and West as intractable opposites entrenched in a monolithic and binary version of the past.

BIBLIOGRAPHY

PRIMARY SOURCES

Adams, Joseph Quincy. *Dramatic Records of Sir Henry Herbert, Master of the Revels, 1623–1673*. Ithaca, NY: Cornell University Press, 1917.

The Alcoran of Mahomet, Translated out of Arabique into French; By the Sieur du Ryer, Lord of Malezair, and Resident for the King of France, at Alexandria. London, 1649.

Andreas, Johannes. *The Confusion of Muhamed's Sect, or a Confutation of the Turkish Alcoran, translated into English, by I. N. (Joshua Nostock)*. London, 1652.

Baron, Robert. *Mirza: A Tragedie, Really Acted in Persia, in the last Age*. London, 1655.

Bedwell, William. *Mohammedis Imposturæ; that is a discovery of the manifold forgeries, falsehoods, and horrible impieties of the blasphemous seducer Mohammed; with a demonstration of the insufficiencie of his law ... delivered in a conference had betweene two Mohametans (Sheikh Sinan and Doctor Ahmed) in their return from Mecha. Written ... in Arabicke and ... done into English by W. Bedwell. Whereunto is annexed the Arabian Trudgman ... with an index of the chapters of the Alkoran*. London, 1615.

Bob Ferguson or the Raree-Shew of Mamamouchee Musty. London 1685.

Boyle, Roger, Earl of Orrery. *The History of Henry the Fifth. And the Tragedy of Mustapha, Son of Solyman the Magnificent*. London, 1668.

A Briefe Discourse upon Tyrants and Tyranny. London: 1642.

Calendar of State Papers Domestic Series, 1640–1685. Ed. Mary Anne Everett Green. London: HMSO, 1878.

'Calvin, Bassa'. *News from Vienna, Contained in a Letter from a True-Protestant-Turk*. London, 1683.

Carlell, Lodovick. *The Famous Tragedy of Osmond the great Turk, Otherwise called the Noble Servant*, 1657.

Cleiveland, John. *Character of Mercurius Politicus*. London, 1650.

Davenant, William. *The First Dayes Entertainment at Rutland House: By Declamations and Musick After the Manner of the Ancients*. London, 1657.

————— *The Siege of Rhodes made a representation by the art of prospective in scenes, and the story sung in recitative musick*. London, 1663.

————— 'Preface to *Gondibert*', in *Gondibert: An Heroick Poem*. Ed. David F. Gladish. Oxford: Oxford University Press, 1971.

————— *The Siege of Rhodes*. Ed. Ann-Mari Hëdbáck. Uppsala: Acta Universitatis Upsaliensis, Studia Anglistica Upsaliensia 14, 1973.

Denham, John. *The Sophy*, 1642.

D'Espagne, Jean. *The Joyfull convert: represented in a short, but elegant sermon, preached at the baptizing of a Turke, who ... was baptized in the French Church May 2. 1658*. London, 1658.

The Dictionary of National Biography. Eds. Leslie Stephen and Sidney Lee. 22 vols. Oxford: Oxford University Press, 1921–2.

A Discovery of 29 Sects here in London, all of which, except the first, are most Divelish and Damnable. London, 1641.

Dr Oats's last Legacys and his Farewel Sermon. He being sent for to be high Priest to the Grand Turk. London, 1683.

Dryden John. 'Of Heroique Playes', in *Essays of John Dryden*. Ed. W. P. Ker. 2 vols. Oxford: Clarendon Press, 1900.

Elliot, Adam. *A Modest Vindication of Titus Oates the Salamanca-Doctor from Perjury.* London, 1682.

Evelyn, John. *The Diary of John Evelyn*. Ed. E. S. de Beer. 6 vols. Oxford: The Clarendon Press, 1955.

The Famous Tragedie of King Charles I. London, 1649.

Firth, C. H. and R. S. Rait, eds. *Acts and Ordinances of the Interregnum 1642–1660*. 3 vols. London: Stationery Office, 1911.

Harrington, James. *Commonwealth of Oceana*. In *Political Works of James Harrington*. Ed. J. G. A. Pocock. Cambridge: Cambridge University Press, 1977.

Herbert, Thomas. *A Relation of Some Yeares Travaile, Begunne Anno 1626*. London, 1634.

Hobbes, Thomas. *Leviathan; or the Matter, Forme and Power of a Commonwealth Ecclesiastical and Civill*. Ed. C. B. Macpherson. Harmondsworth: Penguin, 1968.

Hyde, Edward, Earl of Clarendon. *The History of the Great Rebellion*. Ed. W.D. Macray. 6 vols. Oxford: Clarendon Press, 1958.

Kenyon, J. P., ed. *The Stuart Constitution 1603–1688: Documents and Commentary*. Cambridge: Cambridge University Press, 1969.

King Charles his Letter to the Great Turk: the High and Mighty Emperour Sultan Morat Han: Chiefe Lord and Commander of the Ottoman Kingdom. London, 1642.

Knolles, Richard. *The Generall Historie of the Turkes from The first beginning of that Nation to the rising of the Othoman Familie … Together with the lives and conquests of the Othoman Kings and Emperours, etc.* London, 1603.

———— *The Six Books of a Common-Weale. Written by J. Bodin Out of the French and Latin Copies*. London, 1606.

Learne of a Turk or Instructions and Advice sent from the Turkish *Army at* Constantinople*, to the* English *army at* London*. Faithfully and Impartially communicated by M.B. one of the Attendants of the* English *agent there*. London, 1660.

Liberty of Conscience: Confuted by Arguments of Reason and Policie. Delivered in a Discourse betwixt a Turke and a Christian. Occasioned by a Letter written to a Peere of this Realme. London, 1648.

Lord, George Deforest, ed. *Poems on Affairs of State: Augustan Satirical Verse 1660–1714, Volume I, 1660–1678*. New Haven and London: Yale University Press, 1963.

Machiavelli, Niccolò. *The Prince*. Trans. George Bull. Harmondsworth: Penguin, 1981.

Margoliouth, H. M., ed. *The Poems and Letters of Andrew Marvell*. 2 vols. Oxford: The Clarendon Press, 1971.

Marvell, Andrew. *An Account of the Growth of Popery and Arbitrary Government in England. More particularly from the long prorogation, of November, 1675, ending the 15th. of February 1676, till the last meeting of Parliament, the 16th. of July 1677*. Amsterdam, London, 1677.

Mercurius Aulicus (For King Charles II), Communicating Intelligence from all parts, touching all Affairs, Designes, Humours and Conditions throughout the Kingsom. Especially from Westminster *and the Head Quarters*. London, 14–21 August 1649.

Mercurius Politicus. London, 6–13 May 1657.

A Message sent from His Highness the Lord Protector to the Great Turk; with his demands and proposals; and the releasing of the English captives; ... and a narrative of the several proceedings of the English, in order to the French, Dutch and Spaniards. London, 1654.

Milton, John. *Areopagitica*. In *The Complete Prose Works of John Milton*. Ed. D. M. Wolfe. 8 vols. New Haven and London: Yale University Press, 1966.

The Moderate Intelligencer: Impartially communicating Martiall Affairs to the kingdom of England. London, 1648.

Newes from Turkie, or, A True Relation of the passages of the Right honourable Sir Tho. Bendish, Baronet, Lord Ambassadour With the Grand Signior at Constantinople, his entertainment and Reception there. London, 1648.

Osborne, Francis. *Politicall Reflections upon the Government of the Turks*. London, 1656.

Payne, Henry Nevil. *The Siege of Constantinople*. London, 1675.

Pepys, Samuel. *The Diary of Samuel Pepys*. Eds. Robert Latham and William Matthews. 11 vols. London: Bell & Hyman, 1972.

Perrot, John. *A Visitation of Love, and Gentle Greeting of the Turk, and tender tryal of his thoughts for God, and proof of the hearts of his court, and the spirits of the people round about him in his own dominion, and the inhabitants of the earth that are borderers upon his skirts in their declared religious wayes ... To which is annexed ... Immanuel, the Salvation of Israel*. London, 1660.

Pococke, Edward. *Specimen Historiæ Arabum sive Gregorii Abul Faragii de Origine et Moribus Arabum succincta narratio, in linguam Latinam conversa, notisque illustrata: opera et studio E. Pocockii. Arab. and Lat*. Oxford, 1650.

Prideaux, Humphrey. *The True Nature of Imposture fully displayed in the life of Mahomet. With a discourse annex'd, for the vindication of Christianity from this charge, etc*. London, 1697.

A True Relation of what passed in Constantinople, In August last, about the deposing of the Great Emperour Sultan Hibraim, And the crowning of his Sonne Sultan Mehemet in his place. Printed in the year MDCXLIX. London, 1649.

Ralph, Benjamin. *A Critical Review of the publick buildings, statues and ornaments in and about London and Westminster, etc*. London, 1734.

R. D. *The Strange and Prodigious Religions, Customs, and Manners, of Sundry Nations*. London, 1683.

Reeve, Thomas. *God's Plea for Nineveh: or London's precedent for mercy, delivered in certain sermons within the City of London*. London, 1657.

Roe, Thomas. *A true and faithfull relation, presented to his Maiestie and the prince... concerning the death od Sultan Osman, and the setting up of Mustafa his uncle. Together with other memorable occurrents worthy of observation*. London, 1622.

—— *The Negotiations in his embassy to the Ottoman Porte from 1621 to 1628*. London, 1740.

Ross, Alexander. *A Needful Caveat or Admonition for them who desire to know ... if there be any danger in reading the Alcoran*. London, 1649.

—— Πανσεβεια, *or, a View of all Religions in the world, etc*. London, 1653.

Rycaut, Paul. *A Narrative of the Success of the Voyage of the Right Honourable Heneage Finch*. London, 1661.

—— *The Capitulations and Articles of Peace betweene the Majestie of the King of England, Scotland, France and Ireland &c. And the Sultan of the Ottomna Empire… Written and published by Paul Ricaut Esquire Secretary to his Excellencie the Lord Embassadour*. Constantinople, 1663.

—— *The Present State of the Ottoman Empire. Containing the maxims of the Turkish Politie, the most material points of the Mahometan Religion … their military discipline … Illustrated with divers pieces of sculpture, representing the variety of habits amongst the Turks*. London: Starkey and H. Brome, 1668.

Settle, Elkanah. *Cambyses King of Persia*. London, 1671.

—— *The Empress of Morocco. A Tragedy with Sculptures*. London, 1673.

—— *Ibrahim the Illustrious Bassa*. London, 1676.

—— *The Character of a Popish Successor*. London, 1681.

—— *A Narrative of the Popish Plot*. London, 1683.

Sidney, Sir Philip. *The Old Arcadia*. Ed. Katherine Duncan Jones. Oxford: Oxford University Press, 1985.

Smith, Henry. *Gods Arrow Against Atheists*. London, 1656.

Stubbe, Henry. *A justification of the present war against the United Netherlands: wherein the declaration of his Majesty is vindicated, and the war proved to be just, honourable and necessary. … In answer to a Dutch treatise entituled: Considerations upon the present state of the United Netherlands. By an Englishman*. London, 1672.

—— *An Account of the Rise and Progress of Mahometanism with the life of Mahomet And a Vindication of him and his Religion from the Calumnies of the Christians*. Eds. Hafiz Mahmud Khan Shairani. London: Luzac & Co, 1911.

Swinhoe, Gilbert. *The Tragedy of the Unhappy Fair Irene*. London, 1658.

The Tyranny of Tyrannies. London, 1648.

To the Hon. the Commons of England … the humble petition of ministers and other inhabitants in and about London, praying for assistance in the establishment of a lecture in Oriental languages. London, 1648.

Walton, Brian, ed., *Biblia Sacra Polyglotta*. London, 1657.

Warmstry, Thomas. *The baptized Turk, or a narrative of the happy conversion of Rigep Dandulo, the onely son of a Silk Merchant in the isle of Tzio, from the delusions of that great impostor Mahomet, unto the Christian Religion*. London, 1658.

White, Thomas. *A True Relation of the Conversion and Baptism of Isuf the Turkish Chaous, named Richard Christophilus*. London, 1658.

SECONDARY SOURCES

Allen, David. '"An Ancient Sage Philosopher": Alexander Ross and the Defence of Philosophy'. *The Seventeenth Century* 16, no. 1 (2001), 68–94.

Anderson, Sonia P. *An English Consul in Turkey: Paul Rycaut at Smyrna, 1667–1678*. Oxford: Clarendon Press, 1989.

Barbour, Richmond. *Before Orientalism: London's Theatre of the East 1576–1626*. Cambridge: Cambridge University Press, 2003.

Bartels, Emily. *Spectacles of Strangeness: Imperialism, Alienation, and Marlowe*. Philadelphia: University of Pennsylvania Press, 1993.

Beck, Brandon, H. *From the Rising of the Sun: English Images of the Ottoman Empire to 1715*. New York: P. Lang, 1987.

Bevington, David and Peter Holbrook, eds. *The Politics of the Stuart Court Masque*. Cambridge: Cambridge University Press, 1998.

Birchwood, Matthew and Matthew Dimmock, eds. *Cultural Encounters Between East and West: 1453–1699*. Newcastle: Cambridge Scholars Press, 2005.

Black, Jeremy and Jeremy Gregory, eds. *Culture, Politics and Society in Britain, 1660–1800*. Manchester: Manchester University Press, 1991.

Bock, Gisela, Quentin Skinner and Maurizio Viroli, eds. *Machiavelli and Republicanism*. Cambridge: Cambridge University Press, 1990.

Bradley, Jesse Franklin. 'Robert Baron's Tragedy of Mirza'. *Modern Language Notes* 34 (1919), 402–8.

Brenner, Robert. *Merchants and Revolution: Commercial Change, Political Conflict, and London's Overseas Traders, 1550–1653*. Princeton: Princeton University Press, 1993.

Brotton, Jerry. *The Renaissance Bazaar: From the Silk Road to Michelangelo*. Oxford: Oxford University Press, 2002.

Brown, Laura. *English Dramatic Form 1660–1760: An Essay in Generic History*. New Haven and London: Yale University Press, 1981.

Brummett, Palmira. *Ottoman Seapower and Levantine Diplomacy in the Age of Discovery*. Albany, NY: State University of New York Press, 1994.

Butler, Martin. *Theatre and Crisis 1632–1642*. Cambridge: Cambridge University Press, 1984.

——— 'Politics and the Masque: Salmacida Spolia', in *Literature and the English Civil War*. Eds. Thomas Healy and Jonathan Sawday. Cambridge: Cambridge University Press, 1990, 59–74.

Champion, J. A. I. *The Pillars of Priestcraft Shaken: The Church of England and its Enemies 1660–1730*. Cambridge: Cambridge University Press, 1992.

Chew, Samuel. *The Crescent and the Rose: Islam and England During the Renaissance*. New York: Oxford University Press, 1937.

Child, C. G. 'The Rise of the Heroic Play'. *Modern Language Notes* 19 (1904), 166–73.

Coles, Paul. *The Ottoman Impact on Europe*. London: Thames & Hudson, 1968.

Cook, M.A., ed. A *History of the Ottoman Empire to 1730*. Cambridge: Cambridge University Press, 1976.

Corns, Thomas N., ed. *The Royal Image: Representations of Charles I*. Cambridge: Cambridge University Press, 1999.

Daiber, Hans. 'The Reception of Islamic Philosophy at Oxford in the 17th Century: The Pocock's (Father and Son) Contribution to the Understanding of Islamic Philosophy in Europe', in *The Introduction of Arabic Philosophy into Europe*. Eds. Charles Butterworth and Blake Kessel. Leiden: E. J. Brill, 1994, 65–82.

D'Amico, Jack. *The Moor in English Renaissance Drama*. Tampa: University of Florida Press, 1991.

Daniel, Norman. *Islam and the West*. Edinburgh: University of Edinburgh Press, 1958.

Dent, Edward. *Foundations of English Opera*. Cambridge: Cambridge University Press, 1928.

Dimmock, Matthew. *New Turkes: Dramatizing Islam and the Ottomans in Early Modern England*. Aldershot: Ashgate, 2005.

Earle, Peter. *Corsairs of Malta and Barbary*. London: Sidgwick & Jackson, 1970.

Edmond, Mary. *Rare Sir William Davenant: Poet Laureate, Playwright, Civil War*

General, Restoration Theatre Manager. Manchester: Manchester University Press, 1987.

Epstein, M. *The Early History of the Levant Company.* London: George Routledge & Sons, 1908.

Fissel, Mark C. and Daniel Goffman. 'Viewing the scaffold from Istanbul'. *Albion,* 23, no. 3 (1990), 421–48.

Frank, Joseph. *The Beginnings of the English Newspaper 1620–1660.* Cambridge, MA: Harvard University Press, 1961.

——— *Cromwell's Press Agent: A Critical Biography of Marchmont Nedham, 1620–1678.* Lanham, MD: University Press of America, 1980.

Fuchs, Barbara. 'Conquering Islands: Contextualizing *The Tempest'. Shakespeare Quarterly,* 48, no. 1 (Spring 1997), 45–62.

——— *Mimesis and Empire: The New World, Islam and European Identities.* Cambridge: Cambridge University Press, 2001.

Goffman, Daniel. *Izmir and the Levantine World, 1550–1650.* London and Seattle: University of Washington Press, 1990.

——— *Britons in the Ottoman Empire 1642–1660.* London and Seattle: University of Washington Press, 1998.

——— *The Ottoman Empire and Early Modern Europe.* Cambridge: Cambridge University Press, 2002.

Grosrichard, Alain. *The Sultan's Court: European Fantasies of the East.* Trans. Liz Heron. Intro. Mladen Dolar. London: Verso, 1998.

Haley, K. H. D. *The First Earl of Shaftesbury.* Oxford: Clarendon Press, 1968.

Hamilton, Alistair. *William Bedwell, the Arabist 1563–1632.* Leiden: E. J. Brill, 1985.

Hamilton, Alistair and Francis Richard. *Andre Du Ryer and Oriental Studies in Seventeenth-Century France.* Oxford: Oxford University Press, 2004.

Hammond, Paul. 'Titus Oates and Sodomy' in *Culture, Politics and Society in Britain, 1660–1800.* Eds. Jeremy Black and Jeremy Gregory. Manchester: Manchester University Press, 1991.

Harbage, Alfred. *Sir William Davenant Poet Venturer 1606–1668.* Philadelphia: University of Pennsylvania Press, 1935.

——— *Cavalier Drama: An Historical and Critical Supplement to the Study of the Elizabethan and Restoration Stage.* New York: MLA, 1936.

Harris, Tim. *London Crowds in the Reign of Charles II.* Cambridge: Cambridge University Press, 1987.

Harris, Tim, Paul Seward and Mark Goldie, eds. *The Politics of Religion in Restoration England.* Oxford: Basil Blackwell, 1990.

Healy, Thomas and Jonathan Sawday, eds. *Literature and the English Civil War.* Cambridge: Cambridge University Press, 1990.

Heinemann, Margot. *Puritanism and Theatre: Thomas Middleton and Opposition Drama under the Early Stuarts.* Cambridge: Cambridge University Press, 1980.

Hill, Christopher. *The World Turned Upside Down.* Harmondsworth: Penguin, 1975.

——— *Antichrist in Seventeenth Century England.* London & New York: Verso, 1990.

——— *A Nation of Change and Novelty: Radical Politics, Religion and Literature in Seventeenth-Century England.* London: Routledge, 1990.

Hirst, Derek. *Authority and Conflict: England 1603–1658.* London: Edward Arnold, 1986.

——— *England in Conflict 1603–1660: Kingdom, Community, Commonwealth*. London: Arnold, 1999.

Holt, P. M. *A Seventeenth-Century Defender of Islam: Henry Stubbe (1632–76) and his Book*. London: Dr Williams's Trust, 1972.

Hotson, Leslie. *Commonwealth and Restoration Stage*. Cambridge, MA: Harvard University Press, 1928.

Hughes, Derek. *English Drama 1660–1700*. Oxford: Clarendon Press, 1996.

Hume, Robert D. *The Development of English Drama in the Late Seventeenth Century*. Oxford: Clarendon Press, 1976.

Hutton, Ronald. *The Restoration: A Political and Religious History of England and Wales, 1658–1667*. Oxford: Clarendon Press, 1985.

——— *Charles the Second: King of England, Scotland and Ireland*. Oxford: Oxford University Press, 1991.

Inalcik, Halil and Donald Quataert, eds., *An Economic and Social History of the Ottoman Empire, 1300–1916*. Cambridge: Cambridge University Press, 1994.

Jacob, James R. *Henry Stubbe, Radical Protestantism and the Early Enlightenment*. Cambridge: Cambridge University Press, 1983.

Jardine, Lisa, and Jerry Brotton. *Global Interests: Renaissance Art Between East and West*. London: Reaktion, 2000.

Johnson, Samuel. 'The Life of John Denham', in *The Works of the English Poets, from Chaucer to Cowper*. 21 vols. Vol 7. London: J. Johnson et al., 1810.

Jones, J. R. *The First Whigs: The Politics of the Exclusion Crisis 1678–1683*. London: Oxford University Press, 1961.

——— *Britain and the World 1649–1815*. Brighton: Harvester Press, 1980.

——— *Charles II: Royal Politician*. London: Allen & Unwin, 1987.

Jose, Nicholas. *Ideas of the Restoration in English Literature, 1660–1700*. London: Macmillan, 1984.

Kenyon, John. *The Popish Plot*. London: Heinemann, 1972.

Kinross, Lord. *The Ottoman Centuries: The Rise and Fall of the Turkish Empire*. London: Jonathan Cape, 1977.

Lane, Jane. *Titus Oates*. London: Andrew Dakers, 1949.

Longino, Michèle. *Orientalism in French Classical Drama*. Cambridge: Cambridge University Press, 2001.

Loomba, Ania. *Colonialsim/Postcolonialism*. London: Routledge, 1998.

MacLean, Gerald, ed. *The Rise of Oriental Travel: English Visitors to the Ottoman Empire, 1580–1720*. New York and Basingstoke: Palgrave Macmillan, 2004.

——— *Reorienting the Renaissance: Cultural Exchanges with the East*. New York and Basingstoke: Palgrave Macmillan, 2005.

McCarthy, Justin. *The Ottoman Turks: An Introductory History to 1923*. London: Longman, 1997.

McGowan, Bruce. *Economic Life: Ottoman Europe: Taxation, Trade and the Struggle for Land, 1600–1800*. Cambridge: Cambridge University Press, 1981.

McJannet, Linda. 'Bringing in a Persian'. *Medieval and Renaissance Drama in England* 12 (1999), 236–67.

Maguire, Nancy Klein. *Regicide and Restoration: English Tragicomedy, 1660–1671*. Cambridge: Cambridge University Press, 1992.

Mansel, Philip. *Constantinople: City of the World's Desire, 1453–1924*. London: John Murray, 1995.

Matar, Nabil. 'The Barbary Corsairs, King Charles I and the Civil War'. *Seventeenth Century*, 16, no. 2 (1993), 239–58.

——— *Islam in Britain 1558–1685*. Cambridge: Cambridge University Press, 1998.

——— *Turks, Moors and Englishmen in the Age of Discovery*. New York: Columbia University Press, 1999.

Miller, John. *Popery and Politics in England, 1660–1688*. Cambridge: Cambridge University Press, 1973.

——— *Charles II*. London: Weidenfeld & Nicolson, 1991.

——— *After the Civil Wars: English Politics and Government in the Reign of Charles II*. Harlow: Longman, 2000.

Morrill, John. *The Nature of the English Revolution*. London: Longman, 1993.

——— *After the Civil Wars: English Politics and Government in the Reign of Charles II*. Harlow: Longman, 2000.

Murray, Nicholas. *World Enough and Time: The Life of Andrew Marvell*. London: Little, Brown, 1999.

Nethercot, Arthur H. *Sir William D'Avenant: Poet Laureate and Playwright-Manager*. New York: Russell & Russell, 1938.

Norbrook, David. *Writing the English Republic: Poetry, Rhetoric and Politics, 1627–1660*. Cambridge: Cambridge University Press, 1999.

Orgel, Stephen. *The Illusion of Power: Political Theater in the English Renaissance*. Berkeley: University of California Press, 1975.

Orme, William. *Memoirs of the life, writings, and religious connexions of John Owen, D.D., Vice-Chancellor of Oxford and Dean of Christ Church, during the Commonwealth*. London, 1820.

Orr, Bridget. *Empire on the English Stage 1660–1714*. Cambridge: Cambridge University Press, 2001.

Owen, Susan Jane. *Restoration Theatre and Crisis*. Oxford: Clarendon Press, 1996.

——— ed., *A Companion to Restoration Drama*. Oxford and Malden, MA: Blackwell, 2001.

Parker, Gerald D. 'History as Nightmare in Nevil Payne's *The Siege of Constantinople* and Nathaniel Lee's *Lucius Junius Brutus*'. *Papers on Language and Literature* no. 21 (1985), 3–18.

Parker, Kenneth, ed. *Early Modern Tales of Orient: A Critical Anthology*. London: Routledge, 1999.

Parr, Anthony, ed. *Three Renaissance Travel Plays*. Manchester: Manchester University Press, 1995.

Pailin, David A. *Attitudes to Other Religions: Comparative Religion in Seventeenth and Eighteenth-Century Britain*. Manchester: Manchester University Press, 1984.

Patterson, Annabel. *Censorship and Interpretation: The Conditions of Writing and Reading in Early Modern England*. Berkeley: University of California Press, 1987.

Pierce, Leslie P. *The Imperial Harem: Women and Sovereignty in the Ottoman Empire*. Oxford: Oxford University Press, 1993.

Pincus, Steven C. A. 'Republicanism, Absolutim, and Universal Monarchy: English Popular Sentiment during the Third Dutch War', in *Culture and Society in the Stuart Restoration*. Ed. Gerald MacLean. Cambridge: Cambridge University Press, 1995, 241–66.

Playfair, R. L. *The Scourge of Christendom: Annals of British Relations with Algiers Prior to the French Conquest*. London: Smith, Elder & Co, 1884.

Potter, Lois. *Secret Rites and Secret Writing: Royalist Literature, 1641–1660*. Cambridge: Cambridge University Press, 1989.

——— 'Pirates and "turning Turk" in Renaissance Drama', in *Travel and Drama in Shakespeare's Time*. Ed. Jean-Pierre Maquerlot and Michèle Willems. Cambridge: Cambridge University Press, 1996, 124–40.

Randall, Dale B. J. *Winter Fruit: English Drama 1642–1660*. Lexington: University Press of Kentucky, 1995.

Raymond, Joad. *The Invention of the Newspaper: English Newsbooks 1641–1649*. Oxford: Oxford University Press, 1996.

Rice, Warner Grenelle. 'Turk, Moor, and Persian in English Literature from 1550–1660 with Particular Reference to the Drama'. PhD Dissertation, Harvard University, 1927.

Rouillard, C. D. *The Turk in French History, Thought and Literature 1520–1660*. Paris: Boivon & Co., 1940.

Routh, E. M. G. *Tangier, England's Lost Atlantic)utpost, 1661–1684*. London: John Murray, 1912.

Russell, G. A, ed. *The 'Arabick' Interest of the Natural Philosophers in Seventeenth-Century England*. Leiden: E. J. Brill, 1994.

Said, Edward. *Orientalism*. London: Routledge & Kegan Paul, 1978.

Savory, Roger. *Iran under the Safavids*. Cambridge: Cambridge University Press, 1980.

Schwoebel, Robert. *The Shadow of the Crescent: the Renaissance Image of the Turk, (1453–1517)*. Nieuwkoop: B. de Graaf, 1967.

Scott, Jonathan. *Algernon Sidney and the English Republic, 1623–1677*. Cambridge: Cambridge University Press, 1988.

——— 'England's Troubles: Exhuming the Popish Plot', in *The Politics of Religion in Restoration England*. Eds. Tim Harris, Paul Seward and Mark Goldie. Oxford: Basil Blackwell, 1990, 107–32.

Setton, Kenneth M. *Venice, Austria, and the Turks in the Seventeenth Century*. Philadelphia: The American Philosophical Society, 1991.

Sharpe, Kevin. *Criticism and Compliment: the Politics of Literature in the England of Charles I*. Cambridge: Cambridge University Press, 1987.

——— *The Personal Rule of Charles I*. New Haven and London: Yale University Press, 1992.

Siebert, Frederick Seaton. *Freedom of the Press in England 1476–1776: The Rise and Decline of Government Control*. Urbana: University of Illinois Press, 1965.

Slagle, Kenneth C. 'Robert Baron, Cavalier Poet'. *Notes and Queries* 169 (12 October 1935), 254–6.

Smith, Byron Porter. *Islam in English Literature*. Ed. S. B. Bushrui and Anahid Melikian, and a foreward by Omar A. Farrukh. Delmar, NY: Caravan Books, 1977.

Smith, Nigel. 'Exporting Enthusiasm: John Perrot and the Quaker Epic', in *Literature and the English Civil War*. Eds. Thomas Healy and Jonathan Sawday. Cambridge: Cambridge University Press, 1990, 248–64.

——— *Literature and Revolution in England, 1640–1660*. New Haven and London: Yale University Press, 1994.

Spurr, John. *England in the 1670s: 'This Masquerading Age'*. Malden, MA and Oxford: Blackwell, 2000.

Strong, Roy. *Splendour at Court: Renaissance Spectacle and the Theatre of Power*. London: Weidenfield & Nicolson, 1973.

Thaler, Alwin. 'Heywood, D'Avenant, and *The Siege of Rhodes*'. *Publications of the Modern Language Association* no. 39 (1924), 624–41.

Thorp, Willard. *Henry Nevil Payne, Dramatist and Jacobite Conspirator*. Princeton: Princeton University Press, 1935.

Toomer, G. J. *Eastern Wisedome and Learning: The Study of Arabic in Seventeenth-Century England*. Oxford: Clarendon Press, 1996.

Twells, Leonard. *The Theological Works of the Learned Dr. Pocock ... To which is prefixed, An Account of his Life and Writings never before printed*. London, 1740.

Varley, Frederick John. *The Siege of Oxford: An Account of Oxford During the Civil War, 1642–1646*. Oxford: Oxford University Press, 1932.

Vaughan, Dorothy M. *Europe and the Turk: A Pattern of Alliances 1350–1700*. Liverpool: Liverpool University Press, 1954.

Vitkus, Daniel, 'Turning Turk in Othello: the Conversion and Damnation of the Moor'. *Shakespeare Quarterly* 48, no. 2 (Summer 1997), 145–76.

——— ed. *Three Turk Plays From Early Modern England*. New York: Columbia University Press, 2000.

——— *Turning Turk: English Theater and the Multicultural Mediterranean, 1570–1630*. New York: Palgrave Macmillan, 2003.

Wann, Louis. 'The Oriental in Elizabethan Drama'. *Modern Philology* 12 (January 1915), 163–87.

Wiseman, Susan. *Drama and Politics in the English Civil War*. Cambridge: Cambridge University Press, 1998.

Wood, Alfred C. *A History of the Levant Company*. Oxford: Oxford University Press, 1935.

Worden, Blair. 'Marchamont Nedham and the Beginnings of English Republicanism, 1649–1656', in *Republicanism, Liberty, and Commercial Society, 1649–1776*. Ed. David Wootton. Stanford: Stanford University Press, 1994, 45–81.

Zwicker, Steven N. *Lines of Authority: Politics and English Literary Culture 1649–1689*. Ithaca and London: Cornell University Press, 1993.

INDEX

Index

Index

Studies in Renaissance Literature